Refugees, Women, and Weapons

Refugees, Women, and Weapons

International Norm Adoption
and Compliance in Japan

PETRICE R. FLOWERS

Stanford University Press
Stanford, California

Stanford University Press
Stanford, California

Printed in the United States of America
on acid-free, archival-quality paper

Library of Congress Cataloging-in-Publication Data

Flowers, Petrice R.
  Refugees, women, and weapons : international norm adoption and
compliance in Japan / Petrice R. Flowers.
      p.   cm.
  Includes bibliographical references and index.
  ISBN 978-0-8047-5973-1 (cloth : alk. paper)
  1. Japan—Foreign relations—1945–   2. Treaties.   3. International
obligations.   4. International law.   5. International relations.
I. Title.
  DS889.5.F56   2009
  327.52—dc22   2008055816

Typeset by Westchester Book Group in 10.5/12 Bembo

For my nieces and nephews who fill
my life with hope and joy:

Donté
Princess
Monae
Sydnei
Myles
Dalon
Brice
ArreAnna
Nia

Tell me, what is it you plan to do
With your one wild and precious life?
—Mary Oliver, "The Summer Day"

Contents

Illustrations

Acknowledgments

IN RESEARCHING AND WRITING this book, I have incurred many personal and intellectual debts. I have been fortunate to have had the support of many people along the way, and although I cannot mention each individually, I offer my heartfelt thanks to all of them. I owe special thanks to Kathryn Sikkink, who has provided excellent guidance and encouragement during the first years of my career. Kathryn, Dick Price (now of the University of British Columbia), Bud Duvall, Allen Isaacman, and other mentors in the Department of Political Science and the MacArthur Program at the University of Minnesota greatly contributed to my intellectual development, teaching, and scholarship. I am grateful for funding from the Japan Society for the Promotion of Science that enabled me to conduct research from 2002 to 2004 at the University of Tokyo. In Japan, I am indebted to Iwasawa Yuji for graciously agreeing to host me during my stay at the University of Tokyo. I would also like to thank Yamashita Yasuko, Ishikawa Eri, Omi Miho, and Hayashi Mika for their assistance at various stages of this research. I left Tokyo in 2004 for a position at the University of Hawai'i at Mānoa, where I am fortunate to have great colleagues in the Department of Political Science and at the Center for Japanese Studies. I want to give special thanks to Helen Kinsella, Susan Loveland Lett, Ann Towns, and Kristin Willey for their company as great friends and intellectual companions. Thank you to Cyndy Brown for her editorial skills. The book is much stronger because of the hard work of Jessica Walsh and Stacy Wagner at Stanford University Press and the thorough reading, thoughtful comments, and helpful suggestions of two anonymous reviewers. I am also grateful to Charles Eberline for his skillful copyediting. Finally, Noa Matsushita deserves recognition for doing a last-minute check of Japanese names.

My achievements are always heavily dependent on the collective energy of those outside the academy who help me restore my perspective, rejuvenate my spirit, and keep me centered. I appreciate the encouragement of my large extended family. My parents, Ronald and Sheila, and my sisters and brothers, Sharice, LaRonne, LaNice, Ronice, LaDonne, and Lakisha, helped me stay grounded and kept me motivated. Calvin and Francis Washington and the rest of my Washington family's warm concern gave me great comfort. I am especially gratified to have had a number of awesome women in my grandmothers, Sarah and Isadora, and the sisters—Pearl, Leomi, Ethel, Easter Mae, Ruby, Zipporah, Laverne, and Hilma—who taught me to live with grace and dignity without extinguishing my fire. Finally, I want to thank Kevin, an amazing man with whom I have the privilege of making an incredible journey.

Refugees, Women, and Weapons

Introduction

WHY SHOULD WE CARE about international norms and international law? For many years, international relations scholars neglected their role. The assumption was that they were not important determinants of state behavior and did not tell us much about patterns of interaction between states. But world events began to offer challenges to this view.[1] The primary question in this book is how international norms and international law affect domestic policy change. I investigate the counterintuitive adoption of and compliance with three treaties whose international normative framework conflicted with Japan's domestic norms: the International Treaty Concerning the Status of Refugees and the Optional Protocol (*nanmin no chi'i ni kansuru jōyaku oyobi ni giteisho*) (ratified in 1981), the Convention for the Elimination of All Forms of Discrimination Against Women (CEDAW) (*joshi sabetsu teppai jōyaku*) (ratified in 1985), and the Convention on the Prohibition of the Use, Stockpiling, Production and Transfer of Anti-Personnel Mines and on Their Destruction, the Ottawa Convention or Landmine Treaty (*taijin jirai kinshi jōyaku*) (ratified in 1998). I explain how conflict between international norms and domestic norms was negotiated to result in successful adoption of the international norms, and I trace the effects of this conflict on efforts to ensure compliance. In a world seemingly dominated by considerations of material and security threats, this book analyzes the significance of international norms and identity in understanding state behavior and explains why Japan defied obvious material and security interests in its decisions to adopt the three treaties investigated here.

In international relations literature, Japan is viewed as a "hard case" by those who argue that international norms matter. Asia is understood as a region where international norms and law are least influential. Scholars such as Miles Kahler argue that when Asian countries adopt international agreements, they are more likely to be trade agreements.[2] Historians of Japan and other serious observers know better; I return to this issue in Chapter 2.

Widely accepted assumptions that human rights instruments are diffi-cult to adopt because they conflict with Asian cultural norms lead us to expect that Japan would not have adopted these three treaties, especially CEDAW and the Refugee Convention. The third treaty considered in this study affected Japan's security by requiring changes that invalidated traditional threat perception and understandings of how best to defend Japan against attack. This third case is especially challenging to tradi-tional international relations theory because the treaty posed a threat to Japan's security alliance with the United States; the centrality of the bi-lateral relationship with the United States, especially with regard to secu-rity, suggests that Japan would be keen to avoid any challenges to that relationship.

Although constructivist[3] international relations scholars focus on the process of norm adoption, and international law scholars such as Anne-Marie Slaughter Burley (1993) identify compliance as a common area of study for scholars of international relations and international law, such questions as when and how states comply with these norms are understud-ied by international relations scholars. This book analyzes compliance within a constructivist framework. After establishing the reasons for adop-tion of international norms on women's employment, refugee policy, and land-mine policy, I follow the processes of norm compliance. I address how the processes of identity and interest formation that are key in norm adoption affect compliance. There is general agreement in compliance lit-erature that full compliance is the exception rather than the rule. I build on Chayes and Chayes's (1993) managerial approach to understanding com-pliance as a process along a continuum in order to focus on how greater or lesser degrees of compliance are attained. This helps makes it possible to anticipate the actual impact of international agreements and possibly in-crease levels of compliance. I return to this point in Chapter 2.

Based on extensive fieldwork in Japan, this book analyzes the degree of conflict between international and domestic norms and law, the strength of domestic advocates for both international and domestic law, and the state's desire for international legitimacy. More specifically, the three trea-ties studied here offer challenges to what it means to be Japanese, appro-priate roles for women in society, and the most effective ways to defend the country. Traditional explanations of Japan's reactions to international agreements rely on Japan's "distinctive" culture or the power of economic interest groups. Both of these explanations fail to answer why Japan continues to adopt international treaties that are clearly contrary to its domestic norms.

My research illuminates how even highly contested norms are adopted and reveals the particular strategies that domestic advocates use to influence both adoption and compliance. My theoretical contribution is twofold. First, I offer a more comprehensive model to test the explanatory power of two factors that emerge as important explanations of norm adoption in the constructivist literature on norms in a non-Western state: (1) the degree of conflict between international and domestic norms and (2) the strength of nonstate actors. Although these factors are present in most cases of norm adoption and compliance, the way they interact has not been studied. Instead, each element has been isolated and analyzed independently. This approach is insufficient for a sophisticated understanding of their interaction and of the relationship between international and domestic politics. Furthermore, studies of norm adoption and norm compliance have conventionally been split so that insights gained from studying adoption are too often lost when compliance is the subject of analysis. Second, I theorize a third factor, international legitimacy, which has not been adequately incorporated before. Analysis of this factor advances understanding of the social aspects of state behavior, including the role of state identity, in norm adoption and compliance. I argue that both domestic and international concerns determine which norms matter. Norms that promise to enhance international legitimacy will be adopted even when they conflict with domestic norms. Domestic advocates are essential in institutionalizing norms and ensuring compliance and therefore facilitate the shift in identity necessary for full compliance.

Alternative Explanations and Approaches

Rationalist approaches such as neoliberal institutionalism and *gaiatsu* (foreign pressure) offer alternative explanations. According to neoliberal institutionalist theory, international institutions mitigate the problem that anarchy poses for international relations and state interests and identities are pregiven and orginate from within the state. Although the neoliberal institutionalist perspective does not specifically address the issue of norm adoption or compliance, it does focus on explaining cooperation in situations in which states have incentives and disincentives to cooperate.[4] Neoliberal institutionalist theory states that the main obstacle to cooperation is cheating. Accordingly, institutions can produce cooperation by establishing rules that prevent cheating.[5] Increased interaction, issue linkage, and access to information reduce transaction costs of individual agreements because institutions make cooperation more efficient and therefore reduce the effort of states in cooperation. These changes reduce cheating by raising its costs and providing avenues for the victim to retaliate.

The primary shortcoming of this perspective is the implicit assumption that states would gain some material benefit from cooperating if only the barriers to cooperation were reduced or eliminated. Under explicitly normative international law, this is not always the case. Not only are the issues that these laws seek to address normative, but also the laws themselves often impose normative obligations on states that endorse them. These obligations do not always coincide with either domestic or international material interests. Furthermore, when states make normative commitments, the benefits they reap are not necessarily material. Legitimacy, credibility, and status are important to state survival and state interests at home and abroad. States that are opposed to a norm may adhere quickly during a norm cascade "for reasons that relate to their identities as members of an international society."[6] As members of international society, states seek to increase their credibility and legitimacy and establish a good reputation among other states to maintain their positions as members of the community. International legitimacy also has consequences for a government's domestic basis of legitimacy and its ability to remain in power.[7] Chapter 2 further discusses the theoretical dimensions and empirical significance of legitimacy.

The work of constructivists who argue that norms shape state interests and preferences, and that identity and interests are mutually constituted—that is, neither identity nor interests are pregiven, but each has a role in defining the other through evolving social and political practices—helps answer the question why Japan, in the cases investigated here, agreed to arrangements that imposed international and domestic obligations without any obvious material benefit. For example, Finnemore (1996a, 1996b) argues that international norms have a direct effect on domestic policies by shaping state preferences. Her study explains the adoption of the same norm in different countries even when such norms appear not to be in the state's interest. Constructivist approaches to the study of norms locate the origin of state interests in "an international structure of meaning and social value."[8] In these approaches the role of international organizations in socializing states and constructing state interests is important in the argument that the international system changes states by changing their behavior, not by constraining them. Although her study challenges the assumption that the source of state preferences is located inside the state, Finnemore acknowledges that sometimes domestic politics are important in determining state interests. Nevertheless, she argues that domestic politics cannot explain all state interests or policy choices, especially those policies that seem to contradict or conflict with state interests. She argues that "preferences are strongly influenced and often constituted by social norms, culturally determined roles and rules, and historically contingent discourse."[9] Finnemore does not discount the importance of domestic context and agents in shaping preferences, but she does suggest that there is a dynamic relationship between structure and agents in both international and domestic politics. This is the relationship I explore. Although domestic politics cannot explain all state interests or policy choices, domestic politics do interface with the international system to shape, guide, and influence how the state responds. By arguing that domestic politics cannot explain those policy choices that conflict with state interests, Finnemore assumes that domestic politics do not influence state interests and that the two are always in agreement. This assumption limits the influence of domestic politics to state borders and does not allow for the possibility that domestic and international political interactions take place independent of the state.

Arguments that consider the role of foreign pressure in Japan's foreign policy choices usually focus on the U.S.-Japan relationship and read Japan as occupying a subordinate or dependent position in its relationship with the United States.[10] These arguments also depend on rationalist cost-benefit analysis to explain Japan's actions. As we will see, rationalist explanations do not adequately account for state action on these issues. To develop a more complete understanding of the dynamics involved, it is important to situate Japan in relation to other states in an international context where duties and obligations are defined by a state's identity, as well as its position within the international community. This allows us to broaden our understanding of foreign pressure to include identity-based pressure. Through statements of individual actors, opinion leaders, and politicians, we see that in the case of refugee policy, for example, Japanese politicians were attempting to create an identity based on what they wanted to be true about Japan as a state, what would be acceptable internationally, and what would help fulfill its international duty.

The argument I develop does not discount the role of foreign pressure in Japan's decisions to adopt international legal norms that conflict with domestic norms. Indeed, one of the contributions of my research is to show how foreign pressure is effective in Japan by focusing on the often unacknowledged fact that foreign pressure is not limited to material pressure, as most of the existing *gaiatsu* literature assumes, but that these external pressures include identity pressures that are essential in explaining adoption.

Three Issues: Refugee Policy, Women's Employment, and Antipersonnel Land Mines

My goal in focusing on international agreements is not to argue that they alone determine domestic behavior, but rather to explore how international and domestic political practices interact and under what conditions international norms and law can contribute to domestic policy change. Because domestic norms are filters through which we gain meaning, international norms and law must accord with domestic norms in order to limit tensions and contradictions and to improve the chances that a norm will be adopted and implemented and that some level of compliance will be obtained. My research shows that when there are strong domestic interests in support of implementing the international norm, there is a greater chance that the norm will be adopted and some level of compliance achieved, regardless of its amount of discord with domestic norms.

On the issue of women's employment, there was a high degree of conflict between the international and domestic norms concerned. Before ratification of CEDAW, most legislation related to women's employment in Japan was protective legislation that served to limit women's roles in the paid labor force. The only law that concerned employment discrimination was a law that proscribed wage differentials based solely on sex. Domestic advocates on this issue enjoyed a strong position partly because of high-profile women activists who agitated for adoption of CEDAW, a history of discrimination cases decided in favor of the female complainants, and the long history of women's movements in Japan.

On the issue of refugees, there was a very high degree of conflict between international and domestic norms. Before ratification of the International Refugee Convention, there were no laws in place to deal with refugees, and exclusionary laws guaranteed certain benefits only to citizens. These laws indicated a conscious choice to exclude some groups from these benefits. In this case, implementing the norms and moving toward compliance required changing many laws, not just writing new ones. There were no organized advocacy groups active on the issue when it emerged on the political agenda. In fact, the majority of people supported providing material assistance to refugees but opposed allowing them to settle in Japan.[11] In addition, the history of the treatment of ethnic minorities in Japan, especially after World War II, indicates a strong domestic norm of cultural exclusivity. Furthermore, support for offering material assistance surfaced only after extensive media coverage that was sympathetic to the refugees' plight. When nongovernmental organizations (NGOs) were formed to aid refugees, policy advocacy was not a part of their agenda. Some groups are currently doing this kind of work, but they are still a very small minority. Although some op-ed pieces were printed in newspapers on this issue, and many of these articles were critical of the government's action or lack of action, opinion leaders did not frame the issue effectively. Aside from the critique, these articles did not suggest a basis for action. An analysis of Diet committee meetings leads me to conclude that desire for legitimacy was an important consideration in adopting the Refugee Convention. In the end, the discursive production of state identity in these meetings located much of the rationale for action in the state's duty and obligation to the international community.

There was a high degree of conflict between international and domestic norms on the issue of land mines. Strictly speaking, no laws specifically legislated the use of land mines; thus adopting the treaty required the creation of laws to come into compliance with the treaty. Perhaps more important was the entrenched idea that land mines were an essential tool necessary to defend Japan in case of a land invasion. Although it is reasonable to believe that the pacifism and antimilitarism of much of Japan's population indicate a strong domestic norm that would coincide with prohibition of use, most people were not aware that Japan produced and possessed land mines and were not aware of official positions that land mines were necessary for Japan's defense. The domestic advocates on this issue were moderately strong. There was no initiative to call for a ban on land mines, but there was a base of support among the pacifist and disarmament constituencies; thus the public was not hostile to a suggestion to ban land mines. In addition, there was no opposition from the business community because Japan did not export land mines. Given their limited resources, activists working to ban land mines did a very good job of using the print media to educate the public on the issue and what was at stake, to call attention to government action or inaction on the issue, and to mobilize support. The balance and subtlety of the opinion pieces in the *Asahi Shimbun* and the no-nonsense policy orientation of the op-eds in the *Yomiuri Shimbun* were tailored to each paper's readership, and both spurred action.

Methodology: Identity, Actors, and Legitimacy

I use three issues—refugee policy, women's employment, and land mines—in which international law and Japanese domestic norms diverge to analyze the interaction of domestic norms and international law in the complicated process of adoption of and compliance with international norms. By examining three different issue areas in one country, I can explore the factors that account for different levels of influence of domestic and international norms across issue areas.

Checkel argues that those international norms that come into greatest conflict with domestic norms will be the most difficult to adopt and implement. Some might argue that such conflict would prevent norm adoption and implementation. However, my research shows that although conflict shapes how international norms are interpreted and implemented and what level of compliance can be achieved, it does not automatically follow that those international norms will not be adopted. Within the three issue areas, I use process tracing to understand the domestic and international contexts in which the norms emerged. Process tracing is a method often used to establish causality by linking the decision-making process to specific outcomes.[12] Since the emphasis in this book is more on uncovering and understanding as an interpretive project, I do not attempt to establish causality in the strict sense of empiricist social science research. The value of the method is that the detailed attention to process allows us to uncover, understand, and interpret political and social practices (including but not limited to decision making) as well as historical contingencies that lead to certain outcomes. Attention to history is essential to understanding each of these issues. Because norm adoption, implementation, and compliance are partially rooted in international relations, understood not only as political and economic processes but also as social processes, we cannot understand state behavior without understanding the social relations out of which these behaviors are born. I do not make a deterministic argument; rather, I recognize the historical contingency of state behavior studied in this book and argue that the history of Japan's international (social, economic, and political) relations and the meanings attached to them are part of what constitutes Japan's identity and interests. Attention to history thus helps explain why Japan adopted these three agreements that so clearly conflict with its domestic norms.

These three cases—refugee policy, women's employment, and land mines—offer variation in two important ways. First, they form a continuum from primarily domestic normative issues (women's employment) to primarily international security issues (antipersonnel land mines). Second, there is variation among the relative weight of three explanatory variables investigated: the degree of conflict between domestic and international norms, the strength of the domestic advocates associated with each of the issues, and the extent to which adopting the norms would contribute to the state's legitimacy (Table 1). This bilevel variation helps answer which norms matter, how, and to what extent by closely examining the interaction between domestic advocates and identity and the adoption of international law.

To determine the degree of conflict, I first analyzed the text of the relevant international and national laws before adoption to determine if the

TABLE I. Variation of issues across adoption and compliance phases

	Adoption Phase			Compliance Phase	
Issue	*Year ratified*	*State desire for legitimacy*	*Strength of domestic advocates*	*Degree of conflict between international norms and domestic norms/identity*	*Level of compliance*
Refugees	1981	High	Low	High	Low
Women's employment	1985	High	High	High	Medium
Antipersonnel land mines	1998	Low	Medium	High	High

national laws required substantial revision to bring them into compliance with international law. In Japan, international agreements trump domestic law; thus, whenever international treaties are adopted, the entire body of relevant domestic law is often reformed before the treaty is ratified by the Diet. When substantial changes to existing laws, as well as creation of new laws, are necessary, as with adoption of the Refugee Convention, there is a high degree of conflict. Second, I charted the sentiment of newspaper editorials and opinion pages as an indicator of the intensity of public discourse and debate on each of the three issues. A high degree of conflict exists when an international norm contradicts established domestic norms as reflected in values of the broader population or dominant discourses. In such cases, there are no laws or only conflicting laws on the books, a resistance to creating or changing relevant laws, and sometimes a history of legal battles around the issue. A medium degree of conflict exists on issues where there may not be any laws on the books, but where the issue is not domestically contested and no dominant discourse or strong domestic norms have been established. Finally, an issue has a low degree of conflict when international and domestic norms reflect similar values.

To determine the strength of domestic advocates, I interviewed activists involved in each issue, traced and evaluated organizations' ties to the state, and assessed their political mobilization. In the cases of CEDAW and the Ottawa Convention, interviews and analysis of group publications revealed that activists' access to powerful state actors and transnational networks was essential to their success. The strength of domestic advocates is high when highly organized groups are working on the specific issue, when the groups have connections to powerful actors that allow access to or influence over the policy-making process, and when there is high-profile, public advocacy before, during, and after treaty adoption.

Domestic advocates are moderately strong when advocates are organized around related issues but do not coalesce on the specific issue that the international treaty addresses. In this case, they lack a broad coalition but enjoy pockets of strong supporters, including politicians and government officials whom they lobby behind the scenes. A complete lack of organized advocates does not preclude existence of some local organizations dealing directly with relevant service provision, but it does indicate low strength of domestic advocates.

I established the state's desire for legitimacy through an analysis of Diet committee records of the debates on adoption of the treaties, with particular attention to the substance of the arguments for and against ratification. Arguments for adopting the conventions were based on identity and related specifically to Japan's role in the international community. Dissenting voices articulated the domestic norms at stake and confirmed the level of conflict between international and domestic norms. For example, when the Diet was considering CEDAW, statements such as the following made by Minister Abe Shintaro in the May 24, 1985, Foreign Affairs Committee meeting indicate the importance of international legitimacy: "As a country that is trusted in the international community[, Japan] will need to conduct itself as such. So instead of foreign countries pointing out [Japan's] shortcomings, they will focus on Japan's efforts." To further illustrate the point, in that same meeting Minister Abe also stated, "Our country's ratifying a challenging treaty in front of the world will turn our diplomacy toward the twenty-first century. As with other modern countries in the world, trust [in Japan] will increase and this is a great merit [of the treaty]."

By analyzing these three variables, I was able to identify the relative balance of structural constraints (both material and ideational) and collective activism in influencing Japan's adoption of international law. Once the treaties were adopted, I traced the influence of structural constraints and collective activism in ensuring compliance. Because legitimacy is intersubjective, how other relevant states—those that constitute the community of states engaged on a particular issue—perceive Japan influences the state's identity construction. A high state desire for legitimacy results from overt pressure and, in some cases, intense lobbying from powerful states to conform; dominant discourses and values reflected in the issue are framed as "universal" or "fundamental" (rights) issues by states, international organizations, and international NGOs. In such cases, a significant number of major countries have adopted the treaty. On the other hand, when the issue is more contested within the international community and does not deal with human rights issues that have become significant in defining state identity since World War II with the Universal

Declaration of Human Rights, there is a medium-level state desire for legitimacy. In such cases, there may be significant pressure to conform from the United States, but the U.S. position does not reflect that of the larger international community, there may be pressure from core states concerned with the issue, or lobbying by international NGOs and transnational networks. Finally, low state desire for legitimacy results from a situation where there is pressure to conform from a minority of materially and ideationally less powerful international actors, and the issue itself may be of concern only to a minority constituency in the international community. The states involved in this case may not be the ones that have the most influence on a particular issue.

I analyzed op-ed pages of two Japanese-language newspapers and records of Diet committee meetings relating to each of the three issues over a three-year period of critical discourse moments[13]—the year before ratification, the year of ratification, and the year after ratification[14]—to uncover discourses on Japanese state and national identities, to understand other issues at stake in considering the treaty, such as Japanese perceptions of threat, and to uncover reasons why the treaties were adopted.[15] In addition, because adoption of these agreements spans a seventeen-year period, this research offers insight into the evolution of these discourses over time.

Diet records are an excellent place to locate discourses of state identity and legitimacy, mainly because they are not produced for an audience. Committee meetings are used to debate policy, and, to my surprise, I have found that these discussions can be very frank. There are occasions when members offer strong challenges and openly disagree with each other and even with what have become dominant discourses, such as the standard reasons that refugees do not settle in Japan. These proceedings usually appear to be very civil and polite, but this may be partly because of the lack of texture in written documents (for example, one cannot hear the tone of voice). However, even in the written text, or perhaps especially in the written text, I have easily observed that the level of politeness increases greatly as members disagree more strongly. Analyzing discussions of the lower house of the Diet and public opinion related to the three issues helps shed light on the concerns that drove the decision to adopt CEDAW, the Refugee Convention, and the Ottawa Convention, and how domestic laws were modified ostensibly to implement them.

Editorial and opinion pages from the relatively conservative *Yomiuri Shimbun*, the newspaper with the largest circulation in Japan, and from the more left-leaning *Asahi Shimbun* are important sources of information for what Japanese think about these issues and how the issues are framed for the public. Not only are these places where opinions are expressed, but also these opinions shape the views of those who read them and illuminate various aspects of how people understand the state's identity and its role in the world. Broadbent and Kabashima (1986) illustrate the importance of the mass media in Japan because of their power over society and politics. These authors convincingly argue, "Media give prominence to subordinate social groups and so contribute to greater political pluralism."[16] They go on to show that "the power of the mass media in Japan depends upon their influence, not only over key decision makers, but more broadly over society as a whole. Through this influence, the media exercises increasing, if not always planned, indirect political power."[17] Although Broadbent and Kabashima recognize that this power can often serve to legitimate the ruling elite, they find that it also often serves to redistribute power. Thus in Japan, where the power of civil society is often limited by alliances between more powerful actors, restrictive laws, and ideational constraints,[18] attention to the media is important in helping us understand how they can be used as an avenue for movements that may challenge the ideological hegemony of the ruling Liberal Democratic Party (LDP) on some issues.

Plan of This Book

After fleshing out the theoretical framework in Chapter 2, I turn in Chapter 3 to the first of the three case studies and focus on refugee policy. Japan adopted the Refugee Convention in 1981 and reformed legislation to be more in line with international directives. Yet there were no material international pressures and no public support for allowing refugees to resettle in Japan, and there was a high degree of conflict between international and domestic norms on this issue. Although the high degree of conflict that characterized the refugee issue (and later the issue of women's employment) challenged efforts at adoption, it did not prevent them. I argue that the desire for international legitimacy trumped internal conflict. Japan adopted the Refugee Convention on the basis of the state's quest for legitimacy. Analysis of Diet records reveals that government actors believed that if they reshaped Japan's identity to make it more appropriate for a world "economic power" and "developed country," international legitimacy would follow. Adopting the Refugee Convention was seen as appropriate action for such a state. This chapter expands on the work of scholars who recognize that states seek international legitimacy, but who do not explore the theoretical or empirical significance of states' quest for international legitimacy. Although desire for international legitimacy trumped internal conflict in the adoption phase, the conflict proved more difficult to overcome in the compliance phase. This phase is where domestic advocates are particularly influential. It was not until nearly two decades later that compliance with the Refugee Convention became a possibility because of the growing number of domestic advocates for protecting the rights of refugees and the pressure that they exerted on government officials to create a comprehensive refugee policy in Japan.

In Chapter 4, I turn to the issue of women's employment and Japan's adoption of the Convention for the Elimination of All Forms of Discrimination Against Women (CEDAW). There is great disparity between the social and cultural importance of women as mothers and homemakers in Japan and the significance of those roles as conceptualized within CEDAW, but this conflict was once again trumped by the state's desire for legitimacy. On the basis of the conflict between international and domestic norms, norms literature would predict that domestic norms would prevail and CEDAW would not be adopted. If it were adopted, we would expect a low level of compliance. In fact, not only was CEDAW adopted, but it has been progressively institutionalized, and a medium degree of compliance has been achieved. This marked contrast with the case of refugee policy, where there was also a high degree of conflict, raises these questions: How did these two cases differ? How can we understand the process and explain the outcome to secure better compliance with future agreements? A significant difference between the two issues, refugee policy and women's employment, was the strength of domestic advocates. The efforts of domestic advocates account for compliance with CEDAW, and the state's desire for legitimacy explains Japan's adoption of CEDAW. The organization of domestic advocates is a central part of this chapter. State dominance of state-society relations in Japan, along with state suspicion of citizens' organizations, has produced an anemic civil society in which organizations usually suffer from lack of funding and lack of access to power. In this case, women's organizations used a strategy of coalition building, taking advantage of significant social achievements (the thirtieth anniversary of women's suffrage), and connections with high-profile women in the government to strengthen their influence. Explanations of why states adopt international norms that conflict with domestic norms offered by other scholars include the role of transnational networks and norm entrepreneurs (for example, Klotz 1995a, 1995b; Keck and Sikkink 1998). However, this literature focuses specifically on the role of nonstate actors and their activities and ignores the importance of their ties to the state. These ties were an essential component of the influence of women's organizations in Japan. This literature also stresses the importance of transnational networks as an avenue for domestic actors to go outside a resistant state to exert pressure on that state (Keck and Sikkink's boomerang effect). Although Japanese women's organizations did have access to these kinds of networks, they used them to improve their access to information so that they could deal directly with state actors more effectively. Thus my research improves on established theories by illustrating how nonstate actors use their ties to the state to influence both adoption and compliance, and how transnational networks can be used toward that end. Analysis of the ties between domestic advocates and the state illuminates the opportunities and limitations of domestic context that is central to both Checkel (1999) and Evangelista (1995, 1999), who were key in moving the constructivist research agenda forward after earlier studies established that norms matter.

Chapter 5 takes up the issue of antipersonnel land mines, which directly involves state security and thus, according to mainstream international relations literature, should be the most difficult with regard to norm adoption and compliance. Ratifying the Ottawa Convention required that Japan not only override domestic security concerns but also simultaneously oppose its main ally and security partner, the United States. Japan was in the antiban camp until after the Ottawa Convention went into force. From the time when France called for a Convention on Certain Conventional Weapons (CCW) Review Conference in 1993 until Foreign Minister Obuchi Keizo signed the Ottawa Convention in 1997, Japan's position on this issue was attributed to its security relationship with the United States. But as the trend in the international community turned toward an international ban on antipersonnel land mines, Japan's association with the U.S. position threatened to affect Japan's international standing negatively. Therefore, Japan acted to maintain its unique position as a "pacifist" state in an effort to retain international standing. The role of domestic advocates was also crucial. Although the movement to ban land mines came late to Japan—resulting in moderately strong domestic advocates—there was a ready constituency to support a ban, composed of antimilitarists, peace activists, and those who saw the devastating effects of land mines firsthand through their work in NGOs that assisted refugees abroad. In this case, the state's desire to maintain its legitimacy trumped concern for its relationship with its main security partner, the United States.

I present my conclusions in Chapter 6. My findings advance the constructivist research agenda by demonstrating that the state's desire for legitimacy (state identity) leads Japan to agree to arrangements that impose obligations with no material benefit. The state views these actions as necessary to create a more favorable identity through which it will gain increased legitimacy. The cues for what kind of identity is acceptable and what kinds of actions are appropriate are rooted in contemporary discourses of civilization, which determine standards of appropriate behavior for members of the international community.[19] I show that the power of these "logics of appropriateness" produce particular interests and identities that may actually conflict with domestic norms. When domestic advocates are weak, as in the case of the Refugee Convention, the level of compliance is also likely to be low. No matter how intensely the state desires legitimacy or how much the government may pursue reform through implementing international norms, domestic advocates are critical for actually mobilizing international norms and taking action to ensure compliance.

CHAPTER 2

Adoption, Implementation, and Compliance

ADOPTION, IMPLEMENTATION, AND COMPLIANCE are all stages of the larger process of institutionalizing international norms. In this book, adoption refers specifically to ratification of the treaty in question; the adoption phase includes activities leading up to ratification and the period soon after. Because the Japanese government attempts to bring domestic laws in line with international treaties before the treaties are adopted, implementation—the process that puts international agreements into practice through passage of legislation and creation of institutions—is fairly automatic and less contentious and receives less attention here. Compliance is achieved when state identity has been reconstituted and the norm acquires a taken-for-granted status. In this situation, a state bases norm compliance on an internal sense of obligation that comes with its status as a member of the international community and does not experience any conflict in complying, even with norms that were controversial during adoption.[1] Approaching compliance as part of a process and focusing my study on the entire process avoid the problem of emphasizing the endpoint, where norms, rules, and values are already internalized at the expense of understanding how that internalization takes place. Both international relations and international law scholars stress the need to understand the intervening social processes in order to gain a fuller understanding of why states comply with international norms and law.[2]

The question of compliance is most explicitly addressed in research at the nexus of international relations and international law; thus this study of international legal norms is an opportunity to study compliance within a constructivist framework. Many international law scholars offer compliance as an area where bridging international law and international relations could be fruitful. Broadly speaking, international relations and international law studies explain state motivations for compliance by using realist theory, with its explanations of unequal distribution of material power that makes states vulnerable to coercion; neoliberal institutionalist theory that focus on cooperation driven by motivations endogenous to the state, including self-interest, domestic politics, and national identity; and constructivist explanations that elaborate on the constitutive nature of norms, law, and rules with a central focus on how the mutual constitution of identity and interests shapes state preferences. Much of the work on compliance in both international relations and international law favors a neoliberal approach that focuses on institutions. There are at least two reasons why this might be the case. First, Anne-Marie Slaughter Burley's seminal article in which she lays out a "dual agenda" for international law and international relations focuses on regime theory, a neoliberal institutionalist approach to the study of issues relevant for both fields.[3] Also, within the mainstream approaches to international relations, neoliberal institutionalists are more likely to see validity in studying international law.[4] These studies offer insights into state behavior, but their rationalist approach to international law fails to explore the constitutive nature of international law by assuming that preferences, identities, and interests are pregiven and originate within the state.

I approach compliance from a constructivist framework where the question of how we can account for compliance (or lack thereof) in Japan on the issues of women's employment, refugee policy, and land mines is theorized as part of a process that probes how international relations and domestic politics both play a role in constructing state identity and how state identity in turn influences compliance. I attempt to heed Kratochwil and Ruggie's warning that analysis of compliance should avoid preoccupation with norm violation.[5] Therefore, I do not focus on what compliance or noncompliance tells us about the robustness of a norm or the strength of a regime. Rather, I am concerned with how the processes of identity and interest formation that are key in norm adoption unfold and affect compliance. Approaching the issue of compliance in this way makes it possible to focus on process and how greater or lesser degrees of compliance are attained. This approach also enables recognition of the importance of different levels of compliance and moves us toward explaining variation in compliance with different norms. Finally, thinking about process as opposed to outcomes leads to more substantial analysis of what happens during the period leading up to adoption and after. Research by international law scholars on compliance is very useful in pointing us in the right direction.

Chayes and Chayes's (1993) managerial approach to compliance is instructive for constructivists who study legal norms to address the issue of compliance. Japan is often accused of committing to treaties for strategic reasoning when in reality there is no intention to comply. Chayes and Chayes's argument that failure to comply does not usually result from a deliberate decision pushes us to look beyond the assumption that Japan adopts treaties with no intention to comply with them and to focus instead on the possibility that there is more substance to decisions to ratify international agreements.[6] Although the authors recognize that a state may enter into international agreements to appease a domestic or international constituency but has little intention of complying, they argue that this kind of disregard for legal obligation is an infrequent occurrence.[7] One of the three circumstances that they identify at the root of violations, limitations on state capacity to meet obligations, is especially relevant here.[8] Although studies that adhere to a managerial approach to compliance define capacity primarily in material terms,[9] some scholars who study state capacity to govern employ a broader conception that includes the importance of legitimation and consent for a state to exercise authority.[10] On this basis, my analysis expands state capacity to comply with international law to include not only human and material resources but ideational resources as well. I demonstrate that in the case of Japan, limitations on capacity include identity. I argue that Japan's state identity and the related desire for legitimacy were significant in decisions to adopt the three international agreements investigated here. Obligations associated with these agreements have led to varying levels of implementation, defined as "the process of putting international commitments into practice: the passage of legislation, creation of institutions (both domestic and international) and enforcement of rules,"[11] mostly in the form of new laws; however, attaining a significant level of compliance can be hindered by a conflict between international and domestic norms.

The view that international norms are primarily regulative places the managerial approach to the study of compliance squarely in the neoliberal school of thought. Scholars who use this approach recognize that interests and norms support the likelihood that states will comply with international agreements; they point out that states' commitments to international agreements are based on and reflect state interests. Even so, they argue, this does not guarantee compliance because treaty making is influenced by the structure of the international system; thus states are subject to the power relations that exist in that system. Despite the recognition that norms, interests, and the structure of the system influence treaty making and compliance, the managerial approach does not question either how norms and interests are constituted or their constitutive effects. Furthermore, the exclusive focus on material structure ignores normative and ideational aspects—the social aspects—of international structure. I contend, following a constructivist approach, that in addition, treaty making is also subject to the social meaning and values that are key nonmaterial aspects of the structure of the international system. I show that legitimacy, with its close connection to identity and discourses of civilization, affects compliance, and that legitimacy is not pregiven but is constituted through political practices at the domestic and international levels.[12] I agree with the assertion of Chayes and Chayes that because state interests may change from the treaty-negotiation stage to the compliance stage, a state's lack of compliance is not necessarily just the result of intentions to adopt an agreement to appease international or domestic constituencies with no plans to abide by treaty obligations. I push their analysis further to demonstrate how the process, including state-society negotiations, negotiations among different domestic-level constituencies, and negotiations between international and domestic interests, reconstitute state interests and identity, with implications for both adoption and compliance. Because in many states treaty obligations become part of national law, as is the case in Japan, there is a legal obligation for states to obey. In Japan, although this legal obligation does contribute to fairly high levels of implementation, it is not sufficient to secure equally high levels of compliance.

Koh (1997) outlines a model to explain why states comply with international law. Like other theories of compliance,[13] this framework recognizes the importance of repeated interaction between transnational actors and the power of normative discourse, which increases throughout these interactions. Koh's transnational legal process model outlines a constitutive process whereby states interpret global norms and internalize them into domestic law. This process helps reconstitute national interests and national identities.[14] His transnational legal process approach accords with a constructivist model that depends on social learning to change state behavior. This three-step process of interaction, interpretation, and internalization is how "international law acquires its 'stickiness' . . . nation-states acquire their identity, and . . . nations come to 'obey' international law out of perceived self-interest." Koh concludes that repeated "participation helps to reconstitute national interests, to establish the identity of actors as ones who obey the law, and to develop the norms that become part of the fabric of the emerging international society"[15] where compliance is "based broadly on notions of both identity-formation and international society."[16] Thus compliance is the result of social relations that include the intersubjective process of state identity formation.

I use Raustiala and Slaughter's (2002) definition of compliance as "a state of conformity or identity between an actor's behavior and a specific rule."[17] Thus compliance is about identification; to achieve compliance with contested norms, state identity must change. Some might question identity change as a threshold for compliance, especially in the case of refugees, because it is difficult to imagine an identity shift on an issue that challenges such a fundamental domestic norm as what it means to be Japanese. In this case, it is easy to understand why one might question how an identity shift could take place without the presence of large numbers of refugees. It is true that the presence of a large number of refugees in Japan might necessitate extending rights to them. However, Japan's unwillingness even to accept refugees is part of the puzzle presented in Chapter 3, and my research shows that it is highly unlikely that the government would ever face such a scenario. Still, the issue is an important one and is larger than Japan's identity on refugee issues; it cuts to the core of the argument. I recognize that states may adopt norms, in this case by ratifying treaties, for instrumental reasons and may even respond to international pressure to take certain actions. But the argument I develop demonstrates that compliance is a process of identification. It uses theoretical insights from legal scholars, specifically Koh (1997), Chayes and Chayes (1993), Hathaway (2001–2002), and Raustiala and Slaughter (2002), supported by persuasive arguments about the role of legitimacy made by international relations scholars such as Hurd (1999), Hopf (2002), and Miyaoka (2004). The argument is not that identity change is necessary for any level of compliance, but that full compliance (which legal scholars agree is almost never achieved) requires state identification with the norm. Certainly, constructivists have established that state identity is constantly changing and evolving, so mere identity change is necessary but not sufficient for achieving full compliance.

For most international relations scholars, compliance refers to any state action that is in line with international norms. I suggest that compliance is a more complex concept that is distinct from adoption or undertaking certain desired actions. Compliance does require identification with a norm, and this is achieved, as Koh theorizes, through repeated interactions of state and nonstate actors. I bring insights from international legal scholarship on compliance to bear on the question of state compliance with international norms in an attempt to theorize what is meant by compliance, to distinguish it from adoption, and to bridge international relations and international legal scholarship. The role of international organizations and NGOs in shaping state interests and identity has been established (for example, Finnemore 1996a, 1996b; Price 1997; Keck and Sikkink 1998), so although the presence of refugees might have a certain impact on state provision of material needs, it is not necessary for identity change. If normative expectations and obligations are important, how can we explain compliance? By focusing more closely on a specific domestic context, I capture the richness of domestic political processes and their impact on adoption and compliance. Most significantly, however, my research reveals how domestic and international political practices affect the state's identity and desire for legitimacy, and I then analyze how this desire for legitimacy interacts with the two other variables—strength of domestic advocates and degree of conflict between domestic and international norms.

The next section of this chapter outlines the social and cultural underpinnings of adoption and compliance by focusing on the connection between identity, legitimacy, and civilization. The final section demonstrates state desire for legitimacy at work in Japan's adoption of global norms since the nineteenth century. This final section provides the context for the case studies in Chapters 3, 4, and 5 and grounds my argument that the nature of the norms to which the Japanese government has tried to adapt and the kind of identity toward which Japan has tried to move have changed over time.

Legitimacy, Identity, and Civilization

Adoption of international norms has received extensive attention in the international norms literature.[18] Activities of actors such as domestic and international NGOs, transnational activists, international organizations, transnational advocacy networks, epistemic communities, or sometimes a combination of these play an essential role in norm adoption. How can we explain norm adoption in a state such as Japan, where there may not be a broad-based domestic movement or constituency supporting adoption and compliance with the norm? If there is a relevant set of domestic advocates working on the issue, but they are not networked internationally, how does this affect adoption and compliance? Analyzing variation in the strength of domestic advocates on the three issues I study helps address these questions.

Approaches that consider the role of nonstate actors in norm adoption focus more on transnational actors and processes than on domestic actors. Thus at this level of analysis, the extent to which they consider the role of domestic actors is only to say that they go outside the state to influence norm adoption. Significant changes, such as the end of the cold war and the end of apartheid in South Africa, required a crucial linkage between domestic and transnational actors.[19] Keck and Sikkink (1998) develop a theory of the boomerang effect whereby domestic advocates in state A, being unable to effectively exert pressure on government actors because of lack of access or other characteristics of state-society relations, activate their network to have others, including actors in state B, exert pressure on their state actors to pressure state A to respond. But domestic state and nonstate actors are only partially responsible for norm adoption, implementation, and compliance; these processes are also dependent on domestic norms. Cortell and Davis point out two national-level factors that are important determinants of the effects of international norms at the level of domestic political processes: "The domestic salience or legitimacy of the norm, and the structural context within which the domestic policy debate transpires."[20] According to them, the latter has been well developed in the international norms literature, but the former has not been well defined or operationalized. This book illustrates that compliance with international norms often hinges on the domestic legitimacy of the norm as at least partially determined by the degree of conflict with relevant domestic norms.

Within the constructivist approach to the study of norms, there is an increasing focus on cross-country comparisons in an attempt to explain norm adoption; these comparisons give more attention to domestic nonstate actors and domestic structures in their explanations.[21] In Japan, the story of norm adoption differs from the studies mentioned earlier because of a lack of advocates on a particular issue, such as refugee policy, or because domestic actors are linked to but do not mobilize a transnational network to pressure the state, as in the case of those advocating adoption of CEDAW in the 1980s. It is often the case in Japan that domestic advocates working on a particular issue may not even be linked in a national movement; this, of course, hinders a broadly based movement from efficiently networking internationally and limits the ability of transnational networks to influence decision making.[22] Many studies in which the role of domestic nonstate actors figures prominently examine cases where those actors are working in favor of adopting and implementing the norms in question, often by going outside a resistant state to exert pressure on it. In the case of refugee policy in Japan, this model does not apply because there were no real domestic advocates for adoption in the early 1980s. In the case of CEDAW, rather than going outside the state to exert pressure for adoption, nonstate actors used their ties to the state and mobilized a broader set of domestic advocates to achieve their goals. Chan-Tiberghien observes a similar phenomenon in her study of human rights norms in Japan, where, she argues, "Leverage politics through alliance with target domestic politicians" is one of three mechanisms of international norm diffusion in Japan.[23]

When most studies discuss adoption, they do not focus on why international norms that conflict with domestic norms are adopted, and few studies go further to examine compliance with these controversial norms. How do we measure compliance, especially if there are no international enforcement mechanisms to keep track of it? Implementing norms through establishing government institutions, creating new laws or changing existing laws to bring them into line with international commitments, and a general acknowledgment of legitimacy of the norm as indicated by the willingness of actors (state and nonstate) to alter their behavior help move toward compliance, but they are not sufficient conditions to ensure compliance with international norms, especially when those norms conflict with domestic norms. Even if international norms are implemented, compliance can still be hindered by lack of enforcement of laws, weak laws, or refusal of officials or the general public to recognize the commitments as legitimate. Strong laws, law enforcement, and recognition of the legitimacy of international norms are practices that move states toward increased identification with norms and compliance. There are few studies that can help answer the question why these kinds of norms are adopted in the first place. As mentioned earlier, most studies hold that states will be reluctant to adopt norms that conflict with domestic culture, and if these norms are adopted, they will be difficult to implement, if they are implemented at all, but these studies do not actually account for adoption beyond reliance on instrumental reasoning, and they rely on domestic politics to explain norm adoption.

Risse, Ropp, and Sikkink (1999) address the issue of how international norms affect domestic politics by linking these norms to changing state practices in the area of human rights. They develop a socialization model to investigate how ideas and norms on human rights influence domestic human rights practices. This approach recognizes that norm adoption initially may be purely instrumental, but this can change over the course of adoption and implementation. Although instrumental reasoning is a rationalist motivation, it is not necessarily related to a specific material benefit but is connected to a state's desire for international legitimacy. The authors state, "In addition to securing domestic consent and legitimacy, states also seek international legitimacy. . . . Some states are keenly aware of the approval of other states. Through processes of persuasion and socialization, states communicate the emergent norms of international society, create ingroups and outgroups as normative communities, and may convince norm-violating states that the benefits of membership outweigh the costs."[24] Seeking legitimacy is thus seeking to be a part of a community; being a legitimate actor in a community not only requires internalizing an external standard but also depends on intersubjective identity formation with others in the community[25] and differentiating the self from others.[26]

Nonstate actors have successfully used their ability to frame issues and to teach states how to understand issues in a socialization process that continues through both adoption and compliance.[27] Socialization processes are relational. They call our attention to relations between states and within states and to the role of state identity in these relations. In his study of the taboo associated with using chemical weapons in warfare, Price (1997) argues that part of the stigma attached to chemical weapons is the idea that they are the "poor man's" nuclear weapons. Thus many states observe the norm of nonuse of chemical weapons because they are understood as a weapon of the weak. A particular identity—a negative one—is attached to using these weapons. Observing the norm is not the result of the regulative nature of the norm but of its constitutive nature. Practices surrounding use and nonuse help constitute state identity and interests. Even in cases where the weapons have been used, justifications for and initial denial of use legitimize and strengthen the taboo. Tannenwald's (1999) discussion of the nuclear weapons taboo, which, she argues, is part of the contemporary civilization discourse, furthers the idea that the "logic of appropriateness" that most constructivist norms scholars recognize as the underlying motivation for particular state action has a dimension that is only beginning to be adequately explored in the international norms literature. In other words, constructivists who claim that identity is important in norm adoption and that identity and interests are mutually constituted need to explore more explicitly the idea that some identities are more appropriate than others for membership in the international community and the implications of that idea for a state's legitimacy. Who decides what is appropriate, how does this become institutionalized, what are the consequences for inappropriateness, and how does identity affect a state's legitimacy?

Many scholars point out the importance of state identity as one component of determining whether states will adopt international norms.[28] According to Risse, Ropp, and Sikkink, for states, "what I want depends to a large degree on who I am. Identities then define the range of interests of actors considered as both possible and appropriate. Identities also provide a measure of inclusion and exclusion by defining a social 'we' and delineating the boundaries against the 'others.' Norms become relevant and causally consequential during the process by which actors define and refine their collective identities and interests."[29] One essential element missing from this formulation is the process of making and remaking state identity and how this is involved in decisions regarding adoption of international norms. I am not arguing that there is a discreet state identity on each issue; rather, each issue invokes varying components of an integrated state identity. State identity is the result of political practices that constitute the self. With this in mind, I further suggest that sometimes "who I want to be" and "who others think I am" are also important.[30] This intersubjective identity formation contributes to development of a standard of behavior required for states to gain and maintain international legitimacy.

Identity is thus not just who I am but also who I want to become. These decisions are not based on purely instrumental reasoning. Although it is clear that sometimes human rights norms are initially adopted for purely strategic or instrumental reasons, the effect of adoption on domestic structures is that it "sets into motion a process of identity transformation, so that norms initially adopted for instrumental reasons, are later maintained for reasons of belief and identity,"[31] thereby illustrating the mutual constitution of identities and interests. In my analysis of records from committee meetings in the lower house of the Japanese Diet (Japan's parliament) on the three issues I consider, I have found that adoption of international norms that conflict with domestic norms is closely related to identity formation that can be located in the discussions on adoption. To even justify considering adoption, Diet members invoke identity.

Throughout this book, I explore the discursive construction of tension between state identity and international norms, on the one hand, and domestic norms and national identity, on the other, and how advocacy of particular action on the issues I study appeals to one or the other. I draw attention to the domestic/international divide that characterizes much of the scholarship that seeks to explain Japan's adoption of CEDAW, the Refugee Convention, and the Ottawa Convention, as well as norms literature more generally. Appeals to domestic norms that help shape national identity are often, although not always, conservative in nature because they are intrinsically connected to those factors that individuals who are part of a nation understand as the basis for their sameness— those things that according to its members make a national community unique, bind them together as a community, and distinguish them from outsiders. Members of national communities often react in ways that they believe protect that community. Protection is usually based on conservative ideas of more clearly distinguishing the community in question from nonmembers and more clearly defining the lines that separate the two.

Although national identity pressures exert a conservative pull that in effect rejects change and threatens prospects for both adoption of and compliance with CEDAW and the Refugee Convention, there are also state identity pressures that cannot be ignored. As stated earlier, state identity is both subjective and intersubjective. Thus a given state's identity is partly constituted by how others view it. Just as national identity is closely tied to domestic norms, state identity is related to a state's desire for legitimacy in the international arena. Gaining this legitimacy might require a state to be more progressive and, in the cases I consider, adopt international norms that may conflict with domestic norms.

International legitimacy is a key concept because it calls into question the reasons that states sign on to international law and adopt international norms. Some studies recognize that states seek international legitimacy, but the idea that identity and legitimacy are important motivators, sometimes as important as economic interests, is an underlying claim that is not explicitly investigated. If one views international relations as a social activity, it makes sense to examine international legitimacy. At the root of international legitimacy is a sense of community, power, hierarchy, and ambition—there is something to be gained, but that something is not necessarily material benefit. What is at stake is the very identity of a state. State desire for legitimacy is historically contingent, context based, and intersubjective.[32] Not only does it rely on relations between the state in question and other states, international organizations and transnational civil society, but also tense relations with one significant actor on one particular issue, such as trade, contribute to identity shift—often on other issues—in the state that is seeking legitimacy. Thus a state's desire for legitimacy at any given time relies on its relations with others and how those others view it. Many studies of legitimacy and compliance focus on the legitimacy of norms, rules, and institutions. Here I shift the focus to the legitimacy of a particular institution—the Japanese state. Legitimacy of norms partly grows out of the institutions—including states—from which they emerge. There is a dynamic relationship between them and domestic norms. It is thus possible that shaping a state identity that is beneficial for increasing international legitimacy may create conflict with domestic norms.

In the nineteenth and twentieth centuries, international legitimacy of states was closely tied to the "standard of civilization" that was the foundation of modern international society.[33] The standard of civilization reflected the norms of European international order that were rooted in Christianity and set the terms for non-European states entering international society. These included guarantee of basic rights for citizens and noncitizens, establishment of a political bureaucracy to administer the state and the ability to organize self-defense, adherence to international law in addition to maintaining a domestic legal system to protect citizens and noncitizens, maintenance of avenues for diplomacy, and finally, conforming to the "accepted norms and practices of the 'civilized' international society."[34] In order to become a member of international society, states that did not share the norms of European civilization were subject to a civilizing process that used domination, often in the form of unequal treaties, to draw non-European states like Japan into international society. Thus, at the time of its entry into the international system in the late nineteenth century, Japan was a threat to international order precisely because it did not meet the standard of civilization and was outside the international system itself. After Japan was compelled to sign unequal treaties between 1854 and 1858, Japanese leaders focused on consolidating state power and were preoccupied with the push to modernize, industrialize, and civilize Japan.

In today's world, standards of behavior that help constitute state identity and play a role in states' gaining and maintaining legitimacy are present in discourses of civilization. These discourses set the parameters for legitimizing states and state action and have replaced the standard of civilization and the associated unequal treaties. Japan was finally accepted as a civilized country, partly because of its defeat of Russia in the Russo-Japanese War (1904–5). According to Gong, "Even Japan, which consciously and conscientiously made fulfilling the standard of 'civilization' a national goal, found the path to accreditation as a 'civilized' power long and difficult."[35] Even after Japan had fulfilled the standard of civilization, treatment by civilized Western states did not reflect this.[36] Rumelili's (2003, 2008) analysis of Greece and Turkey as liminal states in relation to Europe—states that are both self and other—offers us new insights about Japan's precarious position in the nineteenth-century European world order and today. In the case of Japan, the discourses and practices that are necessary to differentiate civilized from uncivilized states—the very practices that allow Japan to become a member of the civilized states, including adhering to international law—also serve to sustain conflict, with especially significant consequences for a liminal state such as Japan. Suzuki's (2005) analysis of Japan's socialization into European international society at the end of the nineteenth century challenges the view that collective identity norms and cooperation engendered by mutual respect for sovereign independence that were the basis of international society can be credited with providing greater order at the end of the nineteenth century by exploring the connection between the rise of Japanese imperialism and the state's socialization into the European international order. Suzuki is careful to point out that he is not suggesting that Japan's entry into international society was responsible for Japan's colonial pursuits. However, the broader point that studies of international society ignore how the standard of civilization played a role in disciplining states, creating difference, providing justification for imperial projects, and colonizing the "uncivilized" alerts us to the different and multiple interpretations that non-European states may have had of the European standard of civilization. Suzuki argues that Japan's interpretation of European international society called for the state to pursue cooperative policies with "civilized" European states and coercive policies with "uncivilized" states that included Japan's Asian neighbors.[37] The innovative works of Rumelili and Suzuki help us understand how Japan's contemporary identity as both inside and outside Western collective identity makes Japanese officials particularly sensitive to Japan's identity and to identity-based pressures of today's international community.

International Norms, International Law, and Japan

In international relations norms literature, the terms *international law* and *international norms* are often used interchangeably. The theoretical and empirical significance of this issue—whether or not it matters if something is a norm or a law—means that at least some conceptual clarity is important. In this book, I understand international laws as legal norms that are codified while social norms are not. Constructivists differ on whether and how the distinction between social and legal norms matters.[38] In general, both social and legal norms constitute the normative structure within which states act, so there is no distinction between the two on this score. However, Japanese courts have referred to relevant international law in landmark decisions, such as the Ana Bortz[39] antidiscrimination case that was decided in favor of the plaintiff on the basis of the Convention for the Elimination of Racial Discrimination in 1999 and in the Sumitomo cases discussed in Chapter 4. Given that in the past, Japanese courts have been reluctant to refer to international law, recent decisions such as these two cases are significant developments.[40] These decisions suggest that international law may have a new and important role in Japan that is based on a code of legal norms. In Japan, there is a close link between international law—legal norms—and domestic law because treaty adoption usually leads to changes in existing laws or creation of new ones to implement the treaty. The ability of complainants to use international legal norms as a tool is important, but these legal norms also have significant constitutive effects. This does not mean, however, that social norms are any less important in shaping state interests and identity. Indeed, as Gurowitz (2004, 2006) points out, diffuse social norms shape identities of modern states and play a significant role in framing policy arguments for immigrant rights in Japan.[41] In the cases I study, my analysis focuses on adoption of and compliance with international treaties—legal norms. Because, as Reus-Smit (2004) convincingly argues, international law and international politics are mutually constituted, it is impossible to understand international law and international politics without considering the social milieu in which they are both embedded. Social norms are an important part of this milieu. In the case of CEDAW, for example, women's rights and gender equality are the (evolving) social norms that underlie the treaty.

Codified law does not exist apart from interpretations of the law and the goal of achieving norms of behavior that result. Japan's historical encounters with and adoption of global norms since the Meiji era demonstrate the connection between and inseparability of social and legal norms. The 1854 military and diplomatic mission of the United States headed by Commodore Matthew Perry was a decisive point for Japan and continues to loom large in Japanese reflections on the country's modern history—the "forced" opening of Japan is legendary. Although some argue that this encounter was not an "opening" at all, given the history of trading with the Dutch, the Chinese, and others,[42] and therefore not the revolutionary event that it is often made out to be, the encounter with Western military power was significant because it marked a turning point in diplomatic relations between Japan and the West. Perhaps most important is that this mission and the unequal treaties that Japan was forced to sign with the United States, Great Britain, France, Russia, and the Netherlands between 1854 and 1858 established a lasting connection between treaty making and conflict with the West.[43] The extraterritorial rights of these treaties—which were expanded to include other European countries and governed relations between Japan and the West for the next forty years— were the core characteristic of the agreements that were seen as a national humiliation that Meiji leaders worked to undo after the restoration of the emperor to power in 1868. China's defeat in the Opium War (1839–42) and the failure of Japan's Iwakura Mission (1871–73) to the United States and Europe to renegotiate the unequal treaties impressed on Japan the importance of strengthening its international position. Meiji leaders were convinced that the way to accomplish this was by thoroughly adapting to global norms—Westernization—which would establish Japan as a civilized country. "Civilization and enlightenment" (*bunmei kaika*) became the goal of Meiji leaders and the basis of Japan's modernization.

Efforts to Westernize affected all areas of life, including dress and hairstyles, sexual mores, state making and conceptions of state power, measurement of time, education, and diet. These were not superficial changes; they had wide-ranging effects on the legitimacy of the Japanese state both at home and abroad. Cwiertka's (2006) study of the connections between food and social and political transformation in the nineteenth and twentieth centuries demonstrates the important role that Western food and foodways played in Japan's efforts to become a civilized state. According to her analysis, introducing Western food into the emperor's diet served two important functions in the late nineteenth century: first, it strengthened the Japanese government's authority by demonstrating Japan's affiliation with the West; and second, it demonstrated the emperor's status as a modern monarch.[44] Because of the meat-eating taboo, public reports that the emperor regularly ate meat had great symbolic value. Equating meat eating with civilization illustrates the symbolic value of the emperor's reported meat eating—it demonstrated Japan's status as a modern nation.[45]

In the early twentieth century, Japanese beef consumption became closely connected to two other important aspects of Japan's civilization project or adoption of global norms—war and colonization—and nutrition policies designed to strengthen Japan's military by incorporating more meat influenced civilian consumption. Japan's victory in the Russo-Japanese War is noted for the prestige that Japan earned in the eyes of Western countries;[46] less recognized, however, is the importance of Korean beef in fueling Japan's military, both during the Russo-Japanese War and later in Japan's military buildup in China in the 1930s. Once Japan annexed Korea in 1910, the Japanese population could consume beef at cheaper prices, and thus a larger proportion of common people could participate in this marker of Japan's modernity.[47]

The Meiji leaders faced threats both within and outside Japan. The connection between the humiliation of the unequal treaties and the social and political unrest that led to the Meiji Restoration meant that the new political leaders had to deal with the fact that things Western represented modernity, power, insecurity, danger, and threat to the domestic population. In addition to improving their international position, civilizing processes also helped Meiji leaders consolidate their power, establish their legitimacy, extend their authority, and promote social and political cohesion by creating a Japanese national identity. Thus Westernization, civilization, and the adoption of global norms were important both domestically and internationally. The promulgation of the Meiji Constitution in 1889 signaled the adoption of Western norms of governance and added to the symbols of Japan's civilization. Just as Western-style banquets in Cwiertka's analysis were used for the dual purpose of impressing foreign dignitaries with Japan's level of civilization and strengthening the Meiji ruler's domestic authority by manipulating powerful images of the West, the constitutional ceremonies in 1889 had to demonstrate Japan's modernity and civilization to the foreign dignitaries, as well as maintain the legitimacy of the emperor's rule to the domestic audience. In this instance, both of these ends could not be achieved with one ceremony, so there were dual ceremonies—a Western one with all the pomp and circumstance appropriate for establishing a modern constitutional monarchy, and one that observed Japanese customs that established the emperor's legitimacy by reaffirming the ruling house as descended from the sun goddess.[48] Establishing Japan as worthy of a position among the civilized states of the West had to be balanced against securing the legitimacy of the Meiji rulers among the domestic population. European notions of race, progress, and civilization also significantly affected the government's approach to establishing clearly the northern and southern borders through annexation and the imposition of colonial assimilation policies in Ainu lands to the north and the Ryukyus in the south that were essential in establishing national identity and social cohesion.[49]

Morris-Suzuki (1998) points out that an important part of this balancing between international and domestic demands involves Japanese (local) interpretations of international law. These interpretations fill international norms with local content.[50] Through this process unequal treaties not only can result in establishing formal requirements such as extraterritoriality but also can lead to adoption of dietary norms, such as consuming meat, and norms of governance, such as constitutions, among others.

The same themes are present in contemporary international relations studies of the impact of international norms on Japan. In their attempts to explain Japan's adoption of international norms and understand the impact of contemporary international norms on Japan, these studies point to the continuing significance of a nuanced understanding of the relationship between international norms and domestic politics and how both international and domestic political practices make and remake Japan's identity. Studies demonstrate the role of collective identity norms in determining flexibility of Japan's internal and external security policy.[51] They demonstrate how domestic actors mobilize international law protecting refugees to demand recognition of migrant rights,[52] and the role of domestic NGO networks in diffusing human rights norms related to women and children.[53] Other studies move beyond human rights issues while retaining a focus on how international norms shape the development of Japanese civil society organizations working in the area of development assistance; these studies also make significant contributions to uncovering the implications of international norms for changing state-society relations in Japan in the 1980s and 1990s.[54] In many of these studies, especially those that take norm diffusion as their subject, NGOs and other civil society organizations figure prominently. Those studies that deal most directly with questions of identity offer a wider variety of empirical cases, such as global wildlife preservation norms, whose adoption is attributed to collective legitimation of norms of international society.[55] Some of the most creative and insightful research on how international norms affect Japan's domestic political landscape focuses on the creation and contestation of meaning, which is a significant part of the struggle over ideas that accompanies norm adoption in areas as diverse as leisure policy and transnational crime.[56] The Japanese state's role in tourism and leisure policy illustrates its struggle to control the impact of international norms on Japanese identity.[57] Leheny's (2006) excellent study of transnational crime demonstrates how the meanings of international norms created to address transnational crime are reformulated in the domestic context. The three variables I study, strength of domestic advocates, state desire for legitimacy, and conflict between international and domestic norms, and the three issues I examine, appropriate roles for women, what it means to be Japanese, and conceptions of national security, complement existing studies while offering new insights on how international norms affect Japan's domestic political landscape.

CHAPTER 3

Refugees, Identity, and Foreignness in Japan

In 1978, I received a letter from a friend in Canada. The letter said that Japan had not done anything for refugees and that it was a shameful country with a cold heart. I was shocked by the letter and could not sit idle after reading such words. I thought about how we could overcome the misunderstanding and show the traditional goodwill of Japanese people to the rest of the world.
—Soma Yukika (founder of the Association for Aid and Relief [formerly the Association for Aid to Refugees]), *Daily Yomiuri*, October 5, 1999

As a matter of national policy, Japan absolutely does not accept foreigners.
—Immigration Bureau Chief Kosugi Teruo, Ministry of Justice, Judicial Affairs Committee meeting, lower house, November 5, 1980

Beyond Rationalist Foreign Pressure

When Japan adopted the Refugee Convention, there were no material international pressures, no public support for allowing refugees to resettle in Japan, and no domestic advocates lobbying for creation of a coherent policy regarding refugees, and there was a high degree of conflict between international and domestic norms on this issue. Yet Japan adopted the Refugee Convention and reformed legislation to be more in line with international directives. How do we account for this? Given the high degree of conflict between international and domestic norms and the fact that there were no domestic advocates on this issue, state identity does most of the explanatory work in accounting for why and how Japan adopted the Refugee Convention.

We would expect that in the adoption phase, a high degree of conflict, such as that which characterized the refugee issue (and later, women's employment), does indeed offer a challenge. However, in both of these cases, the high degree of conflict was not enough to hinder adoption, although it did impede achieving a high level of compliance. A high level of compliance depends on achieving "a state of conformity or identity between an actor's behavior and a specific rule";[1] in other words, state identity is reconstituted as state interests on a particular issue continue to change and gradually become more settled after a new norm is adopted. Domestic advocates play a particularly important role during this phase. Because adoption does not mean the end of conflict between domestic and international norms, the work of domestic advocates in pushing implementation (defined as formally codifying the norms in question into domestic legislation, creation of institutions, and establishing rules) to ensure compliance is essential. For instance, a state might implement the Refugee Convention by amending necessary immigration laws, but if these laws do not achieve a taken-for-granted quality because judges refuse to hear cases or do not affirm relevant laws in their decisions, the result is a low level of compliance. On the refugee issue, domestic advocates may increase the level of compliance by supporting stronger legislation, demanding greater transparency in decision-making procedures regarding asylum applications to guard against arbitrary decisions, or assisting asylum seekers in bringing cases that require decisions based on established legislation either to confirm authority of that legislation or to illustrate areas where the existing legal instruments are inadequate and ensure that these gaps are addressed. All these actions help move toward identification with the norm and higher levels of compliance.

Before 1975, the year in which Indochinese refugees began arriving in Japan, there was no understanding of the term *refugee* among the Japanese population.[2] What is even more remarkable is that although Japan has large populations of Koreans and some Taiwanese who had been living in Japan for one or two generations, there was no systematic process for granting permanent residence to foreigners. In 1980 a poll showed that only 3 percent of Japanese surveyed were in favor of allowing refugees to resettle in Japan,[3] but in 1981 Japan adopted the International Refugee Convention. In this chapter, I explain why Japan adopted the Refugee Convention despite the challenge that it posed to one of the most powerful and important domestic norms in Japan: what it means to be Japanese.

One obvious explanation is that adopting the Refugee Convention coincided with low unemployment rates and a high demand for labor to continue economic growth. It is true that during the "Indochinese refugee crisis" preference was given to those who had worked for a Japanese company abroad or had studied in Japan. This preference was based on the belief that those who had such experiences would find it easier to adjust to life in Japan and would find work more easily.[4] Yet once the government decided to allow Indochinese to settle in Japan, the numbers accepted were too low to affect the labor market, as I will show later. Furthermore, the government had to offer companies incentives to hire refugees. Another explanation presented in the literature on Japan's foreign policy focuses on the importance of foreign pressure (usually from the United States) in shaping Japan's policies. Foreign pressure as it is narrowly conceived in literature on it provides an incomplete explanation of why Japan adopted the Refugee Convention. Equating foreign pressure with material pressure is especially problematic in this case because there was no material benefit to Japan in signing the convention; in fact, it led to material costs. Moreover, these theories do not satisfactorily explain why foreign pressure is so effective in Japan. My argument focuses on the importance of foreign pressure by taking into account state identity as it is historically constituted and discursively constructed on this issue. Exploring identity-based international pressure helps us better understand the role it plays in shaping Japan's adoption of international norms. In the remainder of this section, I analyze three explanations for why Japan adopted the Refugee Convention. I show why these explanations are inadequate—one even includes the kinds of arguments that assume Japanese uniqueness, which I will argue against—and explicate my own argument.

The few studies that address why Japan adopted the Refugee Convention focus on explanations that include both an international and a domestic component. However, privileging one of these dimensions over the other (Koizumi 1992; Landis 1996), not recognizing or fully exploring the connection between the two (Landis 1996; Mizuno 1990), or failing to examine the roots of the domestic and international processes at work in this case (Gurowitz 1999b) are major shortcomings. Koizumi (1992) argues that Japan adopted the convention to adjust to a more active role in international cooperation under pressure from the United States and Europe. To support this argument, he discusses domestic opposition to refugee resettlement in Japan. He argues that this opposition was based on geographical isolation that resulted in a lack of influence from other nations, the homogeneous ethnic origins and unique language of Japan, and highly restricted immigration in Japan; a limited amount of land to sustain the population; and the origination of the refugees from Asia.[5] A major shortcoming of Koizumi's explanation is that he sets up international and domestic influences in opposition to each other, which hinders an investigation of how the two interacted in influencing Japan's adoption of the Refugee Convention. For example, the point that the refugees were from Asia is important because it tells us something about how Japan positions itself in the international community vis-à-vis Asia and the West, but

Koizumi does not explore this at all. Moreover, he does not discuss how Japan's national identity—especially the myth of homogeneity—relates to the state's identity construction. In fact, he unquestioningly accepts Japan's "uniqueness."

In her assessment of why Japan adopts international norms, Gurowitz (1999b) agrees with Koizumi on the importance of foreign pressure when she writes that being a reactive state "leads to a pattern of adopting necessary international norms, sometimes wholeheartedly, but doing so not because those norms are seen as relating to domestic politics or as an extension of Japanese domestic norms, but because norm adoption is seen as necessary to exist in the outside world. When those norms clash with domestic norms, and when external pressure is not sufficiently strong, the government is reluctant to adopt them."[6] Thus Gurowitz agrees with Checkel (1997) on the importance of the fit between domestic and international norms for norm adoption. My research indicates that this point holds in the cases of the Refugee Convention and CEDAW, but they were adopted in the end. Gurowitz's further point, that norm adoption in Japan is based on necessity, offers an opening to develop new theoretical insights. Her work hints at but does not pursue the importance of foreign pressure as more than just material pressure. Throughout this book, I develop an argument that foreign pressure is effective in Japan insofar as it includes identity pressures that serve to socialize Japan into international society. Although Gurowitz considers the role of nonstate actors in using international norms once they have been adopted, she does not consider how adoption can hinge on their actions (as well as the actions of other domestic advocates). The role of domestic advocates is especially important when there is conflict between domestic and international norms.

Landis (1996), on the other hand, argues that "in the late '70s and early '80s, as part of an effort to counteract its xenophobic global image and demonstrate influence commensurate with its economic power, Japan embarked on a program of internationalization, *kokusaika*, involving the signing of numerous international agreements."[7] This explanation focuses on the international dimension of norm adoption while only implicitly referencing the domestic dimension, but does not engage the latter at all. Mizuno (1990) argues that a combination of international pressure and public sympathy for refugees accounts for Japan adopting the Refugee Convention. Although his explanation bridges international and domestic factors to explain why Japan adopted the convention, he does not recognize the ongoing tension between the two and the effect that this has on compliance. I show that the tension between international and domestic norms on this issue was negotiated in a way that allowed for adoption of the treaty but hindered compliance. I also show that the general public does not influence political decisions, especially controversial ones, as easily as Mizuno would have us believe. In the next chapter, we see how such barriers to compliance can be overcome.

None of these arguments offers a satisfactory explanation of why the Japanese government responds to foreign pressure or why decision makers and the public are concerned with Japan's identity abroad. Most rely on rationalist explanations of power and self-interest. Although these are certainly part of the story, they are incomplete explanations that do little to advance understanding of the production and reproduction of social aspects of world politics that affect state behavior. This chapter traces two conflicting impulses that have shaped Japan's response to international pressures regarding refugees and affected adoption of and compliance with the Refugee Convention. The first impulse comes from the state's identity as a member of the international community, with obligations to act accordingly. Japan understands itself as an "economic power" and a "developed country" and believes that it has international duties based on these identities. Pressure to fulfill these duties is heightened by Japan's hypersensitivity to criticism and embarrassment. The second impulse, in contrast, emerges from Japanese national identity, which conceptualizes the Japanese nation as a biological race. The nation is conceived as a homogeneous one, and this conception has resulted in a history of immigration restrictions and discrimination against non-Japanese to preserve the nation.

Two primary components of Japan's identity are its economic power and its democratic government. As an economic power, Japan has particular international obligations that increased as it became wealthier. The international obligations of democratic countries are a new phenomenon and increase with increasing power. A state does not have power or become a powerful international actor simply by virtue of being a democracy. To some extent, international political power rests on material capabilities and how states understand the normative obligations that accompany these capabilities. Obligations are part of state identity to the extent that they are shaped by the perception of others, and they grow, at least in part, out of meanings that are attached to identity. Japan's identity as a democracy mediates the actions taken to fulfill these obligations. In this case, state desire for legitimacy accounts for why Japan adopted the Refugee Convention. This case illustrates that the degree of conflict between domestic and international norms does not matter as much as the international norms literature assumes that it does during the adoption phase, when desire for legitimacy is high. Although considering state interests and identity helps us understand why Japan adopted the Refugee Convention, it does not address the question of compliance with the convention.

Examining the particular context in which adoption took place, including the perception of foreignness that has developed over the years, helps us see how the understanding of foreignness in Japan informs the understanding of the refugee in a way that highlights the conflict between Japan's impulse to fully participate in international society and its impulse to protect the nation, which hinders compliance with the convention. Both state and national identity thus shape the action taken on the convention. Although the historical roots predate 1945, it is important that we recognize that World War II and the changes in the international political order that have taken place since then heavily influence Japan's contemporary identity.

By the late 1970s, when the refugee issue was on Japan's doorstep, its identity as an international economic power had been established, but the obligations that accompanied this new role were not yet clear. Until this point, Japan's recognition of its new role was limited to providing increasing levels of foreign aid to poor countries and donations to international organizations. In the 1970s there were moves to increase Japan's international legitimacy by adopting international human rights instruments, but these actions were not enough to curb criticism of Japan's treatment of refugees.

The remainder of this chapter is divided into four sections. I first outline historical processes that helped constitute Japan's state and national identity. I then move on to a more specific discussion of Japan's adoption of the International Refugee Convention. The following section will focus on compliance with the convention, and highlight the conflict between state and national identity and the acceptance of refugees. The concluding section reviews the role that identity plays in norm adoption in this case.

Historical Processes and Making the Nation: Conflict Between International and Domestic Norms

The relevant international norms in the area of refugee policy are Articles 24 and 34 of the Refugee Convention. Article 24 of the convention calls on contracting states to treat refugees in the same way as their own nationals with regard to social security benefits. Article 34 deals with the issue of naturalization and calls on the contracting states to "facilitate the assimilation and naturalization of refugees . . . [and to] make every effort to expedite naturalization proceedings."[8] To comply with the Refugee Convention, Japan changed several laws, including the National Pension Law of 1959 (revised in 1982 to abolish the citizenship requirement) and the National Health Insurance Law of 1958 (amended in 1986 to abolish the citizenship requirement).[9] In addition, Japan passed the Immigration

Control and Refugee Recognition Act, which went into force in 1982 to help implement the convention. Despite these legal changes and the fact that Japan increased the number of Indochinese refugees the country would accept four times between 1979 (when it first agreed to accept refugees) and 1985, the Japanese government did not fully comply with the commitments illustrated in Articles 24 and 34 of the Refugee Convention.[10]

The international norms codified in the Refugee Convention directly challenged the domestic norm of what it means to be Japanese and the general understanding of Japan as a homogeneous nation by requiring that the government accept refugees who might choose to stay in Japan and by forcing the Japanese government to change existing laws that discriminated against non-Japanese. These new laws would have the secondary effect of making Japan's invisible minorities more visible. Before signing the convention, Japan still had not extended social security benefits, such as pensions, to the country's Korean permanent residents. In fact, in its first report to the United Nations Human Rights Committee, the Japanese government stated, "The right of any person to enjoy his own culture, to profess and practice his religion or to use his own language is ensured under Japanese law. However, minorities of the kind mentioned in the [International Covenant on Civil and Political Rights] do not exist in Japan."[11] Although in some cases Koreans had been living in Japan for two generations, and Japanese was the first language of many of them, the Japanese government resisted extending any benefits to them because they were still foreigners. Even today, the phrase for permanent Korean residents, *zainichi kankoku chosenjin*, or *zainichi* for short—literally, North and South Koreans temporarily living in Japan—connotes the expectation that this situation is not permanent. Moreover, the question of citizenship for permanent Korean residents had just recently been settled in 1965. Twenty years after the end of World War II, the Japanese and Korean governments finally agreed that Koreans in Japan would be granted "special permanent resident" status and would retain their Korean citizenship if they adopted South Korean citizenship. If the Japanese government had a difficult time fully integrating its permanent residents into society and in fact resisted measures that would move toward accomplishing this, what would be the reaction to accepting refugees into Japan with the possibility that they would want to permanently settle there and perhaps seek Japanese citizenship?

When states establish refugee policies, they are making a statement on how the nation views itself and who can legitimately reproduce the nation.[12] Japan's desire to preserve its identity as a homogeneous nation clearly conflicts with the desires to fulfill the expectations of the country as a world power and to maintain that position in the face of criticism on other fronts (for example, unfair trading practices). Japan's identity as an ethnically homogeneous society is not to be underestimated in terms of its importance as a project of both the state and society.[13] Indeed, many Japanese—including government officials—consider their so-called homogeneity an important part of the economic miracle; this miracle was beginning to pay off just when the numbers of foreigners began to increase. Thus it became necessary to limit the number and kind of foreigners allowed into Japan while reinforcing the homogeneous national identity. Furthermore, the idea of nation as family was upheld by the Meiji reformers with the aim of securing political loyalty to the emperor and hence the state for the purpose of becoming an industrialized country and gaining recognition as a legitimate world power. In other words, the biological basis of the nation was framed as a fundamental motivation for rapid industrialization at the end of the nineteenth century. It is worth recalling that state building in Japan rested on consolidating the nation through processes of domination and exclusion for dealing with social minorities such as *burakumin* (descendents of a social outcaste group of feudal Japan), the indigenous Ainu, and Okinawans.[14]

Japan's exclusive national identity shapes how the government deals with policies regarding the acceptance of outsiders, including the extent to which they can be integrated.[15] In the 1980s, when there was concern about the influx of migrants in many Western industrialized countries in the face of economic slowdowns, Japan was still experiencing high growth and a shortage of workers.[16] Throughout the high-growth period of the 1970s and 1980s, the government and industry devised a number of policies and practices to avoid having to resort to migrant labor to fill worker shortages. These included moving plants abroad, encouraging technological innovation, and employing more women to reduce the need for unskilled and semiskilled labor.[17] Despite these efforts, undocumented migrant workers moved to Japan to fill the demand for labor. As the national debate over the "threat" that foreign workers posed to Japanese society intensified, the Japanese government allowed the employment of *nikkeijin* (descendants of Japanese emigrants), starting in 1990, and instituted policies to facilitate their migration from Brazil and Peru "in the belief that this would relieve the demands of both employers and workers, while emphasizing the importance of cultural uniformity and ancestry. In short, employment of *nikkeijin* was encouraged because they do not 'look like foreign workers.' "[18] Although this preference for foreigners of Japanese ancestry is no different from U.S. immigration law that historically gave preference to North Europeans, the most interesting element of this policy is its roots in the discourse of foreign workers as "threats" even though their numbers were relatively low. This view and the government response to it reveal the importance of the belief in homogeneity for national identity. To go to the trouble of incurring the costs associated with establishing special benefits to encourage *nikkeijin* to move to Japan, thereby setting up a hierarchy of immigrant groups, illustrates the belief that these workers were less foreign, somehow more desirable, and less threatening than others.[19]

The 1938 National Mobilization Act placed Korean material and human resources under Japanese control and allowed the government to forcibly send Koreans to Japan to provide labor needed for the war effort; this forced migration led to the transfer of more than one million Koreans to Japan.[20] Although colonial subjects faced harsh discrimination in Japan, their citizenship status and migration to Japan illustrate the fact that the idea of a homogeneous Japan was not always the hegemonic discourse in defining Japanese national identity.[21] This citizenship status lasted until 1952, when the San Francisco Peace Treaty went into effect. Even those Koreans who chose to remain in Japan after Korea was liberated in 1945 had no right to retain Japanese citizenship. In addition to symbolizing the existence of a "Japanese Empire," forcing Japanese citizenship on Koreans and other colonial subjects served several purposes. It provided a way to overcome problems posed by Koreans as outsiders in Japan, while the presence of these internal others in Japan further strengthened Japanese ethnic and cultural identity. Withdrawing Japanese citizenship with the 1952 Peace Treaty symbolized the failure of the Japanese Empire itself and the impossibility of fully incorporating foreigners into Japanese society.

Once Koreans in Japan were stripped of their citizenship status, many of them remained in a precarious position because they were not citizens and faced discrimination based on their ethnicity. After the war, approximately five hundred thousand Koreans chose to remain in Japan. Even today their descendents are required to carry alien registration cards and until 1991 were required to submit to fingerprinting to renew the cards. "Until a revision in the Nationality Law in 1985, the small number of Koreans who were successful in applying for naturalization were required to, along with all other naturalized citizens at that time, renounce their Korean culture and take a Japanese name."[22] Article 5 of the Nationality Law that required name change was revised in 1985 because it directly conflicted with Article 27 of the International Covenant on Civil and Political Rights, which requires states to allow minorities to maintain their ethnic identity and cultural heritage.[23] Although name change is no longer a requirement, many who choose to naturalize still hide their ancestry to avoid discrimination. The idea that renouncing one's culture and taking a Japanese name would aid in transforming one into a Japanese illustrates the kind of cultural exclusivity that is codified in Japanese laws. It indicates a belief in the idea of an essence of Japaneseness that is transmitted through culture. The open rejection of cultural mixing signals cultural stasis and rigidity; not only is Japanese culture handed down through generations, but the "fact" that it never changes reinforces the unity of the nation.

The postwar period was not only a time to rebuild Japan's political institutions, physical infrastructure, and economy but also a time when the country had to reestablish its identity in the international community. By the 1970s it was clear that Japan's identity would be based on its growing economic power. However, the demands of this identity were not at all clear. Adopting international norms would help establish Japan as a legitimate international actor, but adopting the norms also challenged fundamental domestic norms.

Adopting the Refugee Convention: Government Initiative and State Identity

The first Vietnamese asylum seekers arrived in Japan on May 12, 1975, nine people who had been rescued at sea by an American ship. After the fall of Saigon on April 30, 1975, Japan faced two years of a constant, albeit small, flow of refugees. On September 20, 1977, the Japanese government decided to establish a committee composed of representatives from five ministries that deal with issues related to Indochinese: Foreign Affairs, Justice, Labor, Education, and Welfare. The result was the development of programs and institutions to deal specifically with Indochinese refugees.[24] In general, Indochinese refugees who resettled in Japan received permanent residence status without being recognized as refugees by the Japanese government. The procedures that were established to address the crisis in the mid-1970s to early 1980s indicated the government's belief that refugee flows to Japan would be a temporary phenomenon.

Although the Japanese government began formulating a refugee policy in September 1977, most of the institutional arrangements were created on an ad hoc basis; the government never attempted to take a proactive role in formulating a systematic and comprehensive refugee policy.[25] This lack of a consistent framework is still a major shortcoming of Japan's refugee policy today, and the problem is amplified by an increase in the number of refugees from other parts of the world for whom there is no comprehensive reception policy. Although Japan was not yet a signatory of the Refugee Convention when the first refugees arrived on May 12, 1975, the government decided to comply with the United Nations High Commissioner for Refugees (UNHCR) Resolution no. 3455, Humanitarian Assistance to the Indochinese Displaced Persons. It was not until 1978, when the number of refugees began to strain the Southeast Asian countries to which most of them fled, that European countries and the United States began to heavily criticize Japan, the second-wealthiest country in the world and the wealthiest in the region, for not taking its share of the responsibility.[26]

Some might argue that this supports a foreign-pressure explanation why Japan adopted the Refugee Convention. I maintain that it does not. Of course, pressure from other countries can always be a factor in considering whether to institute certain policies, but the focus of the foreign pressure argument on material pressure, especially from the United States, as an explanation for Japanese foreign policy choices is too simplistic. In this case, willingness to make large financial contributions counters the argument based on material pressure. Given that the Japanese government was willing to spend money to avoid having actually to accept refugees, it is clear that a simple material cost-benefit analysis was not the state's primary motivating factor. It also indicates that financial contributions were not enough in the eyes of the international community. In this case, pressure originated from Japan's peers—other industrialized countries—and the goal was to force Japan to allow more refugees into the country, not to pressure Japan into adopting the convention. Given that the United States stood to benefit from Japan's willingness to spend large amounts of money in lieu of accepting refugees, U.S. pressure was clearly not based solely on material interests. Criticism from other developed countries included identity pressures that made Japan's government aware of what was expected from the world's second-largest economy. In the end, identity pressures were exerted because Japan was a powerful country with its reputation at stake, not because it was weak and inferior—an underlying assumption of the foreign-pressure thesis.

According to Honma (1990), the Japanese government moved to accept refugees because of strong political demand from the United States. After World War II, the United States viewed Japan and South Korea as important allies in the fight against the spread of communism in Asia. The fall of Saigon intensified U.S. concern and led the U.S. government to request that Western countries accept Indochinese refugees. The new fear was that the large flow of Indochinese would create economic and political stress in other Southeast Asian states that would strengthen more Communist movements in the region.[27] Thus the United States was politically motivated to accept Indochinese refugees and to ensure that other countries would as well. Because of increased unemployment, the United States started to place limits on the number of refugees who would be allowed to settle there. Until this point, approximately 70 percent of the boat people who arrived in Japan were sent to a third country, and close to 60 percent of them went to the United States. Once the United States placed limits on acceptance, the number of those who requested permission to settle in Japan increased, at least temporarily.[28]

Tracing the discursive construction of Japan's state and national identity in the *Asahi* and *Yomiuri*'s op-ed pages and committee meetings of the lower house of the Diet from 1980 to 1982 reveals four aspects of state identity that led Japan to adopt the Refugee Convention regardless of the absence of material benefits. These four aspects of state identity are Japan as a developed state, its duties and obligations to international society, the need to avoid embarrassment, and its preoccupation with avoiding isolationist tendencies. The impulse that leads Japan to be an active member of the international community is rooted in these four aspects. At the same time, a counterdiscourse of national identity manifests the second impulse— for Japan to withdraw, put up its guard, and protect the nation.

As a developed state, Japan looks to the West as its model. In the late 1800s, Western states were the models of economic development, industrial modernization, and civilization. This desire to be like the West in order to avoid being dominated by the West played an important role in Japan's political, economic, and social development. After Japan reentered international society on the basis of the democratic regime created after World War II and high economic growth that began to reap benefits in the 1970s, there were more comparisons of Japan's refugee policies, immigration laws, naturalization, and citizenship with those of Western nations. Many Diet members called on Japan to use these countries as models for how to reform Japan's own policies. Diet member Okada Masakatsu appealed to this aspect of identity when he pointed out that about eighty countries had ratified the Refugee Convention, and of the developed countries, only Japan had not ratified the convention.[29] In short, the West represented the gauge against which Japan could measure its own progress even on an issue with such a high degree of conflict between international and domestic norms.

Japan's identity as a developed state increased its sense of duties and obligations to international society.[30] In the 1970s Japan adopted several international human rights instruments. Some argue that these actions were just window dressing based on instrumental reasoning and did not amount to much actual change in Japan. Analysis of government records leads me to conclude that adopting these instruments increased the sense of duties and obligations to fulfill the "spirit" of the agreements. Throughout the records of the committee meetings, there is an appeal to international duties and obligations in the debates over the low numbers of refugees coming to Japan and the slow rate at which refugees were accepted. In 1980 the Judicial Affairs Committee was the first committee to consider the situation of refugees in Japan in its February 15 meeting. In discussions about whether Japan should adopt the Refugee Convention, the members were often sidetracked into issues that focused on the immigration management system, spreading respect for human rights throughout Japanese society, and conditions of refugees at that time. The committee members even seemed reluctant specifically to discuss adopting the convention. Some exceptions exist, such as the March 7, 1980, Budget Committee meeting. After a discussion of the 1948 Universal Declaration of Human Rights and its connection to the treatment of refugees, Diet member Yokoyama Toshiaki declared, "It is regrettable that even now, our country has neglected to ratify the Refugee Convention even though most of the world has."[31] He went on to criticize the "shameful" acts that Japan committed in deporting some asylum seekers. When the question of adoption did arise, discussion of the problems that this would cause for domestic law immediately followed, highlighting the conflict between domestic and international norms on this issue. The response to these concerns centered on Japan's identity as a member of international society and its duty to fulfill the obligations associated with that status.

The discourse on Japan's duties and obligations to international society emphasizes the last two aspects of Japan's state identity as it developed in discussions on refugee policy. First, the need to avoid embarrassment was particularly strong. Some cultural aspects of the aversion to shame probably were involved here, but Japan's identity as an insecure state in international relations with a need to obtain legitimacy in that sphere, discussed in Chapter 2, the criticisms that it faced regarding unfair trading practices, and accusations that it dumps its social problems into other countries were at least equally important. That Japan seems constantly to battle a negative image internationally says something about Japan's position in the international community. Finally, Japan's tendency to withdraw as one way of dealing with such criticism was a constant concern.

The idea of international duties and obligations is linked to discussions of the need to avoid embarrassment and isolation.[32] The need to avoid isolation does not refer just to being ostracized by the states that matter but also includes warnings for Japan to resist reverting to its own isolationist tendencies. The sense of duty does not originate from humanitarian or other moral concerns; it is instead developed from a heightened sense of awareness of Japan's international position. As such, duty is understood as performing behaviors that Diet members and bureaucrats believe a state is supposed to perform as a member of the international community. It is clear from the Diet records that officials believed that they could learn how to behave appropriately by observing "similar" states and following their lead.[33] These similar states were the developed countries of the West, not just other democracies or other Asian countries. Thus the officials were preoccupied with making decisions regarding refugees that were worthy of members of international society, were appropriate for developed countries, and would gain respect for Japan from the international community. In short, they were concerned with improving Japan's international identity and solidifying its international position through taking appropriate action.

One of the main issues in the March 7, 1980, Budget Committee meeting was that the international community had sharply criticized Japan for its strict conditions for refugee resettlement, as reported in the daily newspapers in Japan. The government was accused of focusing on insignificant technical details instead of humanitarian concerns in its decisions on admitting refugees. To counter these accusations, members of the committee proposed loosening the conditions for allowing refugees to resettle in Japan. One member stated that the number of refugees accepted for resettlement in Japan was "embarrassingly low from an international perspective" and argued that the Diet should increase the cap on that number to a level that would be "more acceptable to the international community." He also advocated quick ratification of the convention despite the problems it would cause with relevant domestic laws. The minister of foreign affairs picked up the discussion by suggesting that the Diet learn from other countries and increase the cap on the number of refugees accepted. He recognized that although there was a problem with coordinating all the relevant government offices, every attempt should be made to increase the cap during that year's Diet session. Although there seemed to be a frenzied discussion that would result in prompt adoption of the Refugee Convention, the meeting ended with Diet member Kanda Atsushi criticizing the low number of refugees that Japan agreed to accept, compared with other (Western) countries.[34]

In the discussions analyzed here, there is an awareness of the dangers of both self-imposed isolation and that imposed by others. In a statement to the Judicial Affairs Committee, Minister of Justice Okuno Seisuke stated, "Thirty-five years after World War II, international society has changed, and if Japan is to exist in this changed international society, it has to continue to carry burdens of its international role. Japan has to think hard about how it wants to deal with international problems thirty-five years from now, and we must choose a road to take."[35] Okuno concluded by expressing a wish to investigate thoroughly what measures a "Japan that has international respect must take." His statement recognized the legacy that Japan's actions would leave and the importance of this historical moment in shaping Japan's role in the world. One member noted that "it has been only 113 years since Japan went from national isolation to an open country, but the tendency of national isolation persists" in the country's refusal to open its doors to refugees. This aspect of Japan's identity is most undesirable, but it is especially important because struggles between state and national identity and the conflicting impulses to turn outward or withdraw are most noticeable in it. According to Japan's national myths, one of the reasons that Japan became such a strong country in such a short amount of time—in the late nineteenth century and again after World War II—was the strength of "the Japanese," understood as a homogeneous nation, and the sacrifices that people were willing to make to secure the state and preserve the nation. As in the case of adoption of the International Refugee Convention, these two goals—securing the state and preserving the nation—sometimes conflict. In this case, state identity, which manifests the impulse to secure the state by participating in international relations, won out over the impulse to turn inward. The remainder of this section focuses on how state identity trumped nationalistic concerns during the adoption stage. In the next section, I illustrate the effects of Japan's domestic norms and national identity in hindering compliance with the convention.

Given the divergent political positions of the *Yomiuri* and the *Asahi*, the major themes that emerged in the op-ed pages of the two papers and the positions taken in 1980–82 were surprisingly similar. Criticism of Japan focused on the fact that the extent of Japan's involvement in helping address the situation rested on financial contributions, viewed as an inadequate response.[36] Japan was further criticized for following the United Nations and not using its position to make sure that suggestions from the Association of Southeast Asian Nations (ASEAN) for dealing with the problem were taken more seriously.[37] These criticisms did not extend to direct attacks on or advocacy of specific steps to address the lack of attention to the problem. This omission could be attributed to the possibility that any serious attempt to criticize current measures or offer solutions would require scrutiny of domestic policies and recommendations for change that would inevitably include accepting more refugees and supporting their transition into society. Instead, there were suggestions that Japan be a voice for proposals from ASEAN countries, that the international community engage the leaders of the countries that refugees were fleeing to prevent the flow of refugees from the source, and that wealthy countries pledge more economic support to those countries. These suggestions hint at two important but somewhat audacious roles for Japan. First, the idea that Japan should listen to ASEAN proposals points to the necessity for improved diplomatic and political relations with those countries. This leads to the second point, which suggests that Japan then give voice to ASEAN preferences; in other words, Japan should become a representative for ASEAN internationally. These suggestions recall Japan's desire to be a regional leader in Asia—a very delicate topic.

Japan's UN-centric foreign policy making has been noted since the country was allowed to join the United Nations in 1956. Turning toward the United Nations and away from ASEAN on the refugee issue signals both Japan's preference to align itself with a more powerful organization led by Western states and the difficulty of Japan's relations within Asia. Association with the United Nations offers more international legitimacy than affiliation with and advocacy of ASEAN policy preferences. Membership in the United Nations was withheld from and sought by Japan for one reason: it would signal Japan's acceptance into the international community.

More specific concern for asylum seekers once they reached Japan was also expressed throughout the opinions. This issue was seen as one of concern for "Japanese who live in an international society." The op-eds called for Japanese to fulfill an international responsibility by appealing to a sense of national pride to further "internationalize" Japan. It was—at least superficially—a statement of what it means to be Japanese in its appeal to the sense that Japanese are open minded, worldly, and sophisticated. Where this sense of responsibility actually motivated action, there was pressure for the government to expand the cap on the number of refugees from five hundred to one thousand while recognizing that allowing asylum seekers into the country was just the beginning of the process. If Japan were to fulfill its obligation, the door would also need to be open to allow refugees to work, to allow their children to go to school, and generally allow them to live in and become a part of society. The transition to life in Japan was presented as relatively smooth and easy; and focusing on the refugees' ability to work and learn Japanese made their presence less threatening because it indicated their ability to assimilate. There was no mention of the real problems that refugees faced because of discrimination or their own past trauma.[38]

The first proposals for Japan to adopt the Refugee Convention came in 1969 from the Japan Socialist Party. The government decided not to ratify the convention on the grounds that the definition of refugee was unclear and that the date specifications in the convention made it relevant only to European countries.[39] The Japanese Diet did not agree to adopt the treaty and the Optional Protocol until 1980; after this decision, government officials needed to change relevant laws to bring them into line with the requirements of the convention. When Japan did adopt the convention and the Optional Protocol, the Optional Protocol clearly determined that there were no temporal or geographical restrictions on its application of the Refugee Convention.[40] Analysis of records from meetings of relevant Lower House Diet committees during the period leading up to adoption of the convention reveal that members focused on problems with the treaty, international duties and obligations, and immigration law.[41] Problems centered on social insurance programs were primarily dealt with in negotiations between the Ministry of Foreign Affairs and the Ministry of Justice, which struggled over these issues. The Ministry of Justice took the position that it was impossible to extend benefits to non-Japanese—at least in part because of the cost—but the Ministry of Foreign Affairs insisted that the government reform all laws to avoid criticism from the international community. The author of an opinion piece on the struggle between these two ministries concluded, "Now that Japan has opened up to international society, Japanese have to decide how they will relate to outsiders. Doing this requires not only that they tackle the refugee issue, but they will also have to turn their attention to those foreigners who have already been living in Japan; attention which was lacking when the Diet decided to consider adopting the Refugee Convention."[42] Indeed, much of the discussion of problems with the treaty focused on domestic issues that had to be dealt with before the treaty could be adopted. These problems were identified as revising domestic laws to bring them into line with the tenets of the convention, naturalization requirements, and difficulty understanding the meaning of the term *refugee*.

The most pressing problem that had to be dealt with before Japan could ratify the convention was the citizenship requirement that was attached to social insurance benefits such as the national pension plan.[43] Because parties to the convention were required to extend to refugees the same social welfare benefits that their citizens enjoyed, the citizenship requirement had to be abolished. Because the citizenship requirement had previously excluded the population of non-Japanese long-term residents already living in Japan, its abolition forced the government to figure out how to incorporate them into the system. Once citizenship was no longer a requirement for being included in the national pension plan, *zainichi* became entitled to join the plan. One remaining problem was the requirement that members of the plan pay into the system for twenty-five years until the age of sixty. This meant that government officials had to address a loophole that excluded twenty thousand *zainichi* who were already over the age of thirty-five and would not have paid into the system for the required twenty-five years by the time they reached retirement age. To avoid international criticism, the government decided to make an exception for these people.[44] This decision added to the cost of including *zainichi* in the pension scheme, but more important, it advanced *zainichi* claims to social citizenship. Despite these changes in the laws, Japan's continued lack of a comprehensive refugee policy means that even those recognized as refugees in Japan still do not enjoy the same benefits as Japanese citizens, nor do they enjoy the rights set forth in the convention itself. I will return to this point later.

The most contentious issue by far was the question of naturalizing refugees. In discussions about the possibility of fulfilling the convention's requirement that naturalization be expedited, many members expressed the belief that because there were already problems with citizenship laws, particularly women's inability at the time to transmit citizenship to their children, the question of naturalizing refugees could not be considered because it would only cause further complications. Although this discussion did not broach the subject of how naturalization of refugees should be handled, it does point out members' concerns regarding the possibility of large numbers of foreigners becoming Japanese citizens. These discussions implicitly gender refugees by including them in the category of those who are restricted from making the nation. At least one member advocated following the lead of countries such as France and Germany that previously had systems of blood-based (*jus sanguinis*) citizenship but have since reformed their systems. Any revision of Japan's citizenship laws would also have to establish equality of men and women in their ability to transmit citizenship to their children. There were appeals that Japan "not be left behind the majority of countries in the world."[45]

Even before the convention was adopted, the government capped the number of refugees it would accept at a very low number, still five hundred in early 1980. Some members of the Diet's lower house were disturbed that even this figure was not being achieved. The most common explanation given was that refugees did not want to stay in Japan. Another explanation was that there was a limit to the capacity of the resettlement centers where refugees were placed for the first three months of their stay in Japan to facilitate their transition into Japanese society. Diet member Okada expressed the more controversial view that

refugees decide not to come to Japan because their situation in Japan would be too unstable given that there is no permanent residency available, and even if they are allowed to come for a year, they may not be able to renew their permits after that. It is regrettable that in comparison with other countries, the number of refugees allowed to resettle in Japan is so low, and even those who are allowed to resettle have difficulty obtaining permanent residency. Although we should not go as far as America and Canada do in their policies to admit refugees, we should automatically give permanent residency to those we do accept after they have been in Japan for three years.[46]

This was a radical proposal that would bypass regulations for naturalization that required an applicant to live in Japan for more than five years, demonstrate good behavior, be able to make a living, be in good health, have a guarantor in Japan to vouch for her or his identity, and have a record of her or his past addresses. In effect, it would create a separate system to facilitate naturalization of refugees. Kosugi, the chief of the Ministry of Justice Immigration Bureau, responded by saying that what accounted for the difference in policy between Japan and countries such as the United States and Australia was that those other countries were immigration countries and therefore had policies in place; Japan had no such policy because "as a matter of national policy, Japan absolutely does not accept foreigners."[47] The lack of objection to this statement indicates that it accorded with domestic norms. Although many members expressed support for adopting the Refugee Convention, none were willing to openly disagree with the sentiments Kosugi expressed. Surely many members recognized that many of their constituents shared these sentiments.

Kosugi's unwillingness to consider a separate procedure for naturalizing refugees signals the inability to understand refugees apart from the broader category of foreigners on the basis of their special circumstances and status as vulnerable people who fear persecution if they are returned to their countries of origin. He advocated a policy that would allow refugees to extend their stay for three years after their first year in Japan, but these extensions would be on a case-by-case basis. This proposal, especially the idea that extensions be granted on a case-by-case basis, did not establish transparency in procedures and allowed Ministry of Justice officials to retain a great deal of power and discretion in deciding who got to stay and why. Furthermore, it did not hold these officials accountable for their decisions to deny applications for extensions. In short, such a policy would ensure that the number of refugees in Japan would continue to be arbitrarily restricted.

The committee finally decided that refugees would be allowed permits that would have to be renewed every six months, year, or three years, but that no special procedure would be put into place to expedite naturalization. Refugees would not be prevented from naturalizing, but they would have to fulfill the same requirements applied to other foreigners wishing to naturalize. Even this would not solve the problem of lack of transparency or ensure that refugees would be able to become Japanese citizens because even if the person wishing to naturalize fulfilled all the requirements, naturalization would still be granted on a case-by-case basis.[48] Table 2 shows the numbers of Indochinese who have settled in Japan and become naturalized citizens.

When questions regarding the mandatory five-year waiting period for naturalization arose, one member argued that it seemed long in comparison with the United States, Canada, and Australia, but it was not a long time when compared with the ten-year waiting periods of some European countries. He went on to say that the five years were necessary for foreigners to get used to life in Japan, "to assimilate," and pointed out that it

TABLE 2. Naturalization of Indochinese who had resettled in Japan as of the end of March 1998

Country	Male	Female	Total
Vietnam	133	71	204
Laos	39	50	89
Cambodia	42	56	98
Total	214	177	391

SOURCE: Refugee Headquarters (RHQ), July 1, 1998. Reprinted by permission.

was not a matter of simply living in Japan; they had to have the same rights and obligations as Japanese nationals (*nihon kokumin*). Although *nihon kokumin* is usually translated as "Japanese," the phrase has connotations of exclusivity because it refers to the citizenry of Japan, understood as those who are ethnically, culturally, and linguistically Japanese; this word continues to draw lines between who is and who is not Japanese because so few non-Japanese naturalize. It also views people in relation to their position in the state. Use of this phrase reinforces the biological basis of citizenship and racialization of Japanese identity. The language of the members themselves supports this analysis. In later discussions, when they were referring to residents of Japan, including non-Japanese, they used the more specific phrase *nihon naikokumin*. This phrase is more inclusive, without the implicit connection to citizenship and ethnic Japanese, but it is not commonly used. That members chose to use *nihon naikokumin* indicates that they recognized a need to clearly delineate who was outside and inside the boundaries of "Japanese."

Throughout the discussions of naturalization, comparisons were made with the United States, Canada, and Australia—the leaders in accepting refugees. Even when objections arose and arguments for more appropriate comparisons were made, Japan was compared with smaller Western countries, not with other Asian countries. Given that no other Asian countries had ratified the convention at this time, these comparisons with European countries suggest identification with countries of the world who had at least adopted the convention and where international treaty agreements were more common. In debates over citizenship laws in general, not one person explicitly advocated continuing to restrict women's ability to transmit citizenship to their children. Here too, members pointed out the need to advance their views on citizenship and cited Germany and France as models on which to base legal reforms. These discussions illustrate the discursive construction of Japan as similar to Western states on the basis of their identity as "developed" countries that are members of international society. The constant comparisons, coupled with reminders of Japan's status as a member of international society, highlight Japan's fear of being left behind or ostracized. Japan's interest in securing its position in the international community thus shaped state identity.

Although the committees agreed to accept the definition of refugee (*nanmin*) stated in the Refugee Convention, there was reference to problems in understanding the term because of lack of clarity in this definition.[49] Throughout the Diet committee records, requests to clarify the definition occur, especially with regard to how it differs from the definition of political exiles (*seiji bōmeisha*). This problem is cited as one of the reasons that adoption of the convention was delayed. These discussions usually ended with statements that the convention's definition of refugee would be accepted. The constant debates, however, do highlight the language problems that arise when international agreements written in English are translated into Japanese.[50] The problem is also a conceptual one in which people do not understand why one would need to flee one's own country and seek protection of another government. In the first decade of the twenty-first century, advocates of strengthening Japan's compliance with the convention have expressed concerns about the convention's definition of *refugee*. These concerns focused on the narrowness of the convention definition of *refugee* and the need to recognize that the reasons why people flee are complicated and are not adequately covered in the convention's definition. From the government's view, the narrowness of the convention's definition is preferred because it helps limit the number of people whom the government would be compelled to protect.

One article that was written in 1981 after the Diet adopted the Refugee Convention reported that the revision of the relevant laws had abolished discrimination against Koreans in Japan with regard to the social security system. The article went on to say,

Since last year's international human rights agreement came into effect, Japan's internationalization has continued on through the revision of legislation and systems. There is still much to be studied regarding discrimination between women and men that is rooted in the nationality law, but Japan, which insists on a system based on pure blood, one culture, and a unified ethnicity, opened its doors to foreigners, as is suitable for a member of international society. After the Meiji opening, this can be called the second opening [of Japan].[51]

This author straightforwardly recognized the systemic bias that exists in Japan's laws and practices as they relate to non-Japanese and women; the reference to the Meiji opening of Japan and this as a second opening is especially interesting. Reference to the Meiji opening recalls increasing international exchange of people and technology. Because this first period of internationalization resulted in the modernization of technology in Japan, the economic growth of Japan, and an increased international presence, reference to the Meiji opening carries a positive connotation. On the other hand, because of the link between one of the great traumas and humiliations in Japan's history and the Meiji opening, this reference also has an implicit negative undercurrent. Calling the adoption of the Refugee Convention the second opening of Japan clearly associates it with the expectation of an expanded role for Japan in international relations while also lamenting once again the fact that Japan's position in the international system makes it vulnerable to identity pressure from more powerful states.[52] The analysis in this section shows that politicians, bureaucrats, and popular opinion makers understood state identity and its importance in shaping Japan's interests. We also see how Japan's interest in increasing its international legitimacy by securing a certain status in turn leads to the articulation of Japan's identity through those interests.

Complying with the Convention: The Pull of the Nation

In the adoption phase, once state identity, domestic advocates, or both overcome conflict between international and domestic norms, adoption can proceed smoothly. For purposes of increased legitimacy or identity-based benefits in the international community, adoption is what is important. There is less need to have high levels of compliance, especially if there are weak (or no) mechanisms to monitor compliance. As long as there are no egregious violations, states can maintain the normative benefits gained from adoption without high levels of compliance. But some level of compliance will be achieved because state identity and interests have already been transformed to some degree; higher levels of compliance can only be achieved with higher levels of identification with the norms in question. This may depend on the work of domestic advocates even more than adoption did.

I noted earlier that there were no domestic advocates active on this issue during the adoption phase. Groups concerned with refugee issues did not emerge until after refugees began arriving in Japan. The first organizations to take action were religious groups, such as Caritas Japan, that were already established and had a long-standing interest in social welfare. Thus these organizations focused on providing relief and assistance, not on policy advocacy. As the number of refugees arriving in Japan began to increase between 1975 and 1979, limitations on the capacity of these organizations to provide assistance became apparent, and government decisions to settle refugees in Japan led to the need for some kind of infrastructure to facilitate their transition into Japanese society. A marginalized and heavily regulated civil society meant that the state dominated assistance activities.[53] Once the government established the Refugee Assistance Headquarters (RHQ) in 1979 within the Foundation for the Welfare and Education of Asian People and under the jurisdiction of the Ministry of Foreign Affairs, the program established in 1979 by the NGO International Social Services Japan (ISSJ) to provide assistance to Indochinese was closed that same year.[54]

Hirata cites the Indochinese refugee crisis as one of two events that led to growth in the number of NGOs in Japan.[55] Before the 1980s most NGOs were either Christian organizations or quasi-governmental organizations such as RHQ.[56] The impact of the Indochinese refugee crisis was significant insofar as it spurred the establishment of about twenty NGOs that, in addition to their primary work of providing assistance overseas, also carried out informational campaigns within Japan, but Hirata admits that their impact was limited. Although the increased activity of Japanese citizens working with Japanese NGOs abroad to address the needs of refugees had some effect on domestic civil society, the lack of advocacy or policy-oriented nonprofit organizations (NPOs) in Japan meant that citizen action was limited to individual volunteers helping refugees adjust to their new life through activities such as tutoring in Japanese. In areas such as Kanagawa Prefecture where there was a concentration of refugees, local NPOs oriented to social services were established. One example is the Kanagawa Indochinese Refugee Assistance Organization, renamed the Kanagawa Refugee Assistance Organization in 2003. These organizations usually had only one or two paid staff who coordinated volunteer activities. The names of the organizations indicate their focus on Indochinese refugees because they developed in response to that crisis. In the early 2000s, quasi-governmental organizations such as RHQ and NPOs such as the Kanagawa organization that were established specifically in response to the Indochinese refugee crisis have realized that with the end of family reunification programs, they must reevaluate their organizations and broaden their mandate if they are to continue to exist. Thus since 2000 more organizations have become aware of the issues confronting convention refugees and asylum seekers in Japan.[57]

From 1980 to 1995 the Japanese government conducted twelve surveys related to Japanese people's perceptions of and attitudes toward refugees and foreign workers. More specifically, the surveys conducted in 1980, 1982, 1991, 1993, and 1994 focused on refugees. In the 1980 survey, the majority of the respondents favored giving financial assistance to those Asian countries that accepted refugees and to international institutions that were engaged in refugee relief, but "only 3 percent said that Japan should receive these refugees as settlers."[58] This shift toward supporting refugees—though still not advocating their settling in Japan—was facilitated by two events: Japanese people's realization of their position in the world generally and in Asia specifically (identity), and the sympathetic media coverage of refugee suffering in Thailand in 1979. Official refugee policy making began in September 1977, but public opinion did not turn favorable until the events of 1979. Although Japan agreed to accept Indochinese refugees—with the understanding that the stays were temporary—the government continued to deport asylum seekers who overstayed and were technically in Japan illegally. After the issue was taken to the Ministry of Justice, asylum seekers were allowed to extend their stays because of their special circumstances, but they still were not given any permanent or official status.[59] Furthermore, Japan did not accept refugees for permanent resettlement, and there were restrictions with regard to the character and ability of applicants to support themselves if they were allowed to resettle. As a result, only one three-person family was accepted for resettlement in 1978.[60]

Analysis of the 1980 and 1982 polls helps us understand how Japanese people viewed refugee settlement in Japan. Honma (1990) cautions us about three problems with the polls. First, conducting them at a time when there was great concern for Indochinese refugees may not accurately measure how the public really viewed Indochinese refugees. Second, some respondents may not have found their preferred answer among the choices. Third, there were no questions about refugees from countries other than those in Indochina in the polls, so they provide no sense of how people felt about refugees in general.[61]

The research for the 1980 poll, which was conducted in August 1979, took place when the quota was five hundred, and the 1982 research was done after the quota was increased to three thousand people. In the 1980 poll, 22.8 percent said that the quota should be increased, 38.7 percent considered the quota of five hundred persons appropriate, and 11.4 percent thought that refugees should not be accepted into Japan at all. In the 1982 research, 7.4 percent said that the quota of three thousand persons should be substantially increased, 42.5 percent said that the quota should be increased, and 19.1 percent said that it should not be increased. In the 1982 poll, which was conducted after the news coverage of the 1979 crisis in refugee camps in Thailand subsided, there was a substantial decrease in those who had a positive view of expanding the acceptance quota. Conversely, the negative view toward refugees who had been allowed to settle in Japan increased twofold. In the 1982 poll, in response to the question "Are you concerned about Indochinese refugees?" 10.6 percent of the respondents said that they were very concerned, 55.5 percent said that they were a little concerned, 19.4 percent said that they were not concerned, and 4.6 percent said that they did not know. Overall, people who were concerned at all totaled 66.1 percent, but this does not necessarily mean that there were many who supported allowing Indochinese refugees to settle in Japan. In the 1980 poll, only 2.6 percent said that they should be allowed to settle in Japan.

Many people responded that refugees were warmly accepted by local communities, but the poll results on building refugee settlement facilities nearby were the following: in 1980, 57.3 percent supported such facilities being built in their community, while 13.7 percent were opposed. In 1982 those who said that they would cooperate to the best of their ability totaled 19.2 percent, those who said that they would not support a settlement facility in their area but had warm feelings toward refugees became the majority at 58.4 percent, those who said that it was none of their business were 8.2 percent, and those who flat out opposed the idea constituted 3.7 percent. By the time the 1982 poll was taken, the concern that had been generated by the 1979 crisis had subsided and more Indochinese refugees had been settled in Japan, so many Japanese might have felt that the need had been addressed and that they had done their part. It is also possible that concerns about the threat of foreign workers in Japan made people more hesitant to welcome foreigners who would become long-term residents of Japan.

According to Honma, although there was goodwill toward refugees, as indicated by the poll, the small number of refugees in Japan could be attributed to people feeling that they could not afford to cooperate because refugees would change the way of life in Japan. Honma refers to the widespread concept of Japan as a "village society." This village is closed to refugees and others on the basis of their differences and their presumed lack of knowledge of Japanese customs, culture, and values. The closed nature of society is apparent in the "general agreement" but "particular objection" illustrated in the attitudes reflected in the results of the survey—people generally agree that assistance is necessary but do not want settlement centers built in their communities. When Japanese think of refugees, they have some misgivings because they stereotype them—as other foreigners are often stereotyped[62]—as troublemakers largely responsible for increased crime. Honma asserts that journalists bear a large part of the responsibility for antirefugee views in Japan because of their power over public opinion.[63] Mizuno states the problem more boldly: "Refugee aid drives in Japan raise millions of yen in goodwill contributions, but xenophobic locals repeatedly oppose the opening of refugee resettlement centers in their neighborhoods."[64]

Japanese understandings of what it means to be Japanese conflate ethnicity, culture, and language.[65] When these understandings are combined with the idea of Japanese uniqueness based on the biological fact of being Japanese, the result is a racialization of the distinction between Japanese and others living in Japan, even if they were born in Japan and Japanese is their first language. This understanding of Japaneseness has limited the ability of those who are not ethnically Japanese to naturalize and become Japanese citizens. Until 1985 even children born in Japan of Japanese mothers and foreign fathers were not guaranteed Japanese citizenship. Thus not only was citizenship based on blood, but also it was centered on the father's blood. Being Japanese meant being born of a Japanese father (who claimed the child), being a native Japanese speaker, and being fully immersed in Japanese culture.[66] An exception to Japan's Nationality Act, which was revised in 1985 to comply with CEDAW by granting Japanese mothers the ability to transmit citizenship to their children, is Article 2 of that act, which authorizes the Ministry of Justice to grant citizenship to children born within Japan whose parents are either unknown or stateless.[67] Without citizenship, stateless children can be deprived of the rights to medical care, education, and social security benefits.

Preserving citizenship for those who "just are" Japanese helps maintain the status quo by reifying the interconnection of ethnicity, culture, and language. Restrictions on naturalization of non-Japanese serve to racialize further the biological basis of Japaneseness. "Until 1984, Japanese nationality law essentially designated a child born to a Japanese mother and a foreign father, whether born in wedlock or out-of-wedlock, as illegitimate and, therefore, not sufficiently Japanese to be included as a citizen."[68] The gendered construction of citizenship was codified in the power of men to control the national constituency. This was clearly illustrated when citizenship of children born out of wedlock depended on acknowledgment by the father before the child's birth or by the Ministry of Justice afterward. Now that women have the right to transmit citizenship to their children, men no longer have a monopoly over constituting the nation. However, a fairly recent court case illustrates the continued gendered and racialized nature of citizenship and limits on who is allowed to construct the nation.

In March 1998, the Japanese Supreme Court denied Japanese citizenship to the daughter of an ethnic Korean man and Japanese woman born out of wedlock in Japan in 1948. Although her parents were not married, the woman's father acknowledged her and placed her name in his family registry in what is now a South Korean province. Because of Japan's occupation of the Korean peninsula, the woman's father was a Japanese citizen at the time of her birth, but lost that citizenship when the San Francisco Peace Treaty came into effect in April 1952. The Supreme Court upheld a lower court ruling that the same peace treaty also divested the woman herself of Japanese citizenship. The Court reasoned that

Korean custom at the time of the woman's birth, which mandated entering the name of illegitimate children as well as legitimate children in the father's family registry, should determine her citizenship despite the fact that she was born out of wedlock to a Japanese citizen mother. Thus, gender remains essential to the construction of Japanese citizenship and the nation.[69]

Augustine-Adams (2000) considers the impact that gender has on citizenship by examining how differential laws on the ability of mothers, fathers, married parents, and unmarried parents to transmit citizenship to their children help produce the nation. She argues that the social meaning ascribed to biology—not biology itself—provides the basis for differentially regulating the ability of men and women to construct a nation.[70] This is clearly illustrated when one examines the current laws in Japan and the obstacles to non-Japanese naturalizing. Now that women can transmit citizenship to their children through laws passed to ratify CEDAW, effectively changing who is Japanese, national membership is increasingly restricted to exclude non-Japanese. This reinforces the idea that one cannot become Japanese by choice, even as the range of who is Japanese is expanded.

Just as it exercises power in determining citizenship status, the Ministry of Justice uses its prerogative to allow asylum seekers to stay in Japan legally without granting them refugee status. Thus it is not the case that refugees do not go to Japan, as is often claimed; rather, those who are allowed to reside in Japan often do so without refugee protection.[71] This is achieved by granting the applicant "long-term resident status." Three examples of this include a North Korean soldier who sought asylum in Japan in 1983, eleven Burmese who sought asylum in 1994, and Chinese dissident students who sought asylum in 1989 after the Tiananmen Square incident.[72]

As one former legal officer of the United Nations High Commissioner for Refugees in Tokyo noted, it is extremely difficult to get data on the numbers of asylum seekers who arrive in Japan each year.[73] This is partly because there are thousands who arrive in Japan each year without documentation and are turned away without being informed of their right to apply for asylum. Table 3 is therefore not an accurate picture of the numbers of asylum seekers who land in Japan each year. The numbers in this table, including the low numbers of applications, are surprising to those familiar with the number of displaced people in the world each year. During the crisis period of refugees fleeing Indochina, indicated in this table as the period 1982–88, Japan granted refugee status to only 192 people from a total of 814 applicants. An incredible 461 applications—over half—were denied, and 130 were withdrawn. The period from 1989 through 1995 saw a significant decrease in the number of applications for recognition of

TABLE 3. Number of applications for recognition of refugee status and number of processed applications

Year	Number of applications	Number of processed applications		
		Approved	Declined	Withdrawn
1982–88	814	192	461	130
1989	50	2	23	7
1990	32	2	31	4
1991	42	1	13	5
1992	68	3	40	2
1993	50	6	33	16
1994	73	1	41	9
1995	52	2	32	24
1996	147	1	43	6
1997	242	1	80	27
1998	133	16	293	41
1999	260	16	177	16
2000	216	22	138	25
2001	353	26	316	28
2002	250	14	211	39
2003	336	10	298	23
2004	426	15	294	41
2005	384	46	249	32
Total	3,928	376	2,773	475

SOURCE: Ministry of Justice Web site, www.moj.go.jp/ENGLISH/IB/ib-13.html, June 12, 2002, for 1982–2000; Ministry of Justice Immigration Bureau, 2006 Immigration Report, pt. 1, for 2001–2005. Note that for each year there may have been cases pending that were not decided until later years.

refugee status, but the number of applications that were approved also decreased, including two years when only one person per year was accepted as a refugee. During this period, in every year except for 1989 and 1991, over half the applications were denied. In these same two years, two people and one person, respectively, were granted refugee status. In 1996 the number of people seeking asylum in Japan increased once again, but the number of acceptances did not start to increase until 1998; even then, the numbers remained incredibly low. Overall, the data presented in this table do not illustrate Japanese government compliance with the Refugee Convention.

Because most of the Indochinese who were allowed to settle in Japan came from camps where Japanese officials screened potential settlers or were admitted through family reunification programs and were granted special permission to stay in Japan long term, they are not included in the numbers of asylum applicants listed in Table 3. This process also means that Indochinese asylum seekers had an advantage over others who just showed up in Japan. Those who came from refugee camps through the government screening process had the benefit of staying in a refugee resettlement center in Japan, where they received classes in Japanese language and culture and assistance in finding work free of charge. Because they had to reside in these centers for at least three months, they did not have to worry about eating; having a warm, dry place to sleep; or access to medical care since all these services were provided for them. Once they were ready to leave the center, they also received assistance in finding housing—a valuable service for any non-Japanese living in Japan. In short, until a change of policy came into effect in 2003, only Indochinese refugees received the kind of treatment to which all refugees should have access under the rules of the convention.[74] All these services, as well as aftercare services provided to help deal with problems that arose once they left the center, meant that these people had a smoother transition into Japanese society than those who just arrived in Japan and applied for refugee status. Until changes in the law went into effect in 2005, convention refugees were routinely detained while their applications were being processed. Although the processing time has decreased from three to four years in the early 1990s to one to three years since 1998, this is still too long.[75] Ogata Sadako, the second-longest-serving high commissioner for refugees, served the UNHCR from 1990 to 2000. Table 3 does not indicate that Ogata's tenure in this position had much impact on the numbers of people granted refugee status in Japan during that period. There was, however, a marked increase in the number recognized, beginning in 1999 with sixteen people. We could interpret the sustained rise that culminated in a record forty-six people being granted refugee status in 2005 as related to the growth in the number of domestic advocates in the 1990s; this growth can be partly attributed to Ogata's high-profile position that helped legitimize activities on the domestic front. Certainly her contact with other states regarding issues of protection affected her view of where Japan stood in relation to other states and how its policies could be improved. During her tenure, Ogata came to recognize that attention to refugees fleeing their countries of origin ignored the millions of internally displaced people who fled fighting near their homes but did not cross an international border during their forced migration. This awareness that all protection problems are not satisfactorily addressed in the Refugee Convention coincided with Japan's granting "humanitarian permission to stay," starting in 1991. These were cases where rejected

TABLE 4. Indochinese resettlement in Japan as of the end of February 1998

Country	From domestic camps	From overseas camps	Total
Vietnam	4,154	3,527	7,681
Laos	73	1,233	1,306
Cambodia	44	1,210	1,254
Total	4,271	5,970	10,241

SOURCE: Refugee Assistance Headquarters (RHQ), July 1, 1998. Reprinted by permission.

applicants were permitted to stay in Japan for humanitarian reasons. By 2005 the number of people allowed to stay in Japan under this category was 341, while a total of only 376 people had been recognized as refugees between 1982 and 2005.[76]

The numbers in Table 4 tell a different story. These are the numbers of Indochinese who were allowed to resettle in Japan but were not formally recognized as refugees. Perhaps most important is that Japan had resettled a total of 10,241 people as of the end of February 1998. This number is still quite low, especially when compared with other industrialized countries, but it is more substantial than the 265 people who had been formally accepted as refugees and granted recognition as such since 1982. The 10,241 here were mainly people screened at refugee camps in Southeast Asia by Japanese officials to determine if they were eligible for resettlement. Some of these were accepted for family reunification purposes, and some had already entered Japan as students before political unrest broke out in their country of origin.

Nearly thirty years after Japan's ratification of the Refugee Convention, compliance remains low. Japanese scholars, activists, and refugee lawyers have pointed out many shortcomings of Japan's refugee recognition system, and some have lobbied the government to make changes. Many of the problems result from the way the current system was established. The most basic issue is that there is no comprehensive policy that deals with the treatment and resettlement of refugees. This problem grew out of the 1979 cabinet agreement that allowed refugees into the country. Japan's current policy is the direct result of the Indochinese refugee crisis that spanned the period from about the mid-1970s to the mid-1980s, and this policy was not meant to be applied to others.[77] This cabinet agreement indicates that officials did not intend to create a comprehensive refugee policy in Japan. It did not make clear how far the principles of the Refugee Convention would be applied to the legal status of Indochinese in Japan.[78] Honma goes so far as to say that the only thing that Japan's Immigration Control and Refugee Recognition Act and the Refugee Convention have in common is the definition of refugee.[79] In other words, the principles of the Refugee Convention were not codified in Japan's law regarding refugees or in the agreement that allowed Indochinese to settle in Japan. Some believe that legislative action would have created a more comprehensive policy, and that action by the Diet is necessary to reform existing policies and create a comprehensive refugee policy in Japan.[80]

The focus on creating policies especially to address Indochinese refugee flows in the region meant that the government was in effect creating dual systems, one that applied to Indochinese and one that applied to all other refugees. The differential benefits that these two groups enjoy were mentioned earlier. Here I will turn to specific problems with refugee recognition procedures in Japan. Because Indochinese family reunification programs operated through 2005,[81] those who arrived in Japan through overseas camps were usually not affected by these problems. One issue is that recognition procedures are handled in the Immigration Bureau. According to domestic advocates, the basic problem is that the same authority is responsible for immigration control and refugee protection. Therefore, on the one hand, the bureau serves a policing function, and on the other hand, a protection function. Officials are expected to deal with people illegally residing in Japan in a punitive manner, and when refugees overstay their visa, they fall into that category.[82] Also, the practice of rotating bureaucrats to different sections means that sometimes those who are focused on apprehending irregular migrants one day are charged with protecting refugees the next—not an easy transition, especially given the overall culture of the Ministry of Justice.

Another issue is the lack of transparency in recognition and appeal procedures.[83] Watanabe Shogo, a well-known refugee lawyer in Japan, notes that because the same authority that handled the initial application (and rejected it) is charged with hearing appeals, the number of those who are granted recognition after appeal is low—in 1995 and 1998 only one person each year and in 1999 only three people were granted refugee status after appealing an initial denial. An underlying issue in the initial decision is that the person who conducts the interview does not have the authority to decide the case; an advisory committee makes the decision. According to Watanabe, the regulations of this advisory committee are unclear; it has no legal basis and lacks expertise in refugee law.[84] According to Toki Hinako (2001), people in charge of refugee recognition procedures have no expertise in international human rights law or international refugee law. In her view, inspectors who interview asylum seekers and decide on recognition status should undergo special training. She admits that more of this has been taking place at the end of the 1990s, but there are still no official requirements in place.[85] A 2005 interview with a Ministry of Justice official revealed that the ministry consults with the UNHCR Tokyo office and the ministry has invited UNHCR representatives to give informational lectures to ministry staff.[86]

The most criticized regulation is the "sixty-day rule," which requires those seeking refugee status to submit their applications within sixty days of their arrival in Japan or, if they were already in Japan, within sixty days of becoming aware of the change in the situation that puts them in danger of persecution. In the past, the majority of cases were decided on the basis of this rule, but since the end of the 1990s there has been some easing of the strict application of the rule. In 1998 eight Burmese were recognized as refugees, but five of them submitted their applications after sixty days. In April 1999 three Burmese were granted refugee status on appeal. Their first application was denied on the basis of the sixty-day rule. The main criticism of the sixty-day rule is that it has nothing to do with whether someone is a refugee and in need of protection.[87] The sixty-day-rule was changed in the May 2005 revised Immigration Control and Refugee Recognition Act. The strict time limit was abolished, but if an application is submitted more than six months after arrival or learning of the changed situation in the country of origin, legal status will be granted only at the discretion of the minister of justice.[88]

The legal position of asylum seekers is an important issue in Japan, especially because it is not always remedied when an applicant is granted refugee status. When people apply for refugee recognition, they may be in Japan on various residency permits (for example, a tourist visa or a student visa). If someone has no permission to stay at the time that she or he applies for recognition, that person maintains this status while her or his application is being considered; in Japan this may be one to two years. Thus many asylum seekers have no legal status, so they are not allowed to work legally, they do not have access to the national health insurance program and other social welfare programs, and they may have trouble securing education for their children.[89] Even if temporary permission to stay is granted during the application period, this does not automatically allow the applicant to work. Furthermore, if a person's application for refugee status is denied, she or he loses the temporary legal status that was granted during the application period and becomes an overstayer during the appeal period.[90] Of the sixteen people granted recognition in 1998, eight were from Burma. Of these, only two had residency permits even after they obtained refugee status—one received it at the time of recognition. The other six did not receive any permits. Therefore, although they were recognized as refugees, they still had no legal status in Japan. In addition, because citizenship is still based on blood in Japan, any children born to refugees with no legal status are in danger of being stateless unless they have one Japanese parent.

Domestic advocates assert that the culture of the Ministry of Justice, with its constant focus on investigating illegality, also permeates the Immigration Bureau, which falls under Ministry of Justice jurisdiction. Until now, suspicion of foreigners as illegal entrants and criminals has dominated the ministry and its bureaus. Because decisions on granting residency permits to refugees are left to the discretion of the Ministry of Justice, there is no way for a person who has been granted refugee status to petition for the residency permit on which one's legal status in Japan depends. Lawyers advocate reforms that would guarantee that when someone is recognized as a refugee, that person would automatically be granted residency. Along with other lawyers, Watanabe believes that the problem is that if the Ministry of Justice agreed to that, it would have to stop deportation procedures once someone applied for refugee status and confront the issue of detention.[91]

Strengthening compliance with the convention would require that Japan institute a system whereby residency permits and social welfare benefits are provided at the same time as recognition. Although the Immigration Control and Refugee Recognition Act was established to facilitate the implementation of the Refugee Convention domestically, this law is very basic and does not fully implement the norms of the convention. Without this first step, it has been difficult for contemporary domestic advocates to move Japan toward higher levels of compliance. Even the most basic provisions of travel documents and social welfare benefits are not clearly established in Japan's immigration law.

Because those refugees who arrive in Japan undocumented, those who overstay their visas, and those who enter Japan illegally are treated as criminals first by the Ministry of Justice, refugees are routinely detained and deportation procedures proceed while applications for refugee status are being considered. Starting deportation procedures provides the basis for detention, and these procedures usually commence at the time of application for refugee status.[92] However, it is now standard practice for any deportation order to be held up until the decision on the application for refugee status is decided. Nevertheless, once deportation procedures have been started, the detention period is unlimited. There are cases where people have been detained for one or two years until a decision is made on their applications for refugee status.[93]

The shortcomings of Japan's refugee policy and its lack of protection have also brought criticism internationally. In a March 1993 report, Amnesty International charged that since Japan acceded to the 1951 Convention and 1967 Protocol in 1981, it has failed to fully abide by its obligations towards people arriving in Japan who need protection against forcible return to their countries of origin. Specifically, the government has not ensured that all people fleeing arbitrary arrest or detention, torture, or other serious threats to their life or personal safety, who arrive in Japan will have an opportunity to have their asylum claim considered.[94]

The report focuses specifically on asylum seekers who arrive directly in Japan. Japan's Immigration Control and Refugee Recognition Act does not specify the procedures that should be used in examining applications for asylum. One of the ways that the Japanese government gets around granting refugee status to asylum seekers is by allowing them to stay in Japan on a "designated activities visa." This is an administrative procedure of the Ministry of Justice that does not recognize the fear of persecution that is the basis of asylum claims, nor does it protect that person as a legally recognized refugee would be protected. Because this visa status is an administrative procedure, it can be withdrawn at the inclination of the Ministry of Justice.[95]

Constructing Identity

Given that adopting the International Refugee Convention threatens what it means to be Japanese, how can we account for its adoption in 1981? In this chapter, I have offered an explanation that takes into account Japan's historical position in international relations, state identity, and domestic norms and identity. Through analysis of opinion pages and Diet committee meetings, I have traced the discursive construction of state identity and illustrated how it accounts for adoption of the treaty through the state's desire for legitimacy. This was not a simple, uncontested process; there were points in the discussion when the discourse of national identity conflicted with the impulse to adopt the convention as a way of fulfilling international duties. When these counterdiscourses arose in committee meetings, Diet members did not directly oppose them. This fact illuminates how the idea of Japan as a homogeneous society resonated with members even as they argued for adopting the convention. Consideration of compliance with the convention showed how domestic norms and identity and the understanding of foreignness inform the treatment of refugees and hinder full compliance with the convention. One discourse did not simply become dominant and lead to a straightforward outcome. In this case, the dominant discourse about Japan's international interests encouraged action based on its identity as a member of international society, but the impulses associated with domestic norms and national identity still constrain policy outcomes, implementation, and compliance. These findings are consistent with a sociological institutionalist explanation, which anticipates disjunction between adoption and compliance.[96] This case and those presented in the following chapters further explain under what conditions states will comply; domestic advocates are an important part of the explanation.

Chan-Tiberghien (2004) documents how the 1990s were a time of increased concern with human rights issues in Japan. This greater concern over the treatment of refugees and asylum seekers in Japan that started with Amnesty International's 1993 report has spawned a new generation of activists and advocacy groups committed to this issue. These advocates call attention to the inadequacies and contradictions in laws and procedures governing treatment of those seeking protection and work toward reforming the laws to address these issues. This case clearly demonstrates how international norms can be implemented in ways that allow compliance to be continually thwarted. Activities of NGOs, lawyers' groups, and supportive judges promise to improve compliance—identification between the state's identity and the norm of protection.[97]

Taken together, the epigraphs that open this chapter tell how complicated the issue of refugee policy is in Japan. The first epigraph illustrates the sensitivity of individual Japanese to the opinion of others and can be used as a mirror of the Japanese state's awareness of the importance of conforming to a range of acceptable behavior in the international community. This woman's statement shows that although she was not necessarily hostile to the idea of assisting refugees, it probably was not an issue about which she was concerned until a letter from a foreign friend criticized the Japanese state—and by implication Japanese people—for its inaction. In the face of such criticism, she felt it necessary to do something on behalf of all Japanese to restore their reputation with the rest of the world. Thus she was motivated by a deep sense of understanding of Japanese national identity, which for her includes compassion, goodwill, and kind hearts. She went on to establish one of the first Japanese NGOs for assisting refugees abroad. At the same time, the second epigraph, a statement made in a Judicial Affairs Committee meeting on November 5, 1980, demonstrates a concern for protecting that same national identity by keeping foreigners out. As far as I know, there is no explicit expression of a desire to keep foreigners out of Japan in national policy, but Kosugi's statement demonstrates the spirit in which many laws regarding foreign residents of Japan were created. As we saw later in the chapter, no one challenged his statement. Despite the boldness of the statement, it resonated with many of the government officials present at the meeting. Although domestic norms, national identity, and culture are flexible and changeable, a core belief in what constitutes the nation takes years to change. Clearly, such identities severely limit capacity for compliance with international norms that promote inclusiveness even though legal structures have been formally implemented. Even a desire to conform to acceptable behaviors based on logics of appropriateness for actions in international affairs on the part of state actors cannot ensure that official change will trickle down during the compliance phase. In the next chapter, we see how the presence of strong domestic advocates on an issue significantly improves the level of compliance.

CHAPTER 4

Gender Equality and Women's Employment

It was most unfortunate that "Tokyo Official Ties Birth Decline to Education" (news article, June 14) conveyed a misinterpretation of my statements on the effect of higher education in Japan on the labor market. The article was based on a Japanese newspaper report that misinterpreted a statement I made at a ministerial meeting June 12 on the effect of the aging of Japanese society. Reportedly, my statement at the meeting was that "the reason for an alarming decline in Japan's birthrate is the government's policy of encouraging women to obtain higher education." What I did say was that the ministries of education and labor should initiate a comprehensive study on the relationship between higher education and its impact on employment. . . . In view of the decline in the birthrate and the acute labor shortage in Japan—as well as the increase in the ratio of people seeking higher education regardless of their sex—I stated my belief that it was time for the government, especially the ministries of education and labor, to review higher education policies. I would add that my wife, Kumiko, is a college graduate and that we are happy with our five children, two boys and three girls, from a daughter who just graduated from college to the youngest, who is in the second grade.
—Finance Minister Hashimoto Ryutaro, letter to the editor of the *New York Times*, June 1990

Contested Meaning

Finance Minister Hashimoto Ryutaro's 1990 letter to the editor of the *New York Times* demonstrates that even ten years after Japan signed the Convention for the Elimination of All Forms of Discrimination Against Women (CEDAW) and five years after the Equal Employment Opportunity Law (EEOL) went into effect and the convention was ratified, high-level government officials remained conflicted about the international norm.[1] The outpouring of criticism from Japanese women against Hashimoto's reported comments is significant. What is more remarkable, however, is that Hashimoto, who held an important cabinet position as minister of finance, felt obliged to write a letter to the editor of a major foreign newspaper to explain himself. Even in 1990, Japan was clearly concerned with how it was perceived on the issue of women's rights and gender equality.

Hashimoto denied making the controversial statement and claimed that what he did say was misinterpreted in the original Japanese reports, but his letter to the editor demonstrates that it does not really matter whether he made the statement; what matters is how other, powerful states would judge Japan if they believed that a key government actor did make such statements. In other words, perception matters, and this has very real consequences for Japan's identity and legitimacy. Certainly a statement by a high-profile politician who aspired to the position of prime minister of a major world power that suggests that women should be discouraged from attaining higher education and focus instead on having babies is problematic.[2] Hashimoto's mention of his wife indicates that he believes that women can both earn college degrees and have babies, hardly an enlightened position. Any indication whether his wife has a career outside the home is conspicuously absent. Indeed, women in Japan continue to face social pressure to withdraw from the paid labor market after marrying and having children.[3]

When Japan adopted CEDAW, a significant number of well-connected women's organizations were active on the issue, the Japanese state was under fire for trade-related issues, and there was significant conflict between international and domestic norms on this issue. Conflict between the social and cultural importance of women's roles as mothers and homemakers in Japan and the rejection of such gender-based roles in CEDAW would lead us to expect the convention to have a minimal impact on domestic policies in Japan. One of the main concerns in the area of women's rights in Japan is employment discrimination.[4] In Japan, the long-standing ideal of "men at work, women in the home" has become a deeply embedded domestic norm. The domestic norms at stake on this issue are the conservative cultural beliefs and attitudes about the appropriate role of women and their contribution to national and familial stability. Adopting and complying with CEDAW threatened the social order, which in the 1980s was firmly based on men as wage earners and women as homemakers.

On the basis of the conflict between international and domestic norms, norms literature would expect domestic norms to prevail and CEDAW not to be adopted. If, by some chance, it were adopted, we would expect a low level of compliance. In fact, not only was CEDAW adopted, but also it has been progressively institutionalized, and a medium degree of compliance has been achieved. This marked contrast with the case of refugee policy, where there was also a high degree of conflict, raises the question: what was different in these two cases? How can we understand the process and explain the outcome to secure better compliance with future agreements? A significant difference between the two issues—refugee policy and women's employment—was the strength of domestic advocates. In this chapter, I argue that the efforts of domestic advocates account for compliance with the treaty, and the state's desire for legitimacy, along with the demands of women, explains Japan's adoption of CEDAW. The organization of domestic advocates is a central part of this chapter. Women were highly organized and well connected; they used their ties to the state to push the government to adopt CEDAW. Compliance has been gradual and hard won; it proceeds because of women's diligence and consistent efforts. This chapter demonstrates the key role that organized domestic advocates play in pushing the government to ratify even controversial treaties and in demanding higher levels of compliance through litigation, lobbying international organizations, and advocating for revisions in the EEOL.

State dominance of state-society relations in Japan, along with state suspicion of citizens' organizations, has produced an anemic civil society where organizations usually suffer from lack of funding and lack of access to power. In this case, women's organizations used a strategy of coalition building, taking advantage of significant social achievements (the thirtieth anniversary of women's suffrage), and using connections with high-profile women in the government to strengthen their influence. Support for CEDAW began in 1975 with International Women's Year (IWY); that year also marked the thirtieth anniversary of women's suffrage in Japan. This issue emerged in the same historical context as the refugee issue, when Japan's international image and reputation were suffering despite the country's rapidly increasing economic power. The continuity in women's movements, the personal appeal of individual women, and their networks of government contacts helped women's organizations exercise influence on this issue.

Explanations of why states adopt international norms that conflict with domestic norms offered by other scholars include the role of transnational networks, norm entrepreneurs, and instrumental reasoning. However, this literature focuses specifically on the role of nonstate actors and their activities and ignores the importance of their ties to the state. These ties were an essential component of the influence of women's organizations in Japan.[5] This literature also stresses the importance of transnational networks as an avenue for domestic actors to go outside a resistant state to exert pressure on that state (Keck and Sikkink's [1998] boomerang effect). Although Japanese women's organizations were connected to these kinds of networks, they used them to improve their access to information so that they could deal directly with state actors more effectively. In cases where the state dominates state–society relations, even networks of transnational actors have limited access to the political system. Therefore, it is necessary for domestic advocates to form relationships with those who occupy higher positions in the decision-making structure.[6] This chapter improves on established theories by illustrating how domestic nonstate actors use their ties to the state to influence both adoption and compliance and how transnational networks can be used toward that end. Analyzing the ties between these actors and the state illuminates the opportunities and limitations of domestic context for adoption and compliance.[7]

The steady increase in the number of employed women during the high-growth period that began in the 1970s meant that a large population of women had something at stake in the adoption of CEDAW. Since the 1960s women had been using lawsuits against employers to redress unfair treatment. By the 1980s, although lawsuits remained an important tool, many women wanted a more systemic change for improving their position and future opportunities in the workplace. The implications for improving women's overall position in the workforce were great, and such improvement would challenge the privileges of seniority pay and promotion and lifetime employment that men employed by large companies had come to enjoy and expect. Although these systems were widely credited as the basis of Japan's economic miracle, once women pressured the government to commit to signing CEDAW, government actors recognized the benefits that adopting the convention would have for Japan's identity and its international legitimacy. In the mid-1980s Japan was still facing some of the same identity issues that had plagued it in the early 1980s, when the government was deliberating over the Refugee Convention. These had been exacerbated by trade wars with the United States.[8] Therefore, the government wanted to avoid international criticism for appearing to be opposed to women's rights.

The vast literature examining the EEOL glosses over the process of how women persuaded the Japanese government to adopt CEDAW. If both women and civil society are weak in Japan, the usual assumption, how could they achieve this outcome? As discussed in Chapter 3, much of the scholarship on Japanese foreign policy making focuses on the importance of *gaiatsu* (foreign pressure), on Japan's foreign policy decisions.[9] Although these studies offer valuable insight on how international pressure affects Japanese foreign policy making by illuminating the effect of

Japan's relationship with the United States on policy decisions, they are problematic for several reasons. First, this literature usually comes to the same conclusion: that it is specifically pressure from the United States that often forces a politically weak and vulnerable Japan into reacting to whatever the more powerful United States dictates. Thus it implies that the Japanese government will follow the United States' lead in international affairs, including norm adoption. Yet in the case considered here, the United States did not pressure Japan to adopt CEDAW; the United States itself has not ratified CEDAW. Second, attention to foreign pressure highlights the uneven relationship between the United States and Japan, but it does not tell us how this relationship is produced, how it plays out vis-à-vis other relationships in international politics, and its domestic consequences. Third, foreign-pressure theories do not adequately explain why Japan succumbs to this outside pressure, in part because they exclude other relevant international processes. Finally, focusing exclusively on foreign pressure leads us to ignore the diversity of domestic and international political processes and the impact they have on decision making and state identity formation. Identity issues are obscured because the state's interests are pregiven in the rationalist account of foreign pressure. As we saw in Chapter 3, the aspect of external pressure that is underdeveloped in the literature on Japan's foreign policy but central in understanding why Japan adopts international norms that conflict with domestic norms is external identity pressures. These identity pressures often involve normative obligations and benefits that are not apparent in a material cost-benefit analysis. If we overlook identity pressures, we overlook the meanings associated with both domestic and international norms, and how actors on the ground shape meanings.

Issues of identity-based pressure and ideational benefits are essential to understanding why Japan adopted CEDAW, because it can be argued that Japan's international political position started to shift during the 1970s when the country gained prominence during the economic miracle. This change strengthened Japan's international position, but just when the country had the possibility of a more secure identity, criticisms of unfair trade practices once again increased its vulnerability. To understand why Japan adopted CEDAW and to evaluate the convention's consequences for domestic policy in Japan, it is necessary to focus on the adoption of CEDAW as one historical moment at the intersection of complex domestic and international processes rooted in the social, political, and economic shifts of the late nineteenth and early twentieth centuries discussed in Chapter 2.

In writing about Japan's adoption of CEDAW and related domestic legislation (the EEOL), scholars have tended to focus on the international dimension of this action, with only passing mention of the historic role that domestic advocates played.[10] Parkinson (1989) cites Japan's awareness of its economic dependence on other states and sensitivity to its international image because of past criticism. She concludes that this combination may have made Japan particularly susceptible to international social pressure in the early 1980s.[11] Although Parkinson illustrates the key role that material and social considerations play in Japan's foreign policy decisions, her explanation leaves aside the dimension of domestic politics and the pivotal role of Japanese women in persuading the government to adopt CEDAW. Without domestic pressure, the Japanese government would have been better able to resist international pressure on this particular issue because CEDAW, as an agreement that ultimately seeks to shape culture, is objectionable to many countries. Although Japan was in search of improving its identity and increasing its legitimacy and credibility, these goals could have been met more effectively in other areas. The fact that there is no mention of direct foreign pressure on this issue in either newspaper editorials and opinions or relevant Diet committee meetings between 1984 and 1986 further undermines foreign-pressure arguments that rely only on material pressures to explain Japan's foreign policy decisions.

The United Nations Decade for Women culminated in CEDAW. Japan signed this convention without reservations in 1980, then ratified it in 1985, and therefore has agreed to abide by its rules and strive to implement policies to achieve CEDAW's objectives. The Japanese government did not originally intend to sign CEDAW, but pressure from women journalists in Japan, female Diet members, various women's groups, and international actors forced the government to sign it.[12] Creighton finds that passage of the EEOL and the events leading up to it "reflect [Japan's] desire to participate in international life, rather than an internal shift in Japanese social values regarding women's roles."[13] Although this observation may accurately describe state motivations, it too falls short because it does not recognize the role that women played in the decision to adopt CEDAW and in shaping its meaning to shift social values. In Japan particularly, legal changes have been one way in which the government has mediated and managed social change,[14] so women activists sought to get the law on their side and produce a shift in social values.

Just how domestic and international forces influenced and continue to shape Japan's policies regarding women's equality is not at all clear from a cursory check of the literature on Japan's adoption of CEDAW. In this case, state desire for legitimacy was high; there was a high degree of conflict between the international and domestic norms; and changing relevant labor laws, citizenship laws, and education policies would require agreement of many different constituencies. Although adopting CEDAW would improve the state's international legitimacy, the trouble it would cause at home seemed to outweigh the benefits. Had there not been strong domestic advocates closely tied to the state through the participation of government officials and prominent activists, the government might have stuck with its original decision not to adopt CEDAW. However, once the government decided to adopt CEDAW, the stakes for Japan's state identity increased. In other words, had Japan decided not to adopt CEDAW, there would have been few negative effects for the state's identity, given the controversial nature of the convention itself. But after Japan signed the convention, not to follow through and ratify it would have negatively affected the state's identity.[15] The next section briefly sketches changes in women's work lives and the government's role in actively shaping gender roles. The following three sections focus specifically on the three variables: domestic advocates, state identity, and conflict between domestic and international norms.

Evolution of Domestic Norms on Women's Roles

As in any society, the current position of women in Japan is the result of historical contingencies, as well as social, economic, and political structures. Gender in Japan is actively shaped by the government to fulfill needs created by the economic situation. Indeed, the Japanese government has been active in constructing gender roles since the Meiji era (1868–1912).[16]

Increased industrialization and government policies of the late nineteenth century affected the structure of the household and had a radical impact on the socially acceptable roles of Japanese women. As industrialization increased the size of the middle class, government policies began to target family life in general and middle-class identity in particular with the effect of restricting women's lives.[17] The Meiji Restoration marked the first time that women were viewed as a unified social grouping with gender roles that dictated their social relations, especially with regard to family and the household.[18] Although there were standards of behavior for women and men of differing social status during the Tokugawa period (1603–1868), the reality of how people of the same status lived day to day differed from region to region because there were no standardized social mores. During this period, women's contributions to their families were not limited to their reproductive roles of mother, wife, and daughter-in-law but also included productive work in managing the household, which sometimes included a small family enterprise.

With increased urbanization, industrialization, and education in the late nineteenth and early twentieth centuries, distinctions in appropriate work and arenas of activity for both men and women became more sharply defined. Migration to urban areas, compulsory education for both boys and girls, and industrialization disrupted the "unity of production and reproduction [that] facilitated women's participation in productive labor" that existed before the Meiji Revolution.[19] These changes, however, did not totally remove women's work—both productive and reproductive—from the public sphere. Despite increasing restrictions on women's political activity throughout the Meiji period, women played a key role in the industrial labor force, making up the majority of the workforce in textiles and light industry.[20]

At the same time at which productive work was increasingly moving outside the home, the role of Japanese women was being redefined. There was tension between the vital roles that women played in both the workplace and the household. This tension was often reconciled by constructing a discourse that allowed and encouraged single women to work in factories for their family's survival while at the same time recognizing the pivotal role that married women played in the household as wives and mothers and encouraging these women to center their lives on their home. The slogan that the Ministry of Education created and popularized, "Good Wife, Wise Mother," made women's work in the home a public activity. The Ministry of Education sponsored the publication of *The Meiji Greater Learning for Women* in 1887. This document stated, "The home is a public place where private feeling should be forgotten."[21] In short, household duties associated with being a wife and mother were explicitly seen as productive work for the state rather than private reproductive activities.[22]

In the 1960s and 1970s it became common for women to be employed until they retired upon marriage—usually in their mid-twenties—or became pregnant. It is important to note that the ideal that married women would withdraw from wage labor was not always possible in reality, but those women who could achieve this ideal were held up as models for others. Government policies continue to support a life course for women that encourages them to work until they marry and have children in their mid-twenties to early thirties, stay at home full-time to take care of their children, then return to work that is flexible enough to allow them to continue to take care of their primary responsibility—their families.[23] The pattern of a woman's employment until marriage or the birth of her first child and after her last-born child enters school is supported by a society that recognizes the importance of child rearing and homemaking and that assumes that women are responsible for both of these duties. This assumption creates social pressure on women to fill these roles. In addition to cultural practices that perpetuate this system, structural conditions also discourage women from becoming full-time regular employees.

Some of the policies that support this life-cycle pattern, known as the M curve, and deter women from seeking work as regular employees are pension policies, health insurance policies, and tax policies. The most intriguing deterrent to women seeking full-time employment is the tax policy. In consideration of Japan's initial report in 1988, the CEDAW Committee requested information on the tax system in Japan and whether it facilitates or hinders women's paid work. In reply, Japan's representative stated, "The income tax system encouraged rather than punished women who wanted to work."[24] This answer contradicts what is now widely known about Japan's tax system: it encourages women to limit their earnings so that they can remain their husband's dependents.[25] The benefits of remaining an economic dependent outweigh the costs that would accrue from having to pay for unemployment insurance, make contributions to pension funds, and pay taxes on income if it exceeded the allowed amount. This fact was recognized in Japan's third report to the CEDAW Committee when Japan's representative stated, "Under the present framework of the tax and social security system, many women part-time workers limit their work hours to keep their income within a certain amount in order to be treated as dependents of their spouses. In such cases, the potential of women is not fully utilized."[26] Women who were not employed were encouraged to fill the gap in the part-time labor market. The government representative's comments regarding the first report took for granted that most women were not working in the paid labor force, once again indicating a particular understanding of the appropriate role for women. The committee's probing led the Japanese government to change its rhetorical position on tax policy between 1988 and 1993.[27] This shift took place only as women working full-time outside the home became more of a norm throughout Japan and the world. Although the tax policy may have encouraged women to work in low-wage jobs, it helped preserve the gender division within the household and large companies by discouraging women from entering segments of the labor force reserved for men, thus ensuring that women would remain primarily a reserve workforce. It was in this context that women's demands that the government adopt CEDAW emerged.

Adopting the Convention: Domestic Advocates

Treaties such as CEDAW can be controversial because their normative obligations demand cultural changes. Conservative social forces usually view these treaties as cultural imperialism and appeal to nationalistic feelings to gather popular support to defend domestic norms and oppose adoption. In Japan, women activists succeeded in using their common concerns for family and their ties to the state to unify diverse women behind adopting CEDAW and pushing the government to ratify the convention.

Women were powerful domestic advocates on this issue. In analysis of the impact of women advocates on adopting CEDAW, five key strategies emerge: framing CEDAW in the context of the thirtieth anniversary of women's suffrage, uniting groups with diverse political interests by focusing on the family, relaying information from international conferences to Japanese women on the ground, exploiting the intergenerational nature of the movement, and government/NGO exchange that was often facilitated by ties to the state.

A total of two hundred Japanese participated in the World Conference of the International Women's Year in Mexico City (June–July 1975). These included fifteen government delegates and an advisory group of ten female Diet members; Fujita Taki headed the delegation. Nineteen Japanese delegates—including eight female Diet members—headed by Takahashi Nobuko attended the mid-decade conference, held in Copenhagen in July 1980.[28] Japan signed CEDAW in 1980 under pressure from Japanese women's groups. Among these was a nationwide NGO network created by Ichikawa Fusae, then a member of the Diet's upper house, and several colleagues, including Takahashi. This network represented more than two million women.[29] The final conference of the United Nations Decade for Women, held in Nairobi in July 1985, included seven delegates headed by Vice Minister of Foreign Affairs Moriyama Mayumi, thirteen women Diet members, and seven hundred women from NGOs.[30]

Because women had been organizing around various issues for decades before IWY (1975), they were in a position to exert pressure on the government.[31] Japan was allowed to join the United Nations in 1956; the following year Ichikawa Fusae, a leading feminist, prewar suffragist, and member of Japan's upper house of the Diet, and Fujita Taki, who would later be the Japanese government's representative at the International Women's Year Conference in Mexico City, formed the National Women's Committee of the United Nations, a coalition of ten women's NGOs and twenty-one individual members.[32] Every year this group seeks to maintain the connection between the UN and Japanese women by recommending a woman from outside the government to serve as a member of Japan's delegation to the UN General Assembly.[33] Thus, when the UN declared 1975 International Women's Year (IWY), Japanese women's organizations were poised to play a role. Japanese women activists were particularly energized when 1976–85 was declared the UN Decade for Women. The start of the decade coincided with the thirtieth anniversary of women's suffrage in Japan; the monthly women's magazine *Fujin tenbō* (Women's Perspective) focused on this connection throughout the year.[34]

International Women's Year and the UN Decade for Women strengthened women's movements in Japan. Ichikawa used her own position and
the international movement to improve women's status and to unite various organizations with diverse political perspectives.

At a December 18, 1974, meeting of the board of the National Women's
Committee of the United Nations, Japanese women began planning for
the first meeting of the International Women's Year Japan Conference
(Kokusai Fujinnen Nihon Taikai). The conference was envisioned as a
forum where the goals, activities, and outcomes of the IWY Conference
in Mexico City could be relayed to a broad audience of Japanese women.
Led by Ichikawa, the board members of the National Women's Committee of the United Nations saw the different values and the diversity of
political positions of the various organizations involved as a chance to
exchange experiences and ideas about Japanese women's status and the
conditions of their lives. It took a year of planning to gather the diverse
group of forty-one organizations that had never before met.

In advance of the first IWY Japan Conference, a planning meeting was
held on November 5, 1975, that included women's organizations and government representatives, with Ichikawa as chair. This meeting illustrates
the essential characteristics of women's activities that account for their
influence throughout the Decade for Women: Ichikawa's leadership and
the close working relationship between women's NGOs and the government. Women learned a great deal from the process of planning for and
attending the first IWY Japan Conference. The most important lesson was
that a broad constituency was necessary to have a significant impact. This
required cooperation to discern their shared interests and to overcome
their political differences. Women who had been active in women's movements both before and after World War II attended this first meeting. This
intergenerational character had a profound effect on participants because
the very presence of women like Ichikawa reminded them of the history
of women's movements in Japan; the continued activities of these prewar
women activists connected the current movement for women's equality to
a distinguished past.[35]

The IWY Japan Conference opened with 2,300 participants on November 22, 1975, under the slogan "Let's do away with gender discrimination and increase women's strength." In her keynote speech, Ichikawa,
then a member of the House of Councilors (the upper house of the Diet)
and the chair of the National Women's Committee of the United Nations,
explicitly addressed the relationship between the goals of IWY and the
UN Decade for Women, gender equality, and Japanese society: "In the
thirty years since the new constitution established women's suffrage,
women's (legal) position in society has improved but (social) inequality

between men and women has persisted. This status quo inequality can be attributed to the male-dominated society with a conventional family system that perpetuates systemic conditions where many women have ability but they do not have the opportunity to influence policy decisions that will improve women's position in society."[36] Ichikawa continued, "To achieve the goal of international peace, women and men must be equal and together pursue economic, social and cultural development."[37] The prime minister, the chair of the government's Headquarters for the Promotion of Gender Equality (the Headquarters), and Japan's representative to the IWY Conference in Mexico City, Fujita Taki, were also present at the conference.

The successes of the Decade for Women included Japan signing CEDAW in 1980 and ratifying it in 1985, the Diet passing the EEOL, changing the citizenship law so that women could transmit citizenship to their children, and reforming the education laws so that home economics requirements would be the same for boys and girls. At the third meeting of the IWY Japan Conference on November 22, 1985, the keynote speaker, Kaji Chizuko, reflected on these experiences. She recalled that Ichikawa, who had been jailed and harassed by the government and the police before World War II, eventually had an audience with the emperor and empress and secured government sponsorship of the IWY commemoration meeting. She expressed the inevitability of Ichikawa being the one figure who could mobilize forty-one diverse women's organizations and women's sections of labor unions and organize nongovernmental women on this issue.[38] In reflecting on the Decade for Women, Kaji stated her belief that "the Decade for Women transcended boundaries between government and citizens and between different groups of people. It was global. Other UN actions that protect human rights also protect women's rights and prohibit gender discrimination. Ten years ago, when the UN announced the Decade for Women, women's groups—both those that had existed since before World War II and those that had been established after World War II—were quick to respond."[39]

Because the group was constituted by organizations concerned with different issues related to women's lives and held very different political positions, it decided to organize around five issues: labor, education, women in politics, family issues, and social welfare. In the presentation on women and labor, Kaji pointed out that the main problems facing employed women were that women's work was unstable, and they suffered wage discrimination and lacked opportunities to receive job training. The women present decided on a course of action to encourage the government to address women's concerns. These included adopting relevant International Labor Organization measures; revising Article 3 of the labor standards law to clearly outlaw sex discrimination, not just wage discrimination based on sex; strengthening maternal protections and programs for working mothers, including instituting child-care leave; increasing the number of day-care facilities for babies and toddlers; and establishing an equal employment committee to investigate cases of employment discrimination. They also called for managers to stop differentiating between men and women, and for labor unions to abolish discrimination against women within their organizations and increase the number of women on their boards of directors.[40]

In the closing session of the conference itself, the participants were once again reminded that 1976 marked the thirtieth anniversary of women's suffrage, which in their eyes was based on the guarantee of gender equality in the country's constitution. They reaffirmed their commitment to abolish discrimination in the family, in the workplace, and in society at large; and they committed themselves to working with all women, regardless of their political position, economic situation, or social standing, to achieve these goals. They also agreed on a list of demands to present to the national and local governments. Some of their requests were as follows: (1) that the Headquarters create a Japan Plan of Action based on the World Plan of Action that had been adopted at the Mexico City Conference, that it thoroughly consider the opinions of women activists when doing so, and that it put the conclusion of the sixtieth International Labor Organization (ILO) meeting that called for equality of opportunity for women workers into practice; (2) that national and local government agencies include women in policy decisions, increase the number of women civil servants, and include women on policy discussion and research committees; (3) that women be sent as government representatives to the United Nations and UN-related international meetings; (4) that education requirements be the same for boys and girls (for example, that home economics classes be required for both); (5) that women receive equal pay for equal work, but also that the labor standards law be changed to make working conditions equal for men and women; and (6) that ILO conventions—89, the Night Work Convention; 102, the Social Security Convention; 103, the Maternity Protection Convention; and 111, the Discrimination Convention that protects women from discrimination in employment and occupation—related to women be ratified and that relevant domestic laws be reformed. In a later question-and-answer session in the Diet, Foreign Minister Miyazawa Kiichi was pressed on the issue of appointing more women to UN posts; he responded by promising Ichikawa Fusae, Tanaka Sumiko, and Doi Takako, then leader of the Japan Socialist Party, that he would appoint a woman to the post of Japan's ambassador to the United Nations. He fulfilled this promise in February 1976, when

Ogata Sadako was appointed Japan's ambassador to the UN.[41] Ogata's previous position as director of the Fusen Kaikan (the Women's Suffrage Center in Tokyo) since 1973 meant that she had close ties to NGOs and women activists; her appointment gave them another connection and another high-profile advocate domestically and internationally.

Prompted by IWY activities, the Ministry of Labor opened a consultation room for employed women with regular weekly consulting hours in April 1976. Employed women continued to press their concerns at the Twenty-first Central Gathering of Working Women (Hataraku Fujin no Chuoshū Kai) held on May 18–19, 1976, with 2,200 participants. Women gathered with the goal of establishing employed women's rights. They demanded improved labor standards, an end to pay discrimination, and the right to equal employment opportunities. In the summer of that year, activities inspired by IWY continued to take place. In June the International Women's Year Commemoration Tokyo Liaison Group, which was composed of seventy-nine organizations (thirty-four women's organizations, thirty-nine women's sections of labor unions, and six other organizations), held a convention to commemorate the anniversary of the International Women's Year Conference. The Committee on Instituting the World Plan of Action, composed of thirty organizations, gathered to evaluate and undertake activities to move toward implementing the goals of the World Plan of Action in Japan. Across Japan, many organizations also formed on the prefectural level to draft plans of action for their prefecture and lobby their local governments to undertake these activities.

Activities by women activists and NGOs continued into 1977 when on January 17 the International Women's Year Liaison Group met and agreed on a list of steps necessary for realizing gender equality. After their meeting, a group of five women who represented different organizations within the Liaison Group met with Prime Minister Fukuda Takeo and Chief Cabinet Secretary Fujita (also vice president of the Headquarters) and submitted a list of requests.[42] Probably the largest gathering of women, twenty-five thousand, took place on February 8–9, 1977, at the ninth meeting of Japan Federation of Women's Organizations. The participants focused on a ten-year plan that addressed four areas—environmental pollution, consumer action, home economics education, and welfare issues—to move toward realizing the goals of the IWY World Plan of Action. On March 5, two hundred women attended a meeting of the National Organization of Women's Groups to discuss the inadequacy of the government's Domestic Plan of Action. Takashima Junko of the Japan Labor Alliance chaired the meeting. The problems they cited were that the government's plan illustrated an inadequate awareness of the present conditions of women, used women to advance economic growth without acknowledging gender equality as a basic right, and exhibited a general lack of substance and proactive stance. They requested that the government revise the plan to bring it into line with the IWY World Plan of Action and submitted specific analyses of areas where they thought that the domestic plan was lacking. The women also made sure that the government was aware of their disappointment with a plan that was completely different from what they were expecting.

Perhaps one of the most important aspects of the activities of women's NGOs is the connection that the NGOs have with (often very high-profile) women in the government. In response to a November 3, 1977, Headquarters presentation to the IWY Liaison Group outlining progress of the Domestic Plan of Action, the group held a "Coordination Meeting for the Purpose of Realizing the Resolution of the International Women's Year Japan Conference" on December 8, 1977, at the Fusen Kaikan in Tokyo. The head of the Ministry of Labor's Women and Young Workers' Bureau was invited to a discussion with the members of the NGO. At the conclusion of the meeting, the group decided to present a report on the shortcomings of government actions on the Domestic Plan of Action to relevant ministries. Akamatsu Ryoko, then head of the Women's Issues Office, attended the meeting of the IWY Liaison Group for the first time. Akamatsu later became the minister of education and a strong representative voice for women activists at Diet committee meetings considering ratification of CEDAW. Since retiring from government service, Akamatsu has become a high-profile activist in several women's NGOs that continue to push for increasing levels of compliance with CEDAW.

Cooperation between the government and women's NGOs was not limited to the domestic arena, as was illustrated when Oba Ayako, a member of the IWY Liaison Group, attended the twenty-seventh meeting of the UN Commission on the Status of Women as the Japanese government's representative. The first planning meeting for the 1980 mid-decade conference took place in Vienna on June 15–30, 1978. Akamatsu Ryoko, Japan's representative to the meeting, gave a report of the meeting to women's NGOs at the Fusen Kaikan on July 22. Ogata Sadako, Japan's ambassador to the UN at the time, was also present at the July 22 meeting in Tokyo. On September 13, a send-off party for Takahashi Nobuko was held at the Fusen Kaikan ahead of her departure for New York, where she would represent Japan at the UN General Assembly Meeting. Forty representatives from the National Women's Committee of the United Nations attended, along with Ministry of Foreign Affairs UN Bureau Chief Watanabe. At the party, Ichikawa gave a speech in which she recognized that Takahashi's new position would help women implement the International Plan of Action by facilitating contact with the head of the General Assembly.

The next fall, Oba attended the mid-decade planning conference for the Asia-Pacific region, which was held in New Delhi on November 5–9, 1979, as an NGO representative member of the Japanese government's delegation. According to Ichikawa, the government included Oba in response to requests from the IWY Liaison Group.[43] Allowing representatives from women's organizations to attend the regional planning meetings helped them (1) connect with government representatives of Japan and other countries, (2) get to know and understand the government's position, and (3) quickly respond to government actions. When another regional planning meeting for the mid-decade conference was held in Tokyo in March 1984, Japanese women's NGOs proposed a joint session of government representatives from the region and Japanese women's NGOs to exchange ideas. This gave the NGOs an opportunity to network with government representatives from other Asian countries in an attempt to gain allies and to see where other governments stood on key issues.[44]

The high profile of some key members of women's organizations increased those organizations' influence by giving them access to government actors and expanding their opportunities for networking internationally, as well as nationally. Although these connections did not guarantee that activists achieved all their goals vis-à-vis the government, they did gain access to and cooperation from high-profile government actors, including several prime ministers. If nothing else, this meant that they could often count on government officials to participate in various conferences and meetings. In fact, when politicians did not cooperate with NGOs, they risked criticism; for example, when the prime minister declined an invitation to attend the second IWY Japan Conference in November 1980, Ichikawa publicly criticized him in her speech.

The year 1980 was a busy one for women activists as they made preparations for the mid-decade conference in Copenhagen. Oba represented Japan at the UN Commission on the Status of Women, which was meeting in Vienna in February and March. Subjects under discussion at the meeting included the condition of the World Plan of Action and preparations for the mid-decade conference program. Meanwhile, all the member organizations of the Japan Federation of Women's Organizations, along with women's labor unions (forty-eight organizations in all), met on April 12 to make plans for the mid-decade conference. They agreed to a thirty-seven-article resolution that Ichikawa presented to the cabinet secretary on April 24. Among the articles was a request that the government ratify CEDAW and include women from NGOs in the government delegation to Copenhagen. Their most important request was that the government sign and ratify CEDAW at the 1980 mid-decade conference.

The cabinet secretary responded that "there are conflicts between CEDAW and domestic law, we are researching those issues now and making efforts to do that quickly." On June 9 the Japan Federation of Women's Organizations also submitted a request that the government sign and ratify CEDAW. The request expressed disappointment and dissatisfaction with what newspapers were reporting as the government's plan to pass up the opportunity to sign the convention. It also called for the government to revise related domestic laws to ensure that gender equality would be achieved.

On June 16, 1980, one month before the Copenhagen Conference, the Ministry of Foreign Affairs (MOFA) announced that Japan would not sign CEDAW. This decision provoked strong protests after the decision was reported in the national newspapers. MOFA took the position that Japan could not sign CEDAW until laws that would bring Japanese domestic laws in line with CEDAW were in place. Ten NGO representatives visited MOFA and other government officials with a petition requesting that the government sign CEDAW. The petition indicated that women were surprised by the government's decision because they had been in close contact with government officials, and Japan's actions at UN meetings regarding CEDAW indicated tacit approval of the convention. Takahashi Nobuko, who had served as Japan's representative to the UN General Assembly's discussions of the proposed CEDAW in 1978, was surprised when the government announced that it would not sign the convention.[45] According to Takahashi's account, the Japanese government instructed her to suggest revisions that would "tone down the requirements" of CEDAW so that they would not be so disparate from Japan's own nationality law, labor law, and education law. Of these three, the government was most concerned with the nationality law; it viewed CEDAW requirements to allow women to transmit citizenship to their children as impossible.[46] This desire to weaken CEDAW would allow the government to sign it without having to make major changes in domestic law. Perhaps more important, the government would be able to sidestep the difficult negotiations that such changes would require.

In addition to submission of the petition to the government, Ichikawa visited the cabinet secretary and MOFA's UN Bureau to negotiate Japan's signing of CEDAW. Although no commitments to sign were made at the time, MOFA agreed to reconsider its decision. The final decision was to be made at a July 15 cabinet meeting, two days before the scheduled signing ceremony in Copenhagen. In the end, women activists were relieved when the cabinet decided to sign CEDAW.

The confidence and strength that these activists gained after successfully pressuring the government to sign CEDAW led to their decision to push for quick ratification without reservations. Resolutions of the second IWY Japan Conference (1980) included getting CEDAW ratified quickly and taking steps to change domestic laws so ratification would go forward. Their triumph in the first half of the Decade for Women made women activists realize the importance of building alliances; they knew that this strategy would have to be employed in getting the EEOL passed. Passage of the law would affect not only employed women but also all women's lives because of its effect on the family. Thus women activists sought the cooperation of labor unions and various women's organizations. In an attempt to use the momentum gained from successes of the previous year, NGOs held a question-and-answer session with ten government ministries and agencies on September 17, 1981, to probe representatives on their goals for the second half of the Decade for Women. This meeting was a signal to the government that advocates for change would continue their fight. They used this meeting to express their own thoughts on moving ahead with reform and to make requests for actions that they believed various governmental organizations should take to ensure progress in the second half of the decade. For its part, the government adopted a new Domestic Plan of Action and made a public promise to ratify CEDAW by 1985.[47]

After signing CEDAW, the Japanese government faced pressure to improve the legal status of working women before the 1985 ratification deadline.[48] The Japanese government's preference for administrative guidance over legal sanctions meshes well with CEDAW.[49] The convention required that Japan institute policies to comply with its goals, but how the country accomplished this would be left up to its own decision makers.[50] Furthermore, the fact that Japan's reputation was on the line provided encouragement for the government to seek change even where there was resistance from business and social leaders. Although CEDAW does not provide for third-party dispute resolution, the CEDAW Committee's reports, which can be critical, are one way to pressure states to increase levels of compliance because they threaten the state's reputation through shaming and inviting international scrutiny of domestic practices. The CEDAW Committee criticized Japan when the government submitted its first report without actively soliciting input from NGOs. The committee instructed Japan's representatives to seek significant input from NGOs when preparing future reports.

In subsequent years, Japanese NGOs made the shift from the goal of getting CEDAW adopted to ensuring implementation and increasing compliance. Women's organizations then began to submit counterreports or shadow reports to the CEDAW Committee. The well-organized women's organizations of the beginning of the Decade for Women that evolved into a significant pressure group by 1980 continue to develop the new skills needed to achieve higher levels of compliance with CEDAW. Before the CEDAW Committee discussed Japan's fifth report, NGOs that had written their own individual counterreports decided to form a network, Japan NGO Network for CEDAW (JNNC). JNNC was established on December 23, 2002; because the CEDAW Committee was set to consider the Japanese government's fourth and fifth reports on July 8, 2003, this gave it six months to prepare for the meeting at the United Nations in New York. In May 2003, fourteen NGOs sent reports and nineteen sent summary reports to the United Nations. In July 2003, sixteen NGOs sent fifty-seven women to the meeting in New York. Women's organizations believe that examination and discussion of country reports by the CEDAW Committee ensure that de facto equality is achieved. In other words, the government reports and NGO counterreports help increase levels of compliance by increasing the state's identification with the norms of CEDAW.[51]

Through a history of experience dealing with both the government and the public, Japanese women activists knew how to frame the issue of adopting CEDAW. Their participation in international meetings certainly increased their contact with other transnational actors, but they did not use these contacts to pressure their own state to adopt CEDAW. In their view, they did not have to; if they had, there is a good chance that the strategy would have actually caused a backlash. Given the challenge that CEDAW posed to conservative domestic norms regarding women's roles, it makes sense that women would be more concerned with building a broad domestic coalition to support CEDAW. Success in this effort would not only increase the strength of women activists vis-à-vis the state, but more important, it would also dampen social opposition, which would deprive conservative elements in the government of a social and political constituency on which they could justify opposing CEDAW. This resulted in a situation in which women could use their government contacts more effectively to increase their access and strengthen their ties to the state. The government's last-minute announcement that it would not sign CEDAW should not have come as a shock, given what we know about its general lack of response to civic associations. This conventional wisdom does, however, raise a new puzzle: why the government reversed its initial decision. I contend that the broad base of support and the networks that women activists developed were then used to pressure the government. The state's desire for legitimacy, which is explored in the next section, was essential at this point in the process.

Government Action: State Identity and Desire for Legitimacy

As Hashimoto's letter to the *New York Times* that opened this chapter demonstrates, state identity and desire for legitimacy are ongoing concerns for the Japanese state. Analysis of Diet committee records regarding ratifying CEDAW revealed two main views of CEDAW. On the one hand, there were those who expressed the belief that CEDAW exposes institutionalized inequalities between men and women; thus ratifying CEDAW offers an opportunity to deal with these problems. Those on this side of the issue viewed CEDAW's requirements as a positive opportunity to change and made identity-based arguments that demonstrated a keen awareness of where Japan stood in the international hierarchy of states. On the other hand, there was the more conservative view that CEDAW threatens to unleash domestic problems because of its incompatibility with Japanese culture and society; thus change should be mediated by domestic norms about the role of women. These two views extended to editorials and opinions on the EEOL as well.

In general, arguments for a gradualist and voluntary approach to law in Japan state that in order for law to be a force for social change, it must reflect a consensus of society.[52] Other arguments suggest that the Japanese government uses law to manage social change.[53] Some might argue that the government was using the same strategy in adopting international law. This view would suggest that the government adopted CEDAW despite the conflict with domestic norms to force a change in the latter. What is left unexplained is why the government would perceive a need for such change, especially because, as we will see later, there were many more conservative voices in the government that argued against adoption. Finally, the government's and courts' reluctance to set precedents using international law is evident on both women's rights and refugee issues. Thus it is not likely that the treaties were adopted to help shape social change in Japan. The history of legal support for workplace discrimination cases and previous court decisions indicate that the issue of women's work outside the home was highly contested. One example of an early court case is the 1966 Sumitomo Cement Company case, in which the Tokyo District Court made history when it ruled against the mandatory dismissal of a woman upon her marriage.[54] Sumitomo Cement appealed to the high court, and eventually a settlement was reached.[55]

Discussions of CEDAW in committee meetings of the lower house of the Diet reveal that after Japan signed CEDAW at the Copenhagen meeting in 1980, ratification was taken for granted. This is not to say, however, that Diet members did not express reservations about ratifying the treaty. Indeed, Diet members questioned the compatibility of CEDAW's goals with Japanese culture. There were even suggestions that CEDAW was more reflective of the culture and customs of Sweden and other European countries. Mention of Sweden demonstrates that government actors were aware of gender equality as a discourse of civilization.[56]

Those who welcomed the Women's Convention as an opportunity criticized the proposed EEOL as inadequate; this criticism continued even after the legislation passed. The main concerns were that the proposed EEOL did not go far enough in its effort to ensure equality of opportunity and treatment of men and women workers.[57] Diet member Doi Takako expressed the need to establish a law that protected the rights of women workers; she did not believe that the proposed legislation would do that.[58] Diet member Nakamura Iwao, the representative of the Komeito Party (Clean Government Party), agreed with Doi: "If you come from a position of respecting human rights, you would expect a proposal that prohibits discrimination; even today this proposal remains inadequate. . . . Compared with developed countries of Europe and America, our country's position is passive."[59] Once again, we see the importance of comparing Japan with Western states to establish identification with these states, and that part of this identification is the shared status of being "developed."

For many, the issue of women's status in the workplace was closely related to their role in the home and other systemic issues such as working hours:

Who carries the burden for the household? From now on, of course, it should be both men and women—this kind of spirit is flowing. But when I look at the government's proposal [for the EEOL], it does not address the basic problem, which is that we have to recognize that both men and women need to carry household burdens. We request that Japan recognize that time is short. Japan has not ratified the 1919 Working Hours Treaty or the 1935 treaty regarding the forty-hour work week. So, with long working hours, men have no time for the household and it is left to women. Therefore, I think we need a forty-hour work week with two days off—we have proposed this many times.[60]

This statement draws out other systemic issues that work to maintain the status quo of women being primarily responsible for the home. Such expressions illustrate the earlier point that gender roles evolve as a combination of historical and cultural processes, along with government policies meant to shape society in particular ways. Recognition of this led advocates of CEDAW to view the treaty and new domestic legislation associated with it as a positive source of change.

Those who saw CEDAW as a threat to Japanese culture and social order always countered complaints that the proposed law was not strong enough with claims that it was based on the reality of the situation in Japan.

As the prime minister put it, "While bearing in mind the ideals of the convention, we came up with the proposed EEOL on the basis of the reality of our country's socioeconomic situation; this proposal is the appropriate step based on that reality."[61] In fact, many members recognized that women were largely responsible for the home; they did not view this as problematic but rather as a reason that labor standards needed to "protect" women. This view reflected the sentiments of many women activists as well. Diet member Hamada Takujiro was one legislator who expressed concern about the kinds of social problems that would arise as a result of ratifying CEDAW; this made him determined to "create a Japanese-style gender-equal society where good Japanese traditions can survive."[62] He even questioned whether the international trend toward promoting the norm of gender equality was desirable everywhere. The representative from the Labor Ministry, Saito Kunihiko, reassured Hamada and answered criticism by stating that although the goal of the treaty was to eliminate discrimination between men and women, it was up to each country to decide the appropriate steps to achieve this goal. Therefore, he concluded that the proposed EEOL was sufficient to ratify the treaty. Hamada was not convinced: "Japan has had a long tradition of men working outside and women defending the home. When women are finished raising children, they can work. This system is fine; men and women are happy with it, . . . so why do we have to change just because of a world trend? I see instituting [CEDAW] domestically as causing a lot of problems. Western European developed countries have their way, and we should make our own way."[63] Although no one challenged these views, the overall assumption that CEDAW would be ratified stood. Compared with the discussions of the Refugee Convention where Western states emerged as the norm to which Japan should aspire, Hamada's criticism illustrates the resistance to changing Japan's domestic norms to create a more positive international identity. There was no middle ground that allowed Japan to adopt the Refugee Convention and retain its own way of doing things. Although Japan would gain increased international standing by ratifying CEDAW, the nature of the issue allowed for more active resistance. Refugee issues fit more readily into a human rights frame, and the connection of the issue with World War II enhanced that. In contrast, although many Japanese women activists and CEDAW supporters employed the human rights frame, discursive framing of women's rights as human rights had not yet been established internationally. States thus had less responsibility to the international community on this issue. Also, understanding women's rights and gender equality as issues that were primarily domestic cultural concerns meant that states were less likely to feel obligated to be proactive on these issues. It was enough to be neutral as long as any action taken was not interpreted by the international community as a gross violation of women's rights. Finally, domestic concern for an already-declining birthrate highlighted the importance of encouraging traditional gender roles because careers outside the home were assumed to lead to fewer children.

A cluster of related themes appeared throughout the discussions of CEDAW: the importance of the treaty, its relationship to Japan's constitution, and Japan's identity. Many Diet members reaffirmed the importance of the treaty and what it meant for Japan to ratify it. This importance had both domestic and international dimensions, which related specifically to improving Japanese society and Japan's standing in the international community. Although expressions of the latter clearly showed an interest in the status that Japan would enjoy by ratifying CEDAW, they also focused on the (domestic) responsibility that would come with it. A statement from Minister Abe Shintaro in the May 24, 1985, meeting of the Foreign Affairs Committee perhaps best captures these sentiments:

Concluding this treaty also establishes various domestic systems by which there will be the possibility of equality between men and women. On the basis of this advance, an unusually great vitality will be born in our society. Within this, we can thoroughly expect that social and economic assistance will increase. At the same time, our country's ratifying a challenging treaty in front of the world will turn our diplomacy toward the twenty-first century. As with other modern countries in the world, trust [in Japan] will increase, and this is a great merit [of the treaty].[64]

It was encouraging that the foreign minister was this enthusiastic about CEDAW. In all the discussions analyzed, he stayed the course of not only supporting ratification for the ideational benefits that Japan would reap in the form of increased international status but also welcoming the opportunity to make progress on moving toward gender equality in Japan, which would eventually lead to greater identification with gender-equality norms and compliance with CEDAW. Of course, one cannot overlook the fact that MOFA has an agenda on all treaties. An important part of MOFA's mission is to improve Japan's relations with other countries and to maintain a positive image—in other words, it seeks to influence Japan's international identity positively. It would be incorrect, however, to discount the importance of how Abe framed his support for the treaty. According to Minister Abe, "Ratifying the treaty is carrying out our international responsibility."[65] Even the leader of the Japan Socialist Party, Diet member Doi, agreed that regardless of the inadequacies of the EEOL, the treaty itself was important. In fact, given the criticism of the inadequacies of the EEOL and the desire of the four opposition parties in the government to strengthen the proposal before it became law, it is clear that these criticisms were not attempts to defeat ratification of CEDAW.

Even with these objections, there were no attempts to make reservations to the treaty. Akamatsu Ryoko, then head of the Ministry of Labor's Women's Bureau, said, "It is not possible for us to ratify with reservations. The government has said several times that to the extent possible, there should not be reservations when we ratify. Also, civic organizations have strongly requested that to the extent possible, they do not want reservations on ratification."[66] Advocates of ratification, including Akamatsu herself, believed that not making reservations would ensure periodic reevaluation and revision of relevant laws; thus the level of compliance would be increased over time as Japanese society evolved and there was increasing identification with the norms codified in CEDAW. Akamatsu's specific reference to the preferences of civic organizations reminds us that these organizations had the ear of some government officials; having met with women's NGOs in the past, Akamatsu was one such official.

After successfully pushing the government to sign CEDAW, women's organizations boldly pushed for ratification without reservations. It is well known that Japan attempted to weaken CEDAW as much as possible during negotiations.[67] I suggest that the final version was still a significant challenge to Japanese domestic norms regarding gender roles. Government officials framed the desire to ratify the treaty without reservations as a public commitment to the international community: "If this treaty is ratified, it is a promise from the country, so we must institute its aims; Japan's government will have a great obligation."[68] Once this promise was made, Japan, "as a country that is trusted in the international community, will need to conduct itself as such. So instead of foreign countries pointing out [Japan's] shortcomings, they will focus on Japan's efforts."[69] Framing the issue in this way appealed to Japan's identity concerns and again illustrated the mutual constitution of identity and interests in deciding to adopt international norms. Being trustworthy and living up to promises are obviously necessary to obtain and maintain legitimacy. Throughout the discussions, there were also references to the importance of Japan as an international actor, a developed country, and the number two economic power in the "free world" and the responsibility that accompanied that status. After the decision to pass the EEOL, Diet member Nakamura Iwao saw this position as enhanced when he said, "Now, as a developed country, our country does not have to feel ashamed in front of Europe and America."[70] Taken together, these statements suggest that Japan had been ashamed of its international position and identity in the past and would face shame again if it did not act appropriately on this issue.

Throughout this discussion of Japan's international position as at least partially responsible for ratification of CEDAW, the role of women's groups in pushing the government to sign the convention was conspicuously absent except for Akamatsu's statements. This is in contrast with discussions on ratifying the Landmine Treaty over ten years later, as we will see in Chapter 5.

The Equal Employment Opportunity Law: Conflict Between Domestic and International Norms

The need to create laws to ensure equal employment before ratifying CEDAW was one indicator of a gap between domestic and international norms on gender equality. As stated earlier, the only legislation dealing with this issue was the Labor Standards Law, which outlawed wage discrimination based on sex; the existing legal regime did not address any other issues to ensure gender equality in employment. That the government moved to implement the treaty by passing the EEOL before ratifying the treaty in 1985 was a positive sign. However, we should remember the distinction between implementation and compliance discussed in Chapter 2. Implementation is a first step insofar as it creates laws and other formal institutions. Even states that adopt international law for instrumental reasons might take some steps to implement the laws. Compliance, however, requires a state's identification with international norms. In cases like those considered here where international and domestic norms conflict, a change in identity is required to achieve a significant level of compliance. This means that the norms in question will achieve a taken-for-granted quality that will be evident in the willingness of courts and other relevant actors to use the norms to enforce laws and actually put other relevant institutions to use. Tracing the development of the EEOL will help us see how the level of compliance has changed over time.

Employment discrimination against Japanese women violates the assertion included in CEDAW's introduction that "the role of women in procreation should not be a basis for discrimination." Article 5 and Article 11, paragraphs 1 and 2, are especially relevant sections of the treaty. Normative international law is often criticized for vague language and reluctance to deal with cultural issues. CEDAW's Article 5, however, is very clear about the responsibility of states "to modify the social and cultural patterns of conduct of men and women" and other practices that are based on "stereotyped roles for men and women" or "the idea of the inferiority or the superiority of either of the sexes." Article 11 specifically addresses employment discrimination by requiring states to take appropriate measures to ensure "the right to the same employment opportunities, . . . the right to free choice of profession and employment, [and] the right to promotion, job security," and other benefits. The article goes further to address the issue of balancing women's work inside the home as wives and mothers with that of their paid employment outside the home. State parties are instructed to prohibit dismissal based on pregnancy, maternity leave, or marital status, to "introduce maternity leave with pay" or other such comparable benefits "without loss of former employment, seniority or social allowances, [and] to encourage the provision of the necessary supporting social services," especially child-care facilities, "to enable parents to combine family obligations with work responsibilities."[71]

When CEDAW was signed, the primary characteristic of Japan's state identity was that of the number two economic power in the free world. Japan was still suffering from a negative international image stemming from accusations of unfair trading practices and lack of commitment to international human rights agreements. Thus Japan's desire for international legitimacy was high, but the state did not adopt CEDAW in order to change its identity in a way that would increase its legitimacy. However, women activists took advantage of the state's desire for international legitimacy and its vulnerability to pressure it into signing CEDAW. The last thing Japan needed was to add one more negative characteristic— hostility toward women's rights—to its already-negative image. The Japanese government might have been able to resist pressure from women had there not been such a widespread international focus on women's issues, and had the government not announced that it would not sign the treaty at the 1980 international conference marking the midpoint of the United Nations Decade for Women. Already-strong and organized domestic women's movements took advantage of the international context to increase their power and advance their cause.

By 1990, when Hashimoto made his controversial comments, the economic recession was making it obvious that women were still considered a reserve labor force, and that after the collapse of the bubble economy they were less needed and certainly less welcome in the labor market. The heightened concern over the declining birthrate and the economic slump provided the context within which women were trying to realize the promise of CEDAW and the EEOL.

The EEOL illustrates that quick implementation of a treaty does not mean that the conflict between domestic and international norms disappears at adoption. It also highlights the need for domestic advocates to remain active after adoption to help achieve higher levels of compliance (see Table 5 for a summary of key gender equality legislation). The issues of gender equality and women's employment and the underlying issue of

TABLE 5. Legal changes affecting women, 1980–1999

Year	Action
1980	Japan signs CEDAW
1985	Nationality Law amended to bilineal system
	Equal Employment Opportunity Law passed
	Ratification of CEDAW
1992	Child Care Leave Law enters into force
1995	Child Care Leave Law revised to establish the Family Care Leave System
	Ratification of International Labor Organization Convention 156
1997	Revision of Equal Employment Opportunity Law and related laws
1999	Enactment of the Basic Law for a Gender-Equal Society
	Enactment of the Basic Law on Food, Agriculture, and Rural Areas (stipulating the promotion of women's participation)
	Revised EEOL enters into force

SOURCE: Japanese Government Web site, www.gender.go.jp/english_contents/index, July 16, 2002. Compiled from a list of "Milestones in Advancement of Women Since International Women's Year."

appropriate roles for women are so contested that without strong domestic advocates continuing to challenge the state and conservative domestic norms, compliance would be quite low.

Despite discriminatory policies and practices in the workplace, the numbers of employed women has steadily increased over time, but women are still employed mainly in those sectors that most need part-time, low-cost labor that can be laid off during slow-growth periods.

From 1960 until 1980, women made up 40 percent of those employed; after the mid-1970s more than half of employed women were married. The primary reason that married women gave for reentering the work force was to add to the family budget. After the 1970s the percentage of household income that came from women's income increased,; this money was used for necessary household expenditures, such as home loans and education.[72] With high economic growth and increased urbanization in Japan, the cost of living also increased and often began to require two incomes, especially for those families whose husbands did not work in a large firm that provided family wages. The idea that women's income was supplemental no longer held.

The labor shortage that accompanies declining birthrates and an increasing elderly population compounds the social issues surrounding women's employment and increases women's responsibilities at home. In the past, government and industry policies have been able to successfully shape women's roles, but now the double bind of caring for the home and working for wages is squeezing women tighter than ever. Although the government is trying to once again shape women's roles in society, there is evidence that these efforts are not going to be entirely successful.[73] Even with the calls to increase social service support for women so that they can continue to work both inside and outside the home, there is evidence that more women are delaying marriage as a form of resistance. Although many of these women will marry, the fact that they are choosing to marry later will increase the marriage age, force society to rethink expectations for women's lives, and continue the trend of declining birthrates.[74]

Figure 1 shows a marked increase in the percentage of women in the workforce between 1985, when the EEOL was passed and CEDAW was ratified, and 1990. After 1990 there was a continued increase, but it leveled off and became less noticeable. This can be attributed mostly to the bursting of the economic bubble at the end of the 1980s and the prolonged recession of the 1990s.

The EEOL is the centerpiece of Japanese women's legal recourse in workplace discrimination cases. This law was drafted by the Ministry of

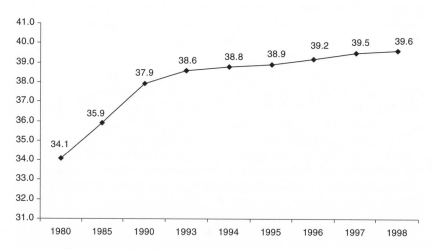

FIGURE 1. Percentage of women in the workforce

SOURCE: Data from the Management and Coordination Agency table "Employees by Occupation," in "Response to the Questionnaire to Government on Implementation of the Beijing Platform for Action: Japan," April 1999.

Labor in April 1984 and submitted to the Diet in May of that year. Passage of the bill was delayed for one year until May 1985 because of opposition from some political parties and business interests.[75] My research supports Parkinson's (1989) finding that the committee that was responsible for making recommendations to the Ministry of Labor regarding the content of the legislation openly recognized that the steps in the EEOL fell short of securing equality for women; it accepted the shortcomings as a reflection of tensions resulting from the need to reconcile the required legislation and women's role in the family. The bill finally passed just before the government's self-imposed deadline to ratify CEDAW before the end of the UN Decade for Women; it went into effect in April 1986. Although the EEOL is a milestone in the fight to secure employed women's rights, it has been heavily criticized within and outside Japan for not having any teeth. Basically, the law asked employers to try not to discriminate against women and lacked any kind of sanctions if they did.[76] Furthermore, the only recourse provided in the law was mediation by the prefectural authorities of the Ministry of Labor, to which the company itself had to agree before the process could begin. These clauses hinder compliance with CEDAW itself because the law does not ensure that there is a move toward identification with the norm of gender equality that is necessary for compliance.

Even after the "duty to endeavor" clauses were strengthened in the 1999 revised law, other shortcomings remained unaddressed. The most egregious shortcoming is a result of the normative framework of the law itself. Although the law seeks to prohibit discrimination against female workers, it does not prohibit discrimination based on sex or gender. The law fails to define what constitutes sex discrimination. Because the EEOL intervenes at the point of hire, it does not attempt to redress past discrimination against women who are already employed and have little or no hope of promotion. Moreover, because the law is aimed at ensuring that women have access to traditionally male-dominated positions, it does not recognize the institutionalized idea that different kinds of work are suitable for different sexes. Thus the law has the potential officially to open the door to management positions for more women without specifically addressing the issue of gender equality, the issue that was the focus of women's NGOs in Japan when they were fighting for the government to adopt CEDAW.

Another shortcoming in the law can be attributed to the lack of attention to the influence of men and women's socialization on women's integration into male-dominated workplaces. Because the EEOL is likely to have the greatest impact on college-educated women trying to enter large companies, it is important to examine how the structure of these institutions and the institutional culture are ill equipped to help women advance in the workplace and often even hinder their advancement. Creighton makes the point that "it raises doubts that legal changes such as the introduction of the EEOL can have any major impact on female employment roles without a corresponding shift in social values."[77] I suggest, along the lines of Upham's argument, that legal changes often precipitate shifts in social values. Creighton finds that the pattern of female work relations may reflect their socialization and not mesh well with the structure of Japanese companies. One example is the central importance of the *senpai-kohai* relationship,[78] a mentoring relationship, where women are at a comparative disadvantage. Failure to address the work culture of large corporations and social institutions such as marriage hinders the achievement of a high level of compliance because the practices that go unexamined are those that impede identification with the norms codified in the treaty.

A third way in which the EEOL is problematic is that in its stated goal of harmonizing career and family for women, it does not mention men; this omission assumes that women are the primary caregivers and that men do not experience conflicts between work and family responsibilities. It is evident in the Diet records discussed earlier and in the popular media examined later that there is a specific realization that although the law focuses on employment, the impact will be felt more broadly throughout society. Many people realize that there are systemic social issues about the nature of work in large Japanese firms that must be addressed before women will have access to equal opportunities in employment without having to sacrifice family life, having to carry a double burden, or becoming stigmatized. In this particular type of firm, men are expected and implicitly required to totally commit themselves to the company. In exchange for lifetime employment, regular promotions, and increases in salary, men are expected to show loyalty to the company by working long hours, participating in late-night socializing with colleagues, and accepting transfers to distant branches within or outside Japan without question.[79] This system depends on a gendered division of labor where a man is able to fulfill his professional and social obligations to the firm by having a wife at home who will tend to his laundry, prepare his meals, take care of the household finances, and rear the children.[80]

Equally important is what this gendered division of labor means for employed women.[81] Because women are expected to give family obligations their primary attention, they become a reserve labor force. When women return to work, they usually do so as part-time workers.[82] Although their hours are more flexible—which is attractive to women with families—they usually do not receive the same benefits as full-time regular workers and can be laid off during tough economic times. The culture of large Japanese firms means that when the EEOL was adopted, employers were not willing to treat women equally, and many women were not interested in becoming a part of large companies until the culture in these companies changed significantly.[83] In an analysis of the kinds of work women do outside the home, Japan's third CEDAW report, which was submitted in 1993, found that in 1992 women held 59.3 percent of clerical positions, 52.6 percent of security and service positions, and only 7.9 percent of managerial positions. The last figure was up from 5.1 percent in 1980. In 1992, of 8,680,000 part-time workers, 68.2 percent were women; 30.2 percent of all employed women were part-time.[84]

Despite the continuation of a gendered division of labor, Japan's third report to the CEDAW Committee stated that many companies had changed their personnel policies to comply with the EEOL. Nevertheless, it also noted, "As the understanding of the purpose of the law is steadily deepening, there is a growing atmosphere in society to utilize women's potential while women themselves become more conscious of their work. However, there are still problems including the existence of recruitment and hiring of 'men only,' especially in the case of engineers. As improvements in practice lag behind the improvements in systems, ensuring de facto equality is a task to be fulfilled."[85] Clearly the substance of the practice lags behind legal progress and there is a lack of state identification with the norms. In addition to a continuation of men-only hiring, the recession also had an impact on women's employment because large companies are less likely to hire women during hard economic times.

Figure 2, a graph of the percentages of women managers and clerical workers, shows the growth in the percentage of women in two work categories over the period 1980–1998. In 1980, the midpoint of the UN Decade for Women and the year Japan signed CEDAW, 51.1 percent of clerical workers were women, whereas only 5.1 percent of managers were women. The rate of change for these two occupational categories has been roughly the same over the nineteen years shown. Even after 1985, when the EEOL was passed and CEDAW was ratified, there was no great increase in the percentage of women managers and officials. Given that the EEOL is designed to address discrimination at the point of hire and that women already made up a majority of the clerical workers before 1985, we would expect a greater rate of increase in the percentage of women holding management positions. Overall, the percentage of women in clerical work increased roughly 8 percent over the entire period, while the increase in managers and officials was only 4 percent. The economic problems that began in the late 1980s when the economic bubble burst, leading to a recession that continued throughout the 1990s and into the first decade of the twenty-first century, affected women's work lives in

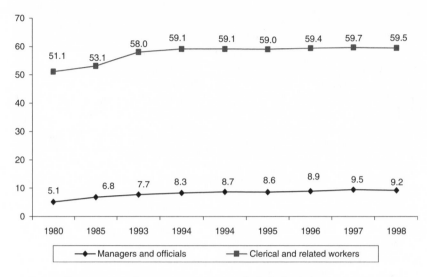

FIGURE 2. Percentages of women managers and clerical workers

SOURCE: Data from the Management and Coordination Agency table "Employees by Occupation," in "Response to the Questionnaire to Government on Implementation of the Beijing Platform for Action: Japan," April 1999.

many ways. Men in large companies faced reduced salaries, and eventually some were laid off from work; more women entered the labor market. However, the economic conditions limited women's options to part-time jobs because the economic downturn reinforced the gendered labor market.

Figure 3 provides information on the percentages of women engaged in work as managers and officials, clerical workers, sales workers, transportation and communication workers, and professional and technical workers from 1980 through 1995. These data confirm the earlier suggestion that there was a minimal increase in the percentage of women in male-dominated occupations during the period after Japan signed CEDAW in 1980, while those occupations that had a large percentage of women at the start of the period grew at equal and often higher rates over the sixteen years shown here. Thus in 1995, ten years after the EEOL and CEDAW went into effect in Japan, the percentage of women in two male-dominated occupations, managerial work and transportation and communication work, were not encouraging. The former increased by a mere 3.5 percent, and the latter actually steadily declined. The percentage of women professional and technical workers, including nurses and teachers, also actually declined over this period. In 1980 women were almost a

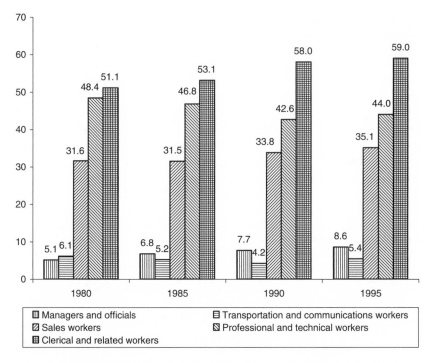

FIGURE 3. Percentages of women workers in selected occupations

SOURCE: Data from the Management and Coordination Agency table "Employees by Occupation," in "Response to the Questionnaire to Government on Implementation of the Beijing Platform for Action: Japan," April 1999.

majority of the workers in this category at 48.4 percent. This declined to 46.8 percent in 1985 and to 42.6 percent in 1990. In 1995 the percentage of women in this category increased to 44 percent, a net decline of 4.4 percent over the sixteen-year period.

On December 17, 1996, the Ministry of Labor announced its intention to reform the EEOL by replacing the "duty to endeavor" provisions of articles with prohibitory language. The report was submitted to the Diet in 1997, and the amended law went into effect on April 1, 1999. In addition to outlawing "men-only" job advertisements, the amended law also recognizes sexual harassment (*seku hara*) in the workplace as discrimination and instructs companies to educate their employees on what constitutes *seku hara*. Recognizing sexual harassment as discrimination moves toward the goal of gender equality because it actually affects women beyond the point of hire, in addition to affecting women working in diverse settings. In addition, the Child Care Leave Law, which entered into force in 1992, and policies designed to encourage rehiring women after child-care leaves have also been enacted. However, by the time the Basic Law for a Gender-Equal Society was enacted in 1999, there was already an overwhelming backlash against issues of gender equality (*jendā furii*).

Despite the shortcomings of the EEOL, my analysis of newspaper editorials and opinions shows that many people supported establishing the law because it would facilitate changing roles in the household, which is necessary if the ultimate goal is to affect gender roles throughout society and change conservative cultural beliefs about gender. This popular support could lead to increasing identification with a norm of gender equality over time. Confidence in the potential for the EEOL to change society was reflected in the editorials and opinions written in the *Yomiuri Shimbun* from January 1984 through December 1986. Although few articles specifically addressed Japan's adoption of CEDAW, the need to adopt the EEOL in order to move forward with ratifying CEDAW was a pervasive theme. Focus on the EEOL and government action to pass the legislation illustrates how the issue of gender equality in Japan was centered on women's employment. Although domestic interest groups did strategically use appeals to Japan's identity and the need to ratify CEDAW as a way to move forward on establishing the EEOL as law, the issue was discussed primarily as a domestic issue, with comparatively low appeal to Japan's identity.[86] Many of the articles remarked on the lack of a societal consensus on the way of achieving equality for men and women, but none opposed equality as a goal. Although the op-eds often grudgingly supported the EEOL, such positions in the more conservative *Yomiuri Shimbun* should not go unnoticed. The editorialists and opinion writers recognized the need for change in women's position in the paid workforce, and their writings show that they knew that change would come only through people making demands on the government to institute a law, a view that supports the idea that the law can produce social change through promoting a change in the way people think about issues.[87] A May 11, 1984, *Yomiuri Shimbun* editorial stated:

I can't help but think that consensus on the EEOL is premature. . . . 70% of Japanese women said that they agreed with the adage "men at work, women in the home" (*otoko shigoto, onna katei*), which is 10% less than a decade ago. Japanese women's consciousness continues to change, but only 30% of European and American women agree with the adage. Under these kinds of conditions, changing men and women's societal and cultural roles that is the ideal of CEDAW is impossible. It is only at our insistence that we will come to this point.[88]

Despite the tone of this statement, the author actually advocated passage of the EEOL and ratification of CEDAW. The primary reason given for supporting these measures was not to change society or improve women's position; instead, the author went on to make vague reference to Japan's identity, which, as stated earlier, is rare in these articles over the three-year period investigated, and to women's increasing levels of education as making passage of the EEOL inevitable: "If we don't ratify CEDAW, our country's international image will probably suffer. Moreover, women will continue to be more and more highly educated, so we should probably institute the EEOL. This will probably change people and companies' thinking on the issue. . . . We need to debate the right way to achieve equality between men and women, given our culture." Even without making specific reference to women's rights or discrimination, the author recognized that to some extent Japan's identity and therefore legitimacy were at stake, but the larger issue was the question of Japanese national identity, which was clearly challenged by both the international and domestic measures proposed to improve the position of women in Japanese society.

According to the logic presented in the two passages just quoted, given the reality of women's own beliefs about their role in the family, the ideals presented in CEDAW will not penetrate Japanese society without intervention. Furthermore, even though a majority of women believe that their primary responsibility is taking care of their families and the home, increasing numbers of women are pursuing some kind of higher education. Given the usual pattern of women working before marriage and after child rearing, the fact that many believe that their place is in the home does not preclude a work life outside the home, especially because the trend of higher education among women is increasing. Thus, according to the editorial, passing the EEOL would not be a radical step but a logical one—maybe even one to be grudgingly undertaken—born out of the circumstances of Japanese women's lives and international expectations. Although these laws will likely change domestic norms about women's roles, Japanese should determine the direction of change—including ratifying CEDAW and instituting reforms associated with it—with respect to cultural norms.

References to CEDAW and Japan's identity are more prevalent in the articles written in 1985, the year in which the EEOL was passed and Japan ratified CEDAW. Minimizing public discussion of CEDAW and the international dimension of women's fight for equality in the op-ed pieces may have helped minimize chances that a potential backlash could find power in rhetoric that would paint women fighting for change as pawns of foreign influence and therefore shift the focus to a more nationalistic concern with defending Japanese culture against outside influences. After the EEOL was passed and the road to ratifying CEDAW was clear, there was more discussion of the influence of the international environment on women's movements inside Japan. One opinion piece stated that establishing the EEOL and ratifying the treaty included an "aim of changing the societal ideal of 'men at work, women in the household.' Not only did the system have to be changed, but society had to be changed as well; thus there was criticism [from within Japan] that [these measures] trespassed on culture."[89] This author also stated, "Our country does not have to worry about being disgraced at the Nairobi Conference that takes place starting June 15. . . . Ratifying the treaty saves face internationally."[90]

The July 27, 1984, commentary used the need to ratify CEDAW as a way to advocate moving forward with the EEOL, which had been bogged down because of conflicting demands made by representatives of labor, on the one hand, and employers, on the other. Because of necessary compromise, the proposed law did not meet the hopes of women activists and led to increasing criticism from labor unions and women's groups. The editorial stated, "CEDAW is an international agreement that will change the relationship between labor and employers and women and men in Japan. If we do not have the agreement, Japanese society will not move toward change."[91] Even with the shortcomings of the legislation, supporters thought that it should be put into effect and revised later. Despite the imperfections of the law, Akamatsu Ryoko, a key government official who played a major role in passing the EEOL and ratifying CEDAW, stated in an interview that because CEDAW was ratified without reservations, the government would have to continue to revise and strengthen the law. Akamatsu went on to insist that regardless of the shortcomings of the law, the original EEOL changed Japanese society because before the law, employers did not even realize that there was anything wrong with their practices.[92] Akamatsu's comments indicate that domestic advocates on this issue understood that they would have to increase Japan's level of compliance with CEDAW gradually. As long as CEDAW was ratified without reservations, improving compliance over time would be possible.

Overall, the articles during the period considered here also stressed the importance of creating an environment where it was possible for women to continue working after marriage and childbirth as one way of moving toward achieving real equality in the workplace.[93] According to the June 6, 1984, editorial, moving toward equality between men and women and extending a child-care leave system both required separating "woman" from "mother." Separating these two identities is at the heart of improving women's status in the workplace. Although the role of mother is idealized in Japan,[94] it is a barrier to advancement for working women and an excuse to relegate women to a lower status in the workplace. The social role of mother is important, but if the only way in which women can be legitimate members of society is in this capacity, the lower status of women in the workplace naturally extends to women throughout society. In short, basing women's social standing on one role or one part of their identity and having that identity be the basis for discriminating against women in different parts of social life undermine the status and respect afforded to the role of mother.[95] This insight is related to two other issues that were addressed in the op-ed pieces. First, they asserted that part of the goal of the EEOL was to establish equality in the household through establishing a norm that men and women should share household responsibilities. Second, many of the articles argued that the basic principle underlying public law as it related to women's employment needed to be changed from "protection" to "equality." This change would require employers and policy makers to change their view of women as individuals in need of protection to that of women as autonomous, capable beings. Through the 1990s—and even today—the EEOL has been disappointing on most measures.

Analysis of the op-ed pages shows that although domestic interests drove the fight for women's equality, it was at least in part fed by the international events of the time. According to the February 26, 1985, editorial, "Because of the UN Decade for Women, the desire to work and to be independent have swelled in women's hearts; after the Decade is over, this will continue. But this kind of change of consciousness does not necessarily mean that society will share this thinking."[96] Thus, the editorial concluded, those fighting for equality would have to change society by creating a desire for and appreciation of women's participation. The conflict between domestic norms and women's fight for equality in employment and the household required that the force for change come from within Japan. However, that same conflict also meant that women would be more successful with support from outside Japan. Japanese women understood this and effectively used the connection between their fight and activities of the UN Decade for Women to bolster their cause while not losing sight of the necessity that their arguments for change be mindful of Japanese domestic norms and their own commitment to what might be called a more maternalist feminism. In short, Japanese women were energized, inspired, and motivated by the international environment, especially the United Nations Decade for Women, but the history of domestic women's movements made it unnecessary for women to rely on international movements.[97]

The Judiciary and Lawsuits as a Force for Change: Pushing for Compliance

The willingness of the judiciary to use domestic and international law in deciding cases is one way to gauge the level of identification—full compliance—with treaties and the norms they embody. In order for the judiciary even to have the opportunity to act, people must be willing to bring lawsuits; thus identification may require challenges to noncompliance on the domestic level.

Although Japanese policy makers have tried to argue that CEDAW is a progressive agreement that requires only gradual change, the position of treaties in the Japanese legal system has supported implementation of the treaty and very meaningful legal reform. In Japan, treaties supersede domestic law but are subordinate to the constitution.[98] This means that each time Japan adopts a treaty, there is an attempt to revise the relevant body of domestic law to reflect the commitments included in the treaty. There are both positive and negative consequences for women's lawsuits as a force for change. Before CEDAW was adopted, there was a first phase of employment discrimination lawsuits from the mid-1960s to the late 1970s that focused on discrimination in wage, retirement, and "reduction-in-force" policies.[99] Decisions in favor of the female plaintiffs in these cases were based on Article 90 of the Civil Code, which states that any "juristic act whose object is such as to be contrary to public order or good morals is null and void."[100] The vagueness of this article suggests that the judges in these cases saw the merits of the cases and searched for a way to support the claims. Interestingly, none of the court cases have referred to Article 14 of the constitution, which prohibits sex discrimination. Adoption of CEDAW and the subsequent establishment of domestic laws related to employment discrimination have given the judiciary a more solid basis for its decisions. The unwillingness of judges to refer to these laws in deciding cases such as the employment discrimination lawsuits discussed shortly is a clear indication that women's employment rights and the norm of gender equality have not attained a taken-for-granted status.

The burden of taking on the legal system and the risk of social stigmatization deter women from pursuing court cases that force adherence to the EEOL.[101] However, Japanese women have continued to use litigation campaigns to achieve gains. Early on, wage discrimination based on sex was one of the few legally sanctioned acts of discrimination that allowed women an opening to pursue legal action. In some cases, plaintiffs have been victorious, but this does not prevent employers from claiming that differential pay rates are due to different kinds of work—most recently, justifications have been based on the two-track system. The legal basis of discrimination lawsuits against employers has evolved with the adoption of CEDAW, the implementation of the EEOL, and the subsequent revision of the law. As far back as its consideration of Japan's initial report, which was submitted in 1988, the CEDAW Committee noted that regardless of the same educational requirements, men's starting salaries were higher than women's. Some of the largest and best-known cases against the Sumitomo Group began in 1994 and have only recently been decided. The women who sued Sumitomo attended the 1994 CEDAW Committee review of country reports at the UN; the experience encouraged them to pursue redress for the discrimination they had faced. After requests for mediation from the Osaka prefectural authorities and help from their local union were rejected, nineteen women filed lawsuits against three companies in the Sumitomo Group for wage discrimination and discrimination in promotion. The women also claimed that the two-track hiring system, whereby men are hired on the managerial track (*sōgō shoku*) while women are hired on the clerical track (*ippan shoku*), violates CEDAW. Article 4 of the Labor Standards Law strictly prohibits wage discrimination based only on sex, but it does not address situations where wage differentials are clearly gendered but are based on the employment system. These were the first discrimination cases that appealed to the relevant international law—CEDAW in this case. In fact, these lawsuits went further in an attempt to change the system by using CEDAW to challenge the legality of dual career tracks.

Osaka prefectural authorities refused to accept the Sumitomo cases for mediation, arguing that the wage differences were due to different career tracks—the employment system—not discrimination. But the women's claim that the system itself was illegal under CEDAW pushed the case forward. The examination of witnesses finally began in 1998. The Sumitomo representative testified that women were not employed on the managerial track because

at that time, since the length of service of women in general was relatively short, [a woman] could not be expected to be trained as a candidate for an executive position who is required to build up business experience. Employees in management positions are expected to often work overtime and during holidays, whereas the maximum working hours of women were legally bound. So it was hard for women to be assigned to more demanding positions, and a transfer to another office was usually beyond the consideration for women, but not for men. In the 1960s, when we hired women, we thought we should be sensitive in our treatment of precious young female workers until they get married. Therefore, even when we had them go on one-day business trips, we tried to not have them go to an unfamiliar place.[102]

This statement illustrates the assumptions that employers make about women's career paths and their commitment to work. In fact, it assumes one career path. Most companies hire women on the assumption that they are only temporary workers who will quit work once they are married or when they have children. Although this is the course that many women choose, the assumption puts other women who are more career minded at a disadvantage because from the time they are hired they are not taken seriously.

There are also economic benefits for the company to perpetuate this cycle of hiring young temporary workers. If there is constant turnover and the new hires are young women with little or no experience, they can be paid low wages. Also, if a woman returns to work after her first child enters elementary school, she too is at an economic disadvantage. Because of a system of seniority-based wages, she may have to accept lower wages as a returning worker than she could have expected had she worked continuously. In a large corporation, she might not be rehired. Finally, the statement from the Sumitomo representative indicates the general view that women must be taken care of. This person reflects the company's paternalistic view that women are not autonomous, independent beings, and the company is doing a service by being concerned about their best interests.

The government representative's testimony protected Sumitomo: "The EEOL was implemented in order to ratify the CEDAW Convention. However, the EEOL does not ban all forms of discrimination based on sex in employment. When a law is enacted, it must not stray from reality. . . . [Because of] the realities—women's occupational consciousness, conventions in Japanese employment practices (and) women's family responsibility—the law should fully reflect our society."[103] In other words, some discrimination is acceptable. This statement illustrates the state's position on how international agreements should be implemented and does not bode well for compliance with CEDAW. In this case, the goal is not to change Japanese domestic norms and social practices by adopting international norms. Instead, the goal is to formally agree to international standards but to limit their scope to preserve the status quo "reality." Despite Foreign Minister Abe's position that viewed CEDAW as an opportunity to move toward gender equality, this representative's testimony demonstrates that there are still some in the government who oppose the norm of gender equality. Under other circumstances, one could argue that the statements of one government official cannot be taken to reflect the state's position on the treatment of employed women, but because these are the statements of the central government's representative at a very high-profile trial, we can assume that they are, at least to some extent, officially sanctioned. Moreover, such statements reflect the tension between the state identity that Japan wants to project and the national identity that it wants to protect.

The cases against Sumitomo Electric and Sumitomo Chemical were decided in July 2000 and March 2001, respectively. The judges ruled against the plaintiffs in all the cases. In the Sumitomo Electric case, the judge decided that although the labor-management practices of the company were in violation of Article 14 of Japan's constitution, which prohibits discrimination based on sex, social norms trumped legal ones: "In the late 1960s [when the women were hired] gender-based division of work was widely accepted in Japanese society and males were expected to be breadwinners of the families and females were expected to get married and concentrate on family matters, raising children and doing house chores. Such labor management is not acceptable at present but in the late 1960s it was an effective and acceptable labor management policy and not against public order and standards of decency."[104]

In response to the plaintiffs' claim that the decision of the Osaka Women's and Young Workers' Office to decline their request for mediation violated CEDAW's requirement that states "take all appropriate measures to ensure the right to the same employment opportunities and the right to promotion, [the court ruled that] 'the CEDAW convention has no retroactive effect.'"[105] Basically, the judge's ruling avoided using CEDAW in any meaningful way to redress the women's complaints and provide the compensation that they sought for the discrepancy in wages.[106] Because the court also ruled that the EEOL is not retroactive and thus did not apply to this case, it left no hope for a decision in favor of the plaintiffs. The ruling quoted much of the ruling in the Sumitomo Electric case but did not make any reference to Article 14 of the constitution. Both of these cases were appealed to the Osaka High Court.[107] The Sumitomo Metals case was the last to be decided; the judge found in favor of the plaintiffs in 2005. In its decision in the Sumitomo Metals case, the court recognized the treatment of the women as unlawfully discriminatory; a total of 63 million yen was awarded to the plaintiffs. The appeal of the Sumitomo Electric Case concluded in 2006; the two plaintiffs were awarded a total of 76 million yen and promotion.

The initial decision was a blow that suggested that compliance was disappointingly low in the early years of the twenty-first century, and that the conflict between domestic and international norms still had not been resolved and would continue to impede identification with the international norm. The women who brought the lawsuits against Sumitomo were supported by an Osaka-based NGO, Working Women's International Network (WWIN), that was formed in 1995 and boasted two hundred members. By 2005 the membership had increased to approximately eight hundred, 10 percent of whom were men. The WWIN used many of the same strategies that women had previously used to pressure the government to adopt CEDAW, including organizing regular symposia to keep members and supporters informed, as well as providing the physical space for supporters to gather, talk, and exchange ideas. Other strategies demonstrate an intensified focus on international networking and public relations. The women appealed to international organizations, including the CEDAW Committee and the United Nations; attended the 1995 Fourth World Conference on Women held in Beijing, where they organized a session on the Sumitomo case and learned that it would be essential for them to establish a Web site and begin organizing through the Internet; worked with Diet members and negotiated with the Ministry of Health and Welfare on what would become the 1999 amendments to the EEOL; and published a newsletter in both Japanese and English. They also publicized their case to the UN, the International Labor Organization, and the European Union as a concrete illustration of sex discrimination in Japan.

In 2003, while the cases in Japan were still under appeal, the CEDAW Committee recommended that Japan revise its EEOL to explicitly prohibit indirect discrimination such as the two-track hiring system. In 2005 WWIN held events every two months that focused on calling for amending the EEOL a second time. In August of that year the group actually submitted a proposal to revise the law directly to the Ministry of Health, Welfare, and Labor. The EEOL was revised a second time in 2006. Women are becoming increasingly bold in their demands for revisions that will truly reflect a move toward gender equality in the workplace. Their demands have led to a medium level of compliance, but full compliance is still a distant goal.

Toward Re-creating Gender Roles

Given the barriers to gender equality in Japan and the economic benefits of maintaining the gendered division of labor, one would imagine that CEDAW would not be implemented in any meaningful way and that compliance would be low. Although the Japanese government cites the end of World War II as a crucial turning point for women because the 1946 Constitution guarantees the equality of men and women, women's status in society has not changed significantly, and equality has not been fully achieved.[108] In addition, the government has not explicitly recognized its role in attempting to shape women's roles in society. One of the greatest barriers to achieving greater gender equity in Japan is that there has been only a slow and reluctant recognition that discrimination exists. Domestic norms relating to gender differences in Japan have roots that have been carefully crafted through government and corporate policies toward women. Although domestic norms surrounding this issue conflict with the norms codified in CEDAW, the domestic advocates also resist and seek to change the domestic norms.

The obstacles that women continue to face in achieving greater gender equality in Japan can be attributed at least in part to the need to change societal expectations of men's and women's gender roles. Despite the changes that have taken place since CEDAW was signed, there is still resistance to redefining gender roles. Even though one of the government's own stated goals is not only to achieve equal opportunities for women in the workplace but also to realize gender equality throughout society, there has been only limited success in creating laws. Of course, it is difficult to legislate equality, but the absence of attention to men's roles and the existence of laws with no sanctions in general reinforce the lack of accountability of employers and men. Furthermore, as long as contradictory laws and other social structures remain untouched, change will be slow, if it happens at all.

Nevertheless, the following statement from Japan's second report to the CEDAW Committee shows that the government recognizes how far it has to go:

It is important to eradicate prejudices, customs, and practices based on stereotyped concepts of roles for men and women deeply rooted in society in order to realize de facto equality between men and women; this is one of the important pillars of Japan's national plan of action. Although Japan has seen considerable improvement in correcting traditional stereotyped sex role concepts in recent years, progress is still insufficient. Japan continues to actively promote information and public relations campaigns and preparation of conditions to facilitate both women's participation in society, especially in policy decision making, and active participation by men in household chores and community activities.[109]

This stated desire to change the actual status of women and men in Japan is directed at the international public. In discussions of gender differences and their impact on the status and position of women, there is often no recognition that in order to positively influence this situation, one must question the underlying social values and be willing to insist that these values be modified to improve the quality of life for all, including men. The conflict between these statements made by a government representative to CEDAW and the statements of the government representative to the Sumitomo trial highlights inconsistencies in statements to international and domestic audiences and indicates that the prescriptive status of the norm of gender equality is very low in Japan.[110] Although many women still feel that they must choose between having a career and having a family, the laws that have been enacted because of CEDAW and the application of these laws by Japanese courts are making great strides to increase women's options. If the legal reforms are observed and enforced, we should see more progress over time.

Although both domestic and international processes are important in understanding how international norms affect domestic policy, we must also recognize that these processes are rooted in a country's history. In the case of Japan, gender ideology was not only shaped by but grew out of the drive to modernize, industrialize, and civilize. Early on, Japan's need to industrialize, consolidate state power, and establish itself internationally resulted in a particular understanding of gender.[111] The consequences of this understanding restricted women's roles, status, and position in society. In the postwar period, Japan's status as an international economic power and its continued attempts to establish an international political position led to the adoption of CEDAW and an opening up of options for women.

Strategic Pacifism

Prime Minister [Obuchi Keizo], I think that throughout
the world, Japan is the Crown Peace Nation.
—Diet member Azuma Shozo in the September 25,
1998, Foreign Affairs Committee meeting

Japan has not used antipersonnel land mines since the
establishment of the Defense Force in 1954. However, the
government for a long time took the stance that land
mines are indispensable means in protecting its long
coast lines.
—*Landmine Monitor Report 1999: Toward
a Mine-Free World*[1]

The Conflict of Security and Identity

Given that the Japanese government viewed antipersonnel land mines (AP
mines) as vital for Japan's defense, why did its representative, then Foreign Minister Obuchi Keizo, sign the Convention on the Prohibition of
the Use, Stockpiling, Production, and Transfer of Anti-Personnel Mines
and on Their Destruction (the Ottawa Convention or Landmine Treaty)
in December 1997 and the Diet ratify it in 1998, especially when this action required that Japan oppose its main ally and security partner, the
United States? Within the international relations and Japanese foreign
policy literatures, there are two strong, related explanations that would
lead us to expect that Japan would oppose the treaty—realist theory and
foreign pressure (*gaiatsu*). The traditional foreign-pressure argument's
focus on material pressures related to security concerns is consistent with
realist theory. However, neither of these explanations is convincing.

When Japan adopted the Ottawa Convention, the United States exerted significant pressure on Japan not to take this action; there were
moderately strong domestic advocates; and there was a high degree of
conflict between international and domestic norms. Of the three issues

studied here, that of AP mines is the only one with a high level of compliance; this was achieved despite the high degree of conflict between
international and domestic norms on this issue. Although Japan eventually adopted the Ottawa Convention, it remained in the antiban camp
until after the convention went into force. Japan's initial position on this
issue was the result of its security relationship with the United States. By
the mid- to late 1990s, Japan's international position was generally more
secure, but the almost decade-long recession and pervasive social unease
certainly meant that the government struggled to remain relevant and to
retain its legitimacy at home and abroad.[2] The state's desire for legitimacy was therefore more closely tied to retaining its relevance and expanding its political influence in international relations. State interests
were clearly focused on establishing Japan as a serious political actor,
especially after the harsh criticism the country faced for its failure to
contribute human resources to the 1990 Gulf War effort. Subsequent
participation in peacekeeping operations signaled a more activist state
identity. In addition, Japan's status as a pacifist country lent it the moral
high ground on the issue of banning land mines. If anything, its association with the U.S. position against the ban threatened to negatively affect Japan's international standing and its identity. As support for the
international ban increased, so did the state's desire for legitimacy; thus
there was interest in maintaining Japan's position and credibility on
banning land mines. Because a significant number of states supported a
ban, the benefits of Japan taking a pro-ban stance could not be over-
looked over the long run.

Although the movement to ban land mines came late to Japan, a
ready constituency was available to support a ban. On the issue of adopting the Ottawa Convention, all three variables—the state desire for legitimacy (low), the level of conflict between international and domestic
norms (high), and the strength of domestic advocates (medium)—
worked together in the adoption phase. Although it is difficult to determine the relative weight of each variable in the decision to adopt the
Ottawa Convention, state desire for legitimacy was very important because of Japan's contemporary quest for a stronger role in international
politics.

Explanations that focus on foreign pressure, especially from the United
States, seem to account for Japan's initial opposition to a ban on land
mines.[3] As mentioned earlier, maintaining the U.S.-Japan security relationship is one of Japan's top priorities.[4] Japan's support of the U.S. position until after the treaty negotiations were complete indicates that this is
a fairly accurate account. However, the fact that Japan did sign the treaty
and later ratified it in the face of U.S. criticism and pressure not to do so

begs the question why this action was taken and, more important, how it was even possible.

On the basis of security concerns, realist theory would lead us to expect that Japan would resist any restrictions on its choice of defense. Diet members were concerned that Japan's security arrangement with the United States could be jeopardized if Japan ratified the land-mine treaty, further threatening Japan's security. By the late 1990s there was great concern that the United States would abandon Japan in the face of the post-cold-war context, and this would have the potential to destabilize regional relations in Northeast Asia.[5] Realists would expect that Japan's general preoccupation with its own vulnerability would be motivation enough to support the United States and oppose a ban. Although the realist argument does accurately describe the situation, it neglects other significant aspects, such as the influence of nonstate actors, relationships among states in the international system, and identity issues, all of which are important in this case.

The conflict between security and identity has been a fundamental tension for Japan, and its shift to an active pacifism—the strategic use of a pacifist identity—on the issue of land mines is a move toward reconciling the two. This identity is reflected in NGO activity, the role of former Foreign Minister and Prime Minister Obuchi Keizo, and Japan's commitment to nuclear nonproliferation. I argue that the need to reconcile the conflict between security concerns and identity pressures was central to Japan's final decision to sign and ratify the convention. In doing so, I recognize that neither security nor identity is a constant, and I posit that one cannot simply be assumed on the basis of the other, but both are continually negotiated. I show how signing and ratifying the Ottawa Convention signals the evolution of Japan's identity through NGOs, the actions of Prime Minister Obuchi, and commitment to and expansion of nonproliferation. Because realist theories conceptualize security as heavily reliant on material capabilities a priori, my argument will challenge the ability of realist theory to account for how states themselves conceptualize security.[6] I also address a deep flaw in the assumption that Japan's postwar security policy is based on its identity as a pacifist country without any reflection on what that identity means, how it was formed, or how it has evolved and continues to evolve. Finally, my argument responds to foreign-pressure literature by showing that Japan is not always a passive follower of U.S. decisions, even on security issues. I demonstrate that Japan strategically used its pacifist identity to gain leverage against U.S. pressure on the issue of AP land mines.[7]

States' identity concerns seriously affect those issues on which states choose to act and the substance of that action. A state is more likely to act on issues that will affect its legitimacy at home or abroad, as well as those issues that are central to its own understanding of self or the self it wishes to establish or project. Japan had both domestic and international motivations for attending to its foreign policy with state identity concerns in mind. It faced a general need to articulate a normative core that would define Japanese foreign policy priorities in a way that offered a more coherent vision of its role in the world. Part of the goal in creating this normative vision was to move Japan toward a more active role in international politics in general and to improve its chances of gaining a permanent seat on the UN Security Council. This took place in a larger international context in which the absence of a constructive or at least a coherent hegemonic interest presented the opportunity for Japan to project its identity.[8] Through its eventual choice to adopt the Ottawa Convention, Japan embarked on an identity-based agenda that would strengthen its legitimacy as an international actor while building a lasting relationship with other states based on shared values. In making an identity-based argument, it is important to point out that identity does not preclude contradictory actions by the state. Thus the Japanese government's willingness to use force through firing on North Korean ships, cooperating with the United States on ballistic missile defense, and sending troops abroad to participate in UN peacekeeping operations (PKO) and the multinational force in Iraq while at the same time espousing a commitment to peace, disarmament, and Japan's role as a pacifist (*heiwashugi*) country does not disprove my argument.

The participation of Japanese Self-Defense Forces (SDF) in UN peacekeeping operations provides a good example of the conflict between security and identity in Japan. Although the government eventually allowed SDF troops to participate in PKO, there was agonizing debate in the Diet, the media, and the public at large on this issue. Many people felt passionately that SDF troops should not participate in PKO. When they were finally allowed to do so, it was in a very limited capacity. The government framed this action in a way that affirmed Japan's identity and its commitment to pacifism. The nature of these peacekeeping operations, it was argued, was in line with Japan's goals of promoting peace throughout the world. The Koizumi government attempted to use the same frame to justify sending SDF troops to Iraq, albeit with less success. Although each of these actions is an interesting and important topic for investigation, I will not take them up here because the goal of this chapter is to attempt to answer the questions set out earlier by critically examining state identity, strength of domestic advocates, and conflict between domestic and international norms.

Building an International Ban on Antipersonnel Land Mines

The use of antipersonnel land mines, primarily as a defensive weapon to deter removal of antitank mines, began during World War I. Their use was not questioned until the 1970s, by which time they were increasingly being used as strategic offensive weapons.[9] In the 1970s attention to the devastation caused by land mines made the issue a concern of international policy that resulted in the ratification of the 1980 Convention on Certain Conventional Weapons (CCW). Protocol II of the CCW focused on the use of land mines. CCW attempted to protect civilians by prohibiting use of land mines in civilian areas. However, exceptions to this prohibition, along with other shortcomings, weakened the prohibition. Internal armed conflicts were not covered by the ban, and even in international conflicts the country where the mines were placed was responsible for their removal, which was usually hindered by lack of resources and removal technology. Finally, Protocol II did not regulate production and transfer of mines.[10] Consequently, NGOs working in mine-infested areas continued to see the damage caused by land mines; moreover, the effects of these weapons often hindered their work. Organizations generally working to provide medical care and those specifically concerned with helping rehabilitate mine victims noticed that after conflicts had ended, the numbers of new victims continued to increase. Those organizations working on repatriating refugees or providing services to them also realized that land mines not only often caused displacement but also inhibited return of refugees to their home and postwar reconstruction efforts.[11] These nonstate actors began to recognize that the damage caused by land mines could be adequately addressed only by banning land mines. In order to facilitate creation of a ban, framing of the issue of land-mine use would have to shift from understanding and dealing with it as a military issue to viewing it as a humanitarian one. U.S. and European human rights and humanitarian aid organizations began organizing to end the use, production, trade, and stockpiling of antipersonnel land mines in the fall of 1992.[12]

NGOs played a crucial role in initiating the process. The 1980 CCW, which entered into force in 1983, was the only treaty that attempted to control the use of AP mines.[13] Ten years later, in 1993, France called for a CCW Review Conference under pressure from two French NGOs, Handicap International and the French Ban Campaign. Workers for Handicap International were spurred to action after they realized that many of the injuries they saw in third-world countries were caused by detonation of land mines long after wars in the area were over. When the

United States announced a moratorium on exporting AP mines and thus gave a boost to the international ban campaign, the time was ripe for a review conference. The CCW Review Conference finally took place in September 1995, and NGOs presented petitions with 1.5 million signatures to the delegates calling for a ban on AP mines. Between the French call for a Review Conference in 1993 and the holding of the conference in 1995, the international ban campaign had made major strides in building a movement. In 1994, under pressure from their national campaigns, both Sweden and Italy called for a ban on AP mines. In May 1993, seventy representatives of forty NGOs attended the first international NGO Conference on AP Mines in London. The second NGO Conference, which was held in Geneva in 1994, marked the beginning of support from various UN agencies. The conference was cohosted by UNICEF, and participation doubled. The third NGO Conference was held in Phnom Penh, Cambodia, in June 1995, just three months before the CCW Review Conference. The founding of the Cambodia Campaign to Ban Land Mines in August 1994 and Cambodia's hosting of the third NGO Conference indicated that this movement was not limited to first-world activists advocating for what is largely a third-world problem. That Cambodia is one of the most mined countries in the world was also important in that it signaled the need to get those countries most affected by mines on board to establish an international ban; a local network to pressure government officials was a step toward achieving this. Another significant milestone was reached in March 1995 when Belgium became the first country to ban use, production, trade, and stockpiling of AP mines; Norway followed suit in June of that year.

The momentum of the third NGO Conference, which had 450 participants from more than forty countries, left activists hopeful that an agreement to ban land mines would result from the upcoming CCW Review Conference in September. However, political disputes, the rules of the negotiating process, and a blocking coalition led by the United States and supported by Japan resulted in a less-than-desirable agreement by the end of the conference. Disappointed by the inability to secure a ban on AP mines, a group of countries that supported a ban and NGOs met before the Review Conference ended. At this meeting they agreed to meet in Canada the next year to continue working toward their goal of establishing a comprehensive ban on antipersonnel land mines. The Ottawa Process, which led to the Ottawa Convention banning the use, transfer, production, and stockpiling of AP mines, was initiated in October 1996 when the Canadian government hosted the conference titled "Towards a Global Ban on Anti-personnel Land Mines." Fifty countries, twenty-four observer states, NGOs, and UN agencies, among others, attended the conference. To the surprise of many, Canadian Foreign Minister Lloyd Axworthy issued a challenge at the conference that participants return to Ottawa in December 1997—a mere fourteen months later—to sign a ban. With that challenge, the Ottawa Process to design, develop, and negotiate an international ban was started.[14] Despite the failure of the CCW Review Conference to produce a ban, the energy and dedication of Canada, the Scandinavian countries, and some other European countries kept the movement going by supporting a ban and giving NGOs access to government actors and the negotiation process. Furthermore, because the negotiations in the Ottawa Process did not have to conform to rules requiring consensus, there was less opportunity for the United States to block progress toward a ban.

When discussions of banning antipersonnel land mines emerged in connection with the CCW Review Conference meeting in 1996, Japan sided with the United States against banning them and maintained this position throughout the Ottawa Process. Japan's position shifted to supporting the Ottawa Convention in October 1997 after negotiations had already been completed, and Jody Williams and the International Campaign to Ban Landmines (ICBL) had been awarded the Nobel Peace Prize. In the end, the United States and Japan were on opposite sides of the issue. Some might argue that Japan acted strategically by supporting the U.S. position when it mattered and then reversing its course after the treaty negotiations were complete, by which time joining a ban became significant internationally; Japan could thus both support its ally and increase its status in the international community.[15] But the fact that the United States continued to pressure Japan and NATO countries that had signed the treaty to delay ratification, and that "senior US officials bluntly reminded Japan of its defense obligations" the day after Japan announced its intention to sign the treaty,[16] counters this argument. Continuing U.S. criticism indicates that Japan's opposition to a ban remained important to the United States.

Domestic Advocates

Analysis of the success of the ban campaign focuses on the importance of transnational civil society and NGOs, especially those affiliated with the ICBL.[17] In fact, given the significance of nonstate actors, some even claim that the Ottawa Process, in which the ICBL exercised great influence, signals democratization of foreign policy decision making.[18] Although this particular issue is outside the scope of this chapter, it points to the importance of considering the role that NGOs played in Japan. The momentum of the treaty negotiations rested on NGOs a great deal, but given the very weak status of NGOs in Japan generally and their inability to shape policy, one would not expect them to exert much significant pressure on Japan's government. In contrast to influential NGOs in the United States and Western Europe, Japan's NGOs are small, relatively powerless, and divided by region and issue. Motoko Mekata, a disarmament expert and steering committee member of the Japan Campaign to Ban Landmines (JCBL), asserts that domestic civil society did not play a significant role in Japan's adoption of the convention.[19]

The status of NGOs in Japan can be attributed to several factors. Social movements in Japan rarely become nationwide; the process for gaining nonprofit status and the benefits that come with it is extremely difficult in Japan; and because these groups, especially those that advocate policy positions, are by definition "outsiders," they usually do not have access to networks of power in Japan.[20] Without broad-based coalitions, it is difficult for domestic advocates to build the winning coalitions that provide transnational networks access to decision-making structures.[21] The status of NGOs in Japan, difficulty in securing funding, and NGO fears of getting pulled into other politicized issues account for late development of the JCBL; therefore, an argument that attributes Japan's adoption of the Ottawa Convention solely to nonstate actors is chronologically suspect. Furthermore, the founding of the JCBL in March 1997, a mere six months before Obuchi announced his intention to sign the convention, calls into question the Japanese campaign's ability to shape and mobilize public opinion in support of the ban in such a short time. Indeed, at the time of the Oslo Conference to finalize the treaty text in September 1997, Japan was still holding fast in its opposition. A more likely explanation is that the JCBL and other domestic NGOs working on this issue had a natural constituency among the large majority of the population who held pacifist ideals and who advocated peace through disarmament or a very limited self-defense force in Japan. Thus public opinion was on the side of those campaigning for the ban; this allowed the JCBL to gather two hundred thousand signatures and present them to the prime minister in an attempt to persuade the government to join the treaty.[22] As the pivotal role of women's organizations in pushing Japan's government to sign CEDAW illustrates, NGOs in Japan are not necessarily powerless, especially if they have access to powerful state actors. Finally, although Japanese NGOs were not totally out of the loop, this case demonstrates a common pattern whereby Japanese NGOs are present in the field responding to the situation on the ground but are not active policy advocates at home.

Variation in the effect that NGOs have on policy change depends on factors such as their level of organization (how well networked they are) and how well they have been able to convince people that their cause is important (their ability to increase their numbers and funds by getting people involved). In the case of women's rights, for example, many groups have large numbers of women working on different areas of this issue, and in specific areas, such as women's employment, disparate groups are forming domestic and international networks. In contrast, groups working on issues related to refugee policy were fewer in number and had not established strong networks with other groups working on this issue domestically or internationally; these groups mainly focused on helping refugees adjust to life in Japan and rarely advocated or initiated drives to change government policies related to refugees. This kind of advocacy work had become a significant goal of Japanese NGOs working on refugee issues at the end of the 1990s; their influence and access to networks of power increased only after September 11, 2001, and the Shenyang incident in May 2002.[23]

In the case of land mines, the NGO movement to persuade the government to sign the treaty came late to Japan. Japan's government held high-level talks with thirty other countries on March 6 and 7, 1997, and the "NGO Tokyo Conference on Anti-personnel Land Mines" hosted by the Association for Aid and Relief (AAR; formerly the Association for Aid to Refugees) took place on March 8 and 9. This international conference included panelists from Japanese NGOs and other NGOs working in areas related to mine clearance or victim assistance, including the ICBL. A follow-up conference was held on January 31 and February 1, 1998, to address how to make the international convention a reality. Jody Williams was a featured keynote speaker at both events, and Foreign Minister Obuchi sent remarks to be read.[24] Until the 1997 NGO conference in Tokyo, there was no Japanese campaign affiliated with the ICBL, although some aid groups were involved in this issue because of their engagement in humanitarian mine clearance. Generally, organizations and individuals concerned with this issue were not organized into the kind of networks that could give them significant political leverage. Yet the momentum of the international movement was essential for Japanese NGOs to gain strength. On the surface, this is the same process that strengthened women's groups working for passage of the EEOL and ratification of CEDAW. Unlike that case, those working toward a ban did not distance themselves from the international movement but closely allied themselves with it. Given the speed at which the campaign to ban land mines took off internationally, it is doubtful that the Japanese NGOs would have gained strength, legitimacy, and momentum without connections to the international movement.

The Association for Aid and Relief/Japan, along with the Japan Council on Disability and Support 21, used the momentum of the 1997 government conference to host the "NGO Tokyo Conference on Antipersonnel Land Mines: Towards a Total Ban on Antipersonnel Land Mines" immediately afterward. This was beneficial because NGOs were allowed to attend only the opening session of the government conference; the NGO conference helped harness the energy of activists who had come to try to rally support from the Japanese government for a ban because Japan was still not in the ban camp at this late date. This conference attracted more than two hundred participants and helped launch the JCBL. In addition, groups with extensive field experience, such as the AAR, that had enjoyed good relations with the government used their connections to gain support from influential people. One of those AAR approached for support was Nakasone Yasuhiro, who had served as both prime minister and director general of the Defense Agency. Nakasone still exercised "enormous influence on both political circles and the Defense Agency. Members of the Liberal Democratic Party [the party in power] admitted that Mr. Nakasone's support for a total ban had a great impact on the government's final decision."[25] Through the election of Fujita Yukihisa, a former board member of AAR, to the Diet in October 1996, NGOs gained an ally who was willing to popularize their concerns about the land-mine issue within the government. Potential support within the Diet increased when the Diet Members League Promoting the Total Ban on Anti-Personnel Landmines was formed in June 1997, with Fujita as secretary general of the group.[26] This organization was instrumental in lobbying the government and served as an intermediary that connected NGOs to politicians. As secretary general, Fujita collected 385 signatures from past and present Diet members, including seven former prime ministers, in support of the convention.[27]

Price (1998b) focuses on the key role of transnational civil society working through NGOs for the ban in socializing states and influencing state interests. The international NGO movement to ban AP mines was headed by the ICBL. Part of the effectiveness of these organizations was their high level of coordination and broad reach around the world. In addition, Jody Williams, the campaign's coordinator, had a very high profile, especially after she and the ICBL won the Nobel Peace Prize.[28] Williams visited Japan and attended the Nagano Olympics in 1998 on invitation from Japanese NGOs.[29] During this visit, Williams praised Prime Minister Obuchi for his leadership on the issue, because it was initially believed that Japan would not sign the convention.[30] Throughout the Diet discussions leading up to ratification of the treaty and afterward (1997–99), members constantly referred to the work of NGOs on this issue and credited them for bringing it into the international spotlight and for the progress that had been made in efforts to ban AP mines.

Because NGOs are outside networks of power, they have to be creative in finding ways to exert pressure on the government. One way is use of the media to educate the public about their issues in hopes of swaying public opinion. One activist with the JCBL said in an interview that "since few countries in Asia had adopted the treaty and the U.S. was against it, there was not much foreign pressure" for Japan to adopt the convention.[31] Thus "more influence came from the domestic debate, [and since] not many people in Japan knew that Japan possessed or manufactured land mines, advocates started to publicize this and got the media to publicize it so that people would be outraged and motivated to press Japan to support the convention."[32] The op-ed pages of the *Asahi Shimbun* and the *Yomiuri Shimbun* from January 1997 through December 1999 illustrate efforts of opinion leaders to educate and sway public opinion. In contrast with the more conservative *Yomiuri Shimbun*, the *Asahi*'s first editorial on the Ottawa Convention appeared on March 8, 1997. The *Yomiuri*'s first editorial did not appear until the treaty negotiations were already completed. The *Asahi* printed more than twice as many op-ed pieces on this issue as the *Yomiuri*; there were an equal number of editorials and commentaries in the *Asahi*, representing a balance between official views of the paper and views from the public.

Most of the op-ed pieces in the *Asahi* gave the basic statistics on the number of deaths caused by land mines. This repetition might have worked to the advantage of those lobbying the government to sign the convention because it reminded the reading public what was at stake on this issue—human lives.[33] Moreover, as many of these articles pointed out, lives of civilians are most affected by land mines because they are more often killed or injured than combatants. Even those op-eds that were not critical of the government had a tone that was supportive of the ban. Some articles praised the government for steps already taken and went on to lay out the next steps that should be taken in a way that made this course of action seem inevitable. Both strategies, not being overly critical and presenting action as a logical sequence that would inevitably lead to ratification, were helpful in gaining support from the general public and the government while avoiding putting the latter on the defensive or polarizing the two. Finally, the articles kept people informed on the Japanese government's stand on supporting or not supporting, signing or not signing, and ratifying or not ratifying, which could help mobilize the public to put pressure on the government.

In addition to these common elements, there were recurring themes in op-ed pieces that appeared between January 1997 and December 1999. First, there was a focus on how Japan and its actions were perceived internationally. A commentary in the *Asahi Shimbun* for October 15, 1997, pointed out that "in an attempt to try to weaken the effectiveness of the treaty, Japan agreed with the U.S. position."[34] According to this commentary, there was a biting response from embassies in Tokyo on Japan's antiban stance, including suggestions that because Japan always sided with the United States on these kinds of issues, it would not need veto power even if it did become a permanent member of the UN Security Council. The article went on to assert, "From the position of international public opinion on banning land mines, Japan is looked upon with scorn."[35] Like other op-ed pieces in the *Asahi*, this pointed out that in the midst of an international movement for a ban on land mines, Japan planned to spend 7 million yen (approximately $700,000) on land-mine production in the next fiscal year. Given that the country was already facing criticism from the international NGO community, this disclosure could add to public fury and government embarrassment. Finally, the author rejected the Defense Agency's claim that "we need land mines to defend our long sea border [because this assertion] has no strength against international public opinion."[36] In fact, throughout this period, many of the articles juxtaposed Defense Agency claims that Japan's long borders required the option of using land mines for security and that without them Japan would be vulnerable with discussions of the destruction caused by land mines and the death of people performing activities related to everyday life.[37]

A commentary published almost a year later, on August 4, 1998, took a more subtle tack by expressing concern that Japan would ratify late because a proposal for ratification still had not been submitted to the Diet because of ongoing bureaucratic investigations of problems related to ratification. This statement, combined once again with the grim statistics of how many people were being maimed and killed by land mines worldwide and the importance of time—"the longer it takes for forty countries to ratify the treaty, the more people die and only thirty-five countries have ratified thus far"—was a subtle way of pressuring the government to get moving on the issue because there was still time for Japan to make a difference by being one of forty countries needed to bring the convention into force. The author went on: "Because of Prime Minister Obuchi's decision to sign the Convention, Japan no longer faces unpopularity in the international community for only following U.S. policy. [However,] Japan will be looked upon with scorn from the world's NGOs" if it did not ratify in a timely manner.[38] Not only was other states' understanding of Japan's identity important, but NGOs and the wider transnational civil society also emerged as important in international politics. This is a significant difference from the issues of women's employment and refugees.

The op-ed articles that appeared in the *Yomiuri Shimbun* were also triggered by an editorial, but the first piece did not appear until after the convention negotiations were completed, a full six months after the first editorial appeared in the *Asahi*. Although this editorial was generally supportive of efforts to move toward banning land mines, and the author recognized that "you cannot ignore the growing support of international public opinion for banning land mines," there was less tone of advocacy in this article than in those printed in the *Asahi*. This September 25, 1997, editorial focused in large part on the requirements of the treaty and its major shortcoming—that the main producer countries had not agreed to sign it. Japan—which was still not in the ban camp at this point—was not mentioned until the end of the article. The article offered subtle praise for Japan's efforts, mixed with pressure to go further and actually commit to signing the treaty The author pointed out that Japan could make a great contribution by removing land mines and supporting victims, but did not insist that this was action that the state should take.[39] It was not until the end of the editorial that its author got to its main point by calling for countries like the "United States, for which signing the Convention is unreasonable, to [still] make efforts to cooperate with banning land mines."[40] This position shifted the focus back to the United States instead of pressing Japan to go forward and sign the ban.

An editorial published the day after Japan signed the convention in December 1997 took the focus back to the evolution of Japan's position on the issue of banning land mines. The author clearly laid out steps that Japan had to take after signing the convention to move toward the goal of abolishing and destroying land mines. In other words, although this editorial praised Japan's action in signing the convention, it acknowledged, "This is not the end of the ban issue but just the beginning of taking positive steps to fulfill the obligations." This approach assumed that signing the convention was not merely a symbolic act, but that it was a sincere action demonstrating the dedication of the Japanese government to solving the problem of land mines and its intention to ratify the convention and comply with its requirements.[41] In comparison with the op-ed pieces in the *Asahi*, the *Yomiuri* articles are aimed less at motivating public action to press the government to act on the issue and more at making recommendations to the policy makers.

Obuchi Keizo: A Pivotal Actor, Government Action, and State Identity

I use the actions and statements of Prime Minister Obuchi in two ways. In addition to analyzing Obuchi's words and actions, I use Obuchi as a lens through which to analyze Japan's state identity. Like individual identity, state identity is neither fixed nor always completely in flux. Instead, like individual identity, state identity is fully integrated but flexible. Using Obuchi as a lens helps illustrate how contradictory actions do not necessarily indicate a lack of commitment to an issue. Understanding identity as flexible and at the same time grounded (by values) allows a more sophisticated understanding of Japan's pacifist identity that addresses the shortcomings of previous readings of this identity as static. In short, my argument does not see Japan's contradictory actions as an indictment of an identity-based argument. Rather, these contradictions are based on a conflict between Japan's security concerns, which lead to dependence on the United States, and its identity, which leads it to resist that dependence. My argument does not place these two in opposition to each other with a possibility that one will win out over the other in the end; rather, it shows how they are reconciled in this particular case.

Understanding the influence of Foreign Minister (later Prime Minister) Obuchi on Japan's adoption of the Ottawa Convention is essential to understanding Japan's actions on the issue. Throughout committee discussions in the Diet, there is constant reference to and praise of Obuchi's leadership on this issue, even in discussions where it is seemingly irrelevant. The decision to sign the treaty was made by Obuchi without undergoing the Ministry of Foreign Affairs' review process.[42] The shift in Japan's position to supporting a total ban depended on a very strong norm entrepreneur and state identity. Obuchi acted as a norm entrepreneur who was empowered by nongovernmental actors and whose high-profile role in the government actually increased these actors' credibility, which increased their support from the public. Domestic NGOs also drew from the rhetorical frames and the increasing willingness and ability of transnational civil society to pressure the government. Because Japanese NGOs had limited access to political power and little chance to affect government decisions directly, they were heavily dependent on Obuchi's support and public opinion. Domestic NGOs' lack of access to policy making made it difficult for transnational civil society actors to affect the Japanese government directly. The one opening to apply pressure was based on Japan's identity concerns. At first, these concerns were strategic and focused on maintaining a "good image." Eventually, the identity concerns became part of a more complex understanding of Japan's focus on human security—

understood in this context as foreign policy based on humanitarian concerns that broaden the way the state conceptualizes security. The fact that there was no consensus among government institutions on this issue was also important. Although Japan's Ministry of Foreign Affairs supported a ban, the position of the Defense Agency was divided between uniformed officials who opposed a ban and civilians who supported one. This, along with the quasi-ministerial status of the Defense Agency, provided opportunities for high-profile supporters like Obuchi to take advantage of the cleavages.

According to Obuchi, when he first became foreign minister and realized that deaths from AP mines in places like Cambodia were not decreasing but increasing, he knew that Japan had to sign the convention. The problem was that there were two seemingly formidable obstacles: belief in the importance of AP mines to protect Japan's coastlines, and the fact that the U.S. military possessed these weapons on its bases in Japan. Although Japan had not used AP mines since the establishment of the SDF, the government remained firmly committed to the idea that land mines were indispensable for protecting Japan's coastlines. Obuchi insisted that the international trend toward banning land mines and Japan's commitment to international peace led to his decision to support the ban.

What motivated Obuchi to take leadership on this issue? Obuchi himself identifies humanitarian reasons based on the effect of land mines, NGO activities, and Japan's international responsibility as the key reasons that he signed the convention. When Obuchi was asked directly why he signed the treaty, he answered, "Thinking about the great deal of damage that land mines do to regular people from a humanitarian point of view, Japan signed the Land Mine Convention in December of 1997. At the same time, activities to get rid of land mines matched up with support for victims to come up with a solution to the land mine problem. As mutually dependent relations deepen internationally, our country has a responsibility to carry out a positive role in advancing world peace and stability."[43] Citing humanitarian concerns as one of the primary reasons for signing the treaty was remarkable because humanitarianism did not play a prominent role in Japan adopting the Refugee Convention. The issue of signing the Refugee Convention could be based on humanitarian concerns, especially because the issue of refugees and concern for them was linked to and embedded in a humanitarian and human rights discourse over many decades before Japan ratified the convention. However, this was not the case in Japan. One might expect protecting women's human rights to spur the government to sign CEDAW on humanitarian grounds, but it did not. Given the controversy over the idea that there is one set of universal rights to which women are entitled, and complaints that such a universalizing norm of gender equality is not appropriate for Japan, where this conflicts with domestic norms and national identity, it is understandable that humanitarianism was not invoked in this case despite the commitment to gender equality in Japan's constitution.

Obuchi's view that Japan had a "responsibility to carry out a positive role in advancing world peace and stability" indicates Japan's initiative and proactive stance on changing the international order. This sense of responsibility is markedly different from the sense of obligation—which indicates the importance of intersubjective understandings—and the obvious lack of concern for humanitarianism that were prominent in Japan's decision to adopt the Refugee Convention. Furthermore, in the September 25, 1998, meeting of the Foreign Affairs Committee, Diet member Azuma Shozo recalled that in an October 13, 1997, Budget Committee meeting Obuchi had urged Japan to deal with the question whether to sign the convention by thinking independently, maintaining that it should not base its decision on the U.S. position. In the 1998 meeting, Azuma asked Obuchi why he signed the convention. Once again, Obuchi replied that the impetus for signing the convention was "humanitarian," but at the same time, he stated that "knowing that our country's defense depended on them and knowing that the U.S. military possessed them on their bases in Japan, I studied the problem." In this case, state identity, domestic norms, and international trends coincided.

While not discounting Obuchi's humanitarian motivations, we must also note that Obuchi recognized a shift in the international system with the increasing power of NGOs on this issue. He knew that taking a stand against land mines could benefit Japan by increasing its legitimacy in the international community. As long as he linked his support for adopting the treaty to already-prevalent domestic norms, he had a chance of overcoming opposition from Japan's security institutions. Although NGOs were not able to directly affect policy making, the strength of transnational civil society was not lost on Japan. Obuchi's leadership is also important because it gave NGO activists in Japan access to what would otherwise have been an area of influence that is usually out of the reach of these kinds of actors. Access to Obuchi reinforced the influential role of public opinion on security issues that has evolved after World War II.[44] However, it is important that we recognize that Obuchi was offering more than leadership. His comments on why he signed the convention clearly bring together the issues of peace, security, and humanitarian action. Instead of simply following the international trend toward banning land mines, Obuchi recognized that this trend offered an opening for Japan to reshape international order by pursuing peace and peace diplomacy. He was quite clear about the necessity of reconciling humanitarian goals and security interests to ensure peace; instead of viewing peace and security in opposition or basing security on weaponry, Obuchi presented peace and security as not only complementary but also inseparable.

The connection between humanitarianism and security is visible not just in the content of the discussions but also in the context in which they took place. One example is that Diet member Nakatani Gen, an LDP member of the Diet Members League Promoting the Total Ban on Anti-Personnel Landmines, stated on September 24, 1998, "NGOs realized their goal of prohibiting inhumane weapons by focusing on building international cooperation around the convention." He went on to "express respect for Prime Minister Obuchi, who made the political decision with a human conscience with regard to peace." These issues frequently permeate contexts where they would be out of place and inappropriate unless we understand them as a broadening of Japan's concept of security, which indicates proactive and strategic use of pacifist ideals from the postwar focus on demilitarization, to include humanitarian concerns and peace as key in conceptualizing security in the post–cold-war period.[45]

Examining the evolution of Japan's pacifist identity through NGOs and a key government actor is helpful in developing a better understanding of what pacifism means as part of Japan's identity and how it has evolved since the postwar period. It is important to consider how Japan's pacifist identity is used and invoked strategically. Furthermore, Japan's pacifism does not mean that Japan is a passive state; indeed, its pacifism is a basis for action. It is a means by which Japan can become a more active state in international politics and at the same time resist U.S. domination of its security. Japan's identity as a pacifist country can be broken down into several different characteristics, all of which are key to this discussion. Some Japanese officials believe that peace diplomacy can work toward achieving Japan's goal of striving for peace throughout the world. An extension of its commitment to peace is the development of its nonnuclear stance whereby Prime Minister Sato Eisaku and his cabinet committed not to possess or produce nuclear weapons or introduce them into Japan.[46] Perhaps most important, many Japanese see the pursuit of peace as an area where Japan can exercise international political leadership. One manifestation of this is Diet members marrying the issue of banning AP mines to the principle of and commitment to nuclear nonproliferation. Price (1998b) points out that the ICBL consciously avoided linking the ban issue to disarmament issues because it would close doors to activists' influence; government officials could claim that the issue was then a matter of national security. Yet in Japan, government officials themselves and other opinion leaders used this connection to strengthen commitment to ratifying the convention within their own body; they also saw it as one possible way to persuade other countries, such as Russia and the United States, to join the treaty.

Negotiating Conflict Between Domestic and International Norms

The international concern for humanitarianism and human rights became part of a discourse of civilization in international relations after World War II, but it has served as the basis for judging the degree to which Japan is civilized at different moments throughout history. The idea of human security has been around since the 1950s as part of a framework of development. Some trace Japan's concern with human security back to 1954 and Prime Minister Yoshida Shigeru. Yoshida believed that ensuring people's well-being was an essential element in obtaining and maintaining political stability.[47] The activities of Japanese humanitarian assistance organizations in Southeast Asia in the 1950s and 1960s reflected this concern for individuals and their role in political stability and economic development. Although there was some variation in a broad understanding of security that had several iterations from the 1960s through the 1980s, including UN-centered foreign policy and comprehensive security, Japan's commitment to human security as part of its foreign policy agenda was not firmly established until the 1990s.

In the changed international political environment of the 1990s, it became clear that an increase in intrastate violence, especially against civilians, demanded new thinking about where people fit into a discourse of national security. The 1993 and 1994 United Nations Development Program (UNDP) reports were instrumental in bringing the idea of human security to the international arena to address the growing concerns. The 1993 report called for a new concept of security that focused not only on national security but also on the security of people; the 1994 report set out a more detailed understanding of the concept of human security.[48] Japan had been searching for a way to take a more active role in international politics, especially international military action, because its unwillingness to dispatch self-defense forces drew heavy criticism from the international community. For Japan, the concept of human security reflected the public's desire to realize pacifist ideals of the constitution and make these ideals a basis for Japan's foreign policy. This concept made it possible for Japan to take a more active international role that it hoped would satisfy demands of the United States and other Western nations and reassure Japan's Asian neighbors that the country's international security activities would not threaten them. From the mid-1990s, each prime minister—Murayama Tomiichi, Hashimoto Ryutaro, and Obuchi Keizo—was a proponent of human security. In Obuchi's case, human security became the core of his vision of Japan's foreign policy.[49] Edström (2003) argues that the 1997 Asian financial crisis contributed to a new regional focus on human security, and that in his 1998 policy speech in Hanoi, Prime Minister Obuchi made human security the central concern of Japan's foreign policy.

Although there is some criticism of shortcomings in the Ottawa Convention, the actual text is clearly written, and the convention allows for checks on compliance. The relevant parts of the treaty include all of Article 1, which states the general obligations of the state parties not to use, develop, stockpile, or transfer antipersonnel mines and requires them to destroy mines in their possession.[50] Article 4 and Article 5, paragraph 1, are also important for my argument because they elaborate on destruction of stockpiled AP mines and of AP mines in mined areas. More specifically, Article 4 requires each state party to undertake "to destroy or ensure the destruction of all stockpiled anti-personnel mines it owns or possesses, or that are under its jurisdiction or control, as soon as possible but not later than four years after the entry into force of this Convention for that State Party."[51] "Destruction of all anti-personnel mines in mined areas under [state parties'] jurisdiction or control" must take place no later than ten years after the convention enters into force for that state.[52] Paragraphs 2 through 6 of Article 6 are also important because they lay out means of and responsibilities for international cooperation and assistance in obtaining the goals of the convention. Paragraph 2 is especially relevant for Japan because in mandating that "each State Party undertakes to facilitate and shall have the right to participate in the fullest possible exchange of equipment, material and scientific and technological information concerning the implementation of this Convention," it directly conflicts with Japanese domestic laws prohibiting the export of military technology and the participation of Japanese self-defense forces in mine clearance. Article 7, paragraphs 1 and 2, and Article 8, paragraph 2, are significant because they relate to measures to ensure and verify compliance. Article 7 basically enumerates required reporting measures. Article 8, paragraph 2, allows one or more state parties "to clarify and seek to resolve questions relating to compliance with the provisions of the Convention by another State Party."[53] Although this is not third-party dispute resolution, this kind of inquiry could increase the likelihood of Japan's compliance. As mentioned previously, Japan is very sensitive to outside criticism and shaming and thus is responsive in situations where another state might question its activities. Finally, Article 9 requires each state to take measures "to prevent and suppress any activity prohibited to a State Party under this Convention undertaken by persons or on territory under its jurisdiction or control."[54] As we will see, interpretations of Articles 5 and 9 and what they meant for U.S. military bases in Japan were issues that contributed to Japan delaying ratification.

Broadening the conceptualization of security shifted Japan's position to one of a leader on moral concerns and questions, which was a way to resist U.S. pressure. This shift is consistent with what de Larrinaga and Sjolander (1998) call the "humanitarianization" of land mines as a counterdiscourse to focus on mines as a security issue—the securitization discourse. According to de Larrinaga and Sjolander, situating the land-mine issue in a humanitarian discourse marginalizes the state security discourse.[55] In Diet committee discussions, the land-mine issue was not understood solely as a humanitarian issue, which was the dominant frame employed by international NGO activists. In Japan, the issue was understood as simultaneously a humanitarian and a security concern because attention to humanitarian issues was seen actually to enhance the country's security. Remarkably, these two were not pitted against each other; instead, Japan's security concerns were reformulated and understood as the quest for peace, which would reconcile security and identity. This reformulation resisted a complete humanitarianization of the land-mine issue in the Diet while also avoiding the wholesale expansion of human security to include concern for the mine issue. The only way to secure Japan would be to move toward ensuring a more peaceful world.[56] Thus banning land mines became just as important as, and did not compete with, the U.S.-Japan Security Treaty for ensuring Japan's security and peace in the region. Furthermore, even if Japan could not rely on U.S. protection in the event of an attack, supporting a ban on AP mines and moving toward disarmament would lead to an even more secure position.

In the Diet, discussions of ratification centered on two issues, each of which represents one side of the conflict between security concerns and identity: how ratification would affect the U.S.-Japan Security Treaty, and the importance of Japan being among the first forty countries to ratify the treaty. As one member pointed out in the February 13, 1998, meeting of the Foreign Affairs Committee, if Japan entered the convention as one of the first forty countries to ratify and therefore shared responsibility for bringing the treaty into effect, it would be awarded international prestige and power, especially because Japan would have to oppose the post–cold-war hegemon to bring this about. This enhanced international status and moral authority would then lead the way for Japan to persuade other Asian countries to ratify. But the framing of these two issues illustrates a deep conflict between Japan's desire to be an independent leader in world politics, especially in Asia, and its dependence on the United States for its security and survival, a conflict that actually delayed ratification.

Japan's precarious position of pursuing international power and status and its subordinate position in the international system relative to Western states have a long history. After World War II Japan could reenter international society only if it no longer posed a threat to its neighbors or to international order; this was achieved through demilitarization. Although demilitarization was a check on the state, the corresponding check on society was the institution of democratic reforms, which included establishing a democratic government and implementing an educational curriculum designed to promote the spread of democratic values throughout society. We can trace this new identity—and the need to civilize on which it rests—from the constitution through Japan's commitment to nuclear nonproliferation and Japan's state-society relations as manifested in the role of NGOs in Japan.

Through international agreements related to warfare, the kinds of weaponry used in war have been incorporated into a measure of the level of a state's civilization. Tannenwald points out that "the nuclear taboo has become part of the contemporary discourse of 'civilization'" and has constitutive effects on "the categories actors use to understand weapons and on the identity of a 'civilized' state."[57] Thus standards of civilization must still be met for a state to be recognized as legitimate in the international system. Although the ICBL avoided linking a ban on AP mines to nuclear nonproliferation, it did make a connection between AP mines and nuclear weapons themselves by arguing that AP mines, like nuclear weapons, are indiscriminate weapons of mass destruction and, as such, are inhumane. Framing the issue in this way implicitly links the issue of AP mines to the norm of nonuse and the nuclear taboo, both of which are part of the contemporary civilization discourse.

Many Diet members link the issues of land mines and nuclear weapons[58] and state that Japan's responsibility to pursue banning both is rooted in its identity as a peace nation (*heiwa kuni*), which is explicitly connected to the bombing of Hiroshima and Nagasaki during World War II only one time in the committee records.[59] India and Pakistan's nuclear weapons tests make this a more prescient argument. Members recognize that these events have great potential for mobilizing people on both issues—nuclear weapons and land mines—because of the threat it poses to the world. As Price and Tannenwald point out with the example of the effectiveness of linking chemical weapons to nuclear weapons to further delegitimize the use of chemical weapons and undermine their status as standard weapons,[60] this could be a very effective strategy. Japan was facing another threat at the time that became all the more pressing when North Korea launched a missile over Japan. Instead of focusing on the need to counter these threats by military strategies, the conversations in the Diet leaned more toward the idea that in the long run, shifting from the position that peace depends on the ability to project force to the belief that abolishing weapons such as land mines would lead to a greater chance for peace.[61] These ideas are more satisfactory in helping us understand Japan's goals than unreflective reference to Japan as a peaceful country. Indeed, throughout the Diet discussions, there is mention of Japan's peace diplomacy and how giving humanitarian and human rights principles precedence over weaponry would increase the credibility and persuasiveness of diplomacy based on the pursuit of peace. In other words, the post–cold-war environment facilitated the state's ability to use pacifist ideals as an instrument for change in international relations.

Interestingly, although Diet members consciously "grafted" the issue of banning AP mines onto disarmament and nuclear nonproliferation—thus making it a matter of national security—there was only one overt mention of the use of nuclear weapons against Japan.[62] This gaping silence on the bombing of Hiroshima and Nagasaki speaks very loudly and parallels the lack of discussion of the taken-for-granted nature of Japan's identity as a pacifist country to which it is intimately linked.[63] Part of what makes it possible to graft banning land mines onto nuclear nonproliferation is that both are seen as indiscriminate weapons of mass destruction—with land mines working in slow motion—and thus they are inhumane.

Linking demilitarization and pacifism was a move more typically made by political leftists in Japan after World War II when there was intense political and ideological struggle over what Berger (1996) calls Japan's political-security culture. Those who advocated this position, including a large portion of the general population, saw demilitarization as a way to realize the pacifist ideals codified in the constitution. The position that won out—at least with regard to controlling the government—was that advocated by Prime Minister Yoshida and became known as the Yoshida Doctrine. Through the slogan "merchant country," Yoshida linked demilitarization with marketization, therefore signaling that postwar Japan would focus its energies on economic development. This linkage allowed the government to ignore the pacifist ideals of the constitution without necessarily contradicting them. Despite the political move to downplay any connection between demilitarization and pacifism, the public at large continued to link the two because after World War II it was clear that people wanted no more war; pacifist ideals embodied in public opinion remained a check on pressures from the United States for Japan to rearm. This attitude is reflected in the public's resistance to changes in security policy such as the establishment of the SDF, expansion of its duties, allowing the SDF to participate in UN peacekeeping operations, and, most recently, deploying the SDF to Iraq. Although right-wing nationalists always supported rearming, mainstream leaders in the LDP were reluctant, mainly because this would take valuable resources away from consumer production and thus limit Japan's economic growth. Despite changes in its post–cold-war security environment and steady growth in relative power, Japan's national security policies continue to "de-emphasize military instruments as a means of achieving national objectives."[64] The Japanese government is content to allow the United States to remain the dominant military power while it focuses on increasing its international position through diplomacy.

Ratifying and Complying with the Convention

One concern raised in Diet discussions of ratifying the Ottawa Convention was whether Japan would be left vulnerable without land mines if the United States had to deploy personnel from bases in Japan to deal with another problem in the region. This concern originally emerged in the 1970s when the U.S. military was seen as having lost its superiority over the Soviet military and U.S. defense spending was decreasing. Furthermore, "the oil crisis in 1973, the American withdrawal from Vietnam in 1975, and finally the planned (but later cancelled) withdrawal of U.S. ground troops from South Korea in 1977 shook Japanese confidence in the American security umbrella, and rising trade frictions with its most important ally added to the concern about the reliability of the American security protection."[65] The 1998 launching of a North Korean missile that could reach Japan heightened this sense of vulnerability; concerns about threats to Japan's security from its neighbors have reemerged and become more valid with successful weapons tests. Others voiced concerns that even if U.S. troops were not otherwise occupied and there was an attack on Japan, the United States might be reluctant to use its own troops because the American public would see the situation as too dangerous without the use of land mines. To support their argument, members cited a U.S. simulation that reported that the rate of casualties would increase by a projected 35 percent if land mines were not in use.[66] This reasoning was quickly dismissed when members pointed out that the effectiveness of AP mines was not the issue; the issue was whether the weapon was inhumane, and if so, whether it should be banned.[67] Invalidating discussion of the effectiveness of AP mines early on also shut down the possibility that security concerns based on fear and danger—a reactionary approach—could be used as a legitimate reason not to ratify the treaty. This move clearly framed the issue as a humanitarian one; realist theories cannot explain how, in a situation like this, humanitarian concerns could trump security concerns. Some might argue that in fact humanitarian concerns did not trump security concerns because AP mines are useful only if an attack on Japan takes the form of a land invasion—a highly unlikely scenario; mines are not important for Japan's security. Although this is a sensible position, what matters is not outsiders' views of what is a more likely scenario or the military usefulness of AP mines but Japan's own threat perception. In the related Diet discussions that took place between 1997 and 1999, members were very worried about both air and sea invasions, especially early on.[68] In this context, those who mattered viewed AP mines as central to securing Japan.

The increased threats to Japan from its own backyard, the post–cold-war environment, and Japan's economic decline meant that the country was at a crossroads. During the cold war, fear of entanglement shaped Japan's security relationship with the United States in a way that distanced the country from American wars in Korea and Vietnam. With the end of the cold war, these kinds of entanglements became less likely, but Japan faced more direct threats such as a missile attack from North Korea or nuclear proliferation in Asia. Furthermore, without the cold war to maintain the fragile status quo in the region, decisive action from Japan became more important. All these issues made a good case for further increasing Japan's arms, but on this issue Japan's decisive action was a turn toward expanding the norm of nonuse of AP mines. Price points out that the end of the cold war has "facilitated the strengthening and expansion of other prohibitionary weapons regimes"; this hospitable environment extends to the possibility of a norm against use of AP mines.[69]

Preserving the U.S.–Japan Security Treaty was still a key concern when officials were deciding whether to ratify the treaty. Although there was some debate over whether researching how NATO countries were handling their commitment to house U.S. bases on their territory was an appropriate comparison, in the end, Diet members decided to study how those countries were establishing their domestic laws in a way that would allow them to honor their commitments to the United States and still ratify the treaty. Much of the investigation focused on Germany. Because Germany was one of the core states that supported a ban early on and ratified the treaty seven months after it signed, we would expect that the information that Japan sought in its investigation would have been available in time for it to be one of the original forty countries to ratify the treaty and bring it into force. However, partly because of India and Pakistan's nuclear weapons tests, the investigation dragged on to the point that close to a year later the Ministry of Foreign Affairs still had not presented a proposal to the Diet for ratification. In the end, Japan followed Germany's lead and decided that mines on U.S. bases in Japan were outside its responsibility. Japan's commitment to prohibit nuclear weapons from passing through its territory could be used as a precedent in this case for not allowing AP mines to be transported through Japan and prohibiting Japanese citizens from handling them.[70] However, some fear that the U.S. military's ability to possess AP mines on its bases compromises the ban in the same way in which the three nuclear principles were consistently transgressed. Thus under the Diet's plan, the U.S. military could keep its mines on bases but was asked not to produce them at the bases. In addition, the Japanese SDF and civilians working on bases would not be allowed to transport or help transport mines. The SDF could, however, possess mines for purposes of research and to train in disarming them. Although Diet members had expressed great interest in being one of the original forty countries to ratify and bring the convention into effect, the Ministry of Foreign Affairs' tardy presentation of a proposal to the Diet made this impossible; Japan was the forty-third country to ratify.

Price (1998a) is instructive in evaluating whether this norm will be effective in the Japanese context in his assessment of compliance with the norm proscribing the use, transfer, stockpiling, and production of antipersonnel land mines. He concludes that "the absolute form of the taboo, its legitimacy, and its relative institutional maturity carry the potential for norm effectiveness over time, though the elusiveness of AP mines for an enforcement regime significantly detracts from immediate prospects of widespread and robust compliance."[71] He goes on to caution against jumping to the conclusion that this norm will suffer from low levels of compliance. In evaluating the possibility for norm effectiveness, he considers factors related to the international context, as well as features of the norm itself. In the case of Japan, a high level of compliance has already been reached; Japan destroyed the remainder of its stockpile ahead of schedule in February 2003.

Unlike the cases of women's employment and refugee policy, there are not many ways to get around destroying stockpiled mines—either the mines are destroyed or they are not. Japan could have stalled on destroying the mines, but given the strict deadline of February 28, 2003, to destroy 985,089 of the 1,000,089 antipersonnel land mines that it possessed at the time of treaty ratification, the country's representatives would have had a difficult time creating an excuse while maintaining its credibility. Japan retained 15,000 mines for purposes of training and producing demining technology. According to *Landmine Monitor 2003 Report*, Japan used 5,387 of these mines between 1990 and the end of 2002, leaving 9,613. As Price points out, the clarity of the treaty language does not leave much room for maneuver. The available evidence supports Japan's commitment to the treaty and shows that the state has been proactive in destroying its stockpiled mines and in the reporting transparency also required by the treaty. By the end of February 2001, Japan had destroyed 220,285 AP mines. One year later, in March 2002, that number increased to 609,000, leaving fewer than 400,000 AP mines to be destroyed. Japan fulfilled its treaty obligation when it destroyed 380,000 mines between March 2002 and February 2003; the last mines of the stockpile were destroyed on February 8, 2003, several weeks ahead of the deadline.

Securing Peace

Adopting the Ottawa Convention was a contentious process in which international and domestic politics were deeply implicated. An analysis focused on realist conceptions of state behavior assumes that Japan would pursue pregiven national interests, continue to follow the United States' lead, and oppose the convention. Japan did not follow this course of action. Japan's adoption of and compliance with the Ottawa Convention is better explained by normative analysis that considers the state desire for legitimacy and the strength of domestic advocates. Domestic advocates were especially important for adoption in this case. Although an organized campaign to ban land mines emerged late in Japan, it benefited greatly from widespread public support and significant backing from powerful politicians. Obuchi Keizo's role was indispensable, since without his unilateral decision to sign the convention, and the legitimacy he lent to nonstate actors, the Ottawa Convention might not have been ratified.

Although the United States was not in favor of the Ottawa Convention, it had over the course of the 1990s demanded that Japan take a more proactive role internationally, especially on security issues. The Japanese government started to view a more active role in international politics as necessary and desirable, but it was difficult to strike a balance that would satisfy the United States and other major international players on the one hand and its Asian neighbors on the other. The Ottawa Convention presented an opportunity for domestic political negotiations that addressed the long-standing conflict between security and identity.

The context of Japan's historically rooted sense of vulnerability, its sometimes precarious position in the "civilized" international system as a non-European state, dependence on the United States for its security, and fearsome neighbors threaten to prevent Japan from asserting a more activist identity internationally. Pursuing its security and a new international order through peace trumps the United States' dominance over Japan in international relations and in ensuring its security; Japan also assuages the fears that other Asian countries have of Japan taking a leadership role and being politically powerful in Asia. Convincing its neighbors that a more politically powerful role will not threaten their sovereignty is not always easy, given how Japan has pursued "stability" in the region in the past. In Diet committee records, the importance of Japan signing the treaty and the goal of being one of the first Asian countries to ratify it were mentioned repeatedly. In the end, policy makers viewed it as part of Japan's international mission to pursue security through peace and to play an important role in "leading Northeast Asia into a new era,"[72] starting with persuading other Asian countries to sign the convention.

CHAPTER 6

Conclusion

Perry came, the black ships came, we civilized (*bunmeika*) and modernized. Japan became Japan; we pursued an extraordinary path.
　　—Labor Minister Sakamoto Misoji, Labor and Welfare
　　　　　　　　Committee meeting, July 17, 1984

Taking Japan Seriously

Japan is often portrayed in a one-dimensional manner that focuses on it either as a purely instrumental actor whose behavior is based only on a calculation of benefits or as an untrustworthy member of the international community. The former view portrays Japan as not taking its international commitments seriously or not being able to commit to anything beyond superficial lip service to agreements. In other words, Japan's actions are selfish, and it is incapable, for whatever reason, of being a fully reliable member of the international community. Another common portrayal is of a Japan that is subordinate to the United States and always willing to follow the U.S. lead in international relations. I have argued that Japan's adoption of and compliance with international agreements can be better understood by considering the degree of conflict between domestic and international norms on the issue at hand, state identity and desire for legitimacy, and the strength of domestic advocates. By taking this approach, we can begin to understand which norms will matter in Japan, how they are institutionalized, and their influence on state behavior.

Analysis of the three cases considered in this book offers insights on why international norms that conflict with domestic norms are adopted, how they are implemented to varying degrees, and how identity can facilitate or limit the state's capacity to comply with the norms. These cases illustrate that Japan's relationships within the international system are not easily explained by theories that do not acknowledge changing historical contexts, the complexity of the international system itself, and the mutual constitution of structures and agents within that system.

Alternative Explanations

The main alternative explanation considered in each of the three cases is the rationalist argument regarding the importance of foreign pressure (*gaiatsu*) on Japanese foreign policy making. In the cases of refugee policy and women's employment, I also considered another rationalist argument that attributes adoption of the Refugee Convention and CEDAW to Japan's need for more workers during the high-growth period that started in the late 1960s and early 1970s and reached a peak in the 1980s.

I have argued that the foreign-pressure explanation is inadequate because of its reliance on the United States as the primary source of foreign pressure and its lack of attention both to Japan's position in the international community vis-à-vis states other than the United States and to relationships with other states based on its identity and the duties and obligations that come with it. In the case of the Refugee Convention, pressure on Japan came from its peers in the international community— other advanced industrial democracies—and not just the United States; it was pressure to accept more refugees into Japan, not to sign and ratify the Refugee Convention. Japan's state identity and the duties that government actors believed came with it formed the basis for acceding to the convention. In the case of CEDAW, the United States has not ratified the convention, and there was no evidence of pressure from other states for Japan to adopt it. In this case, domestic advocates on the issue took advantage of Japan's desire for legitimacy to reverse the state's decision not to sign CEDAW at the 1980 middecade conference in Copenhagen. Once Japan had signed CEDAW, there was strong feeling in the government that it had made a promise to the international community to ratify it; Japan finally did so at the end-of-decade conference in Nairobi. On the issue of banning AP land mines, the United States led opposition to a comprehensive ban and never signed the Ottawa Convention. After siding with the United States until late 1997, Foreign Minister Obuchi of Japan signed the convention despite strong U.S. objections. A rationalist argument easily explains Japan's decision to side with the United States against a ban, given its security interests and U.S. dominance in Japan's security, but this argument cannot explain Japan's later decision to actively oppose the United States, resist U.S. pressure, and adopt the Ottawa Convention.

The argument that links adoption of the Refugee Convention and CEDAW to Japan's need for more labor is also insufficient. As we saw in Chapter 3, the numbers of refugees admitted are so low that they do not make a difference for the country's employers. Women had already been employed in increasing numbers since the end of the 1960s, so it was not necessary to adopt CEDAW to achieve this. Furthermore, adopting CEDAW and implementing it through domestic laws actually posed a threat to the gendered division of labor favored by employers, and women competing with men for jobs in large firms would decrease the number of women available for low-paying jobs, where more of the demand lay.

Summing Up the Cases

As stated in Chapter 2, one of the criteria for selecting these three cases was that conflict existed between domestic and international norms on these issues, but the international norm was nevertheless adopted. All of these cases had a high degree of conflict, but norms were adopted and there was a range of compliance.[1]

Although the level of compliance can be considered the result of a combination of the three variables considered—(1) state desire for legitimacy, (2) strength of domestic advocates, and (3) the degree of conflict between the international and domestic norms—we can draw some conclusions about the relative importance of each. Most notable is that a ranking of high on both or either of the two enabling variables—state desire for legitimacy and strength of domestic advocates—does not guarantee a high level of compliance. By the same token, a ranking of high on the limiting variable—degree of conflict between international and domestic norms—does not necessarily result in no or low compliance. It is not that the degree of conflict is unimportant. On the contrary, it is key, especially in combination with the strength of domestic advocates on the issue. The evidence I have presented shows that strong domestic advocates are necessary to achieve anything more than low levels of compliance, especially when there is a high degree of conflict between international norms and domestic norms and identity. Let us turn to more specific consideration of the cases in light of these insights.

There was a high degree of conflict between the domestic and international norms on all three issues, but the levels of compliance are drastically different. Because refugee policy and women's employment ranked high in the state's desire for legitimacy, the strength of domestic advocates emerged as most significant in explaining the difference in levels of compliance on these two issues. Low strength of domestic advocates on the refugee issue, combined with the high degree of conflict between international norms and domestic norms, accounts for the low level of compliance with the Refugee Convention. In contrast, in the case of CEDAW, a high strength of domestic advocates has, to some extent, overcome the degree of conflict between international norms and domestic norms and identity, resulting in a medium level of compliance. Also, in the case of women's employment in particular and the social position of women more generally, we must not overlook the fact that medium compliance has been a significant accomplishment, despite the great gap that still exists between men's and women's status and pay. Furthermore, it is difficult to capture the vast difference in levels of compliance on the Refugee Convention and CEDAW by using the terms *low* and *medium*; I refer the reader back to Chapters 3 and 4.

Interestingly, the only issue that achieved a high level of compliance was banning AP land mines. In contrast to the other two issues, the state's desire for legitimacy on the land-mine issue was low in the adoption phase. The strength of domestic advocates was medium, but we must keep in mind that domestic advocates did not emerge on this issue until just six months before negotiations were complete in late 1997. At first glance, the low ranking in the state's desire for legitimacy may be surprising, but when we consider the context, it makes more sense. Compared with some other states, Japan was in the unusual position of having little involvement with land mines. Because laws established after World War II prohibited the export of military technology, the country actually used all the mines it manufactured within its own borders. In some ways this made it easier for Japan to comply with the treaty requirements once it was ratified, but Chapter 5 shows that the road to ratification was still challenging. This issue touched the core of every state's concerns—security. Japan's alliance with the United States in the blocking coalition actually made it subject to criticism from the international community. Even before the Ottawa Process began, the number of states, including advanced industrial states that Japan considers its peers, that supported the ban was sufficient to suggest that if Japan's primary motivation was increasing its international legitimacy, it would have joined the pro-ban states during the CCW Review Conference in 1995, when the ban was first considered. Once the Ottawa Process began and a majority of the core industrialized democracies took a pro-ban stance, Japan continued to side with the United States. This decision to remain in the antiban camp illustrates the critical nature of Japan's security concerns. It was not until Obuchi Keizo took over as foreign minister and after domestic advocates became more organized that Japan changed its position.

It can be argued that late in the adoption phase and on into the compliance phase, Japan became more interested in positively shaping its identity on this issue. This is illustrated by sensitivity to the influence of the international NGO community on this issue; government actors expressed a clear desire to establish and maintain a positive image with these groups.

To some extent, this helps account for the strength of domestic advocates on this issue because some government actors, including Obuchi Keizo, actively sought to improve Japan's international image on this issue by working cooperatively with domestic NGOs. In addition, this issue is unique among the three because the community from which Japan sought to increase its legitimacy was not limited to the core industrialized states. In this case, taking a proactive stance to promote peace through disarmament and military restraint was important in Japan's efforts to gain the trust of its Asian neighbors and improve its chances for becoming a political leader in the region. In its overall attempts to increase its international political role, Japan has also sought to build positive relations with the European Union.

My research shows that a high degree of conflict between international norms and domestic norms can be at least partially overcome by the strength of domestic advocates on the issue. Domestic advocates are important because they work to frame the issue in a way that responds to the limiting role that domestic norms and identity can play in compliance. In the case of women's employment, long-established women's movements were in place and able to mount an immediate protest when the Japanese government announced that it would not sign CEDAW. Although international action on this issue energized Japanese women, they were careful to frame the issue in the media as one focused on domestic norms. Their success depended on their understanding that issues related to women's status in the workplace could not be separated from questions of national identity. The importance of domestic norms and identity as a limitation on this issue is illustrated even more clearly when we consider that when Japan ratified CEDAW in 1985, its primary international identity was as an economic power. Japan's high economic growth continued to result in a shortage of labor. Women could fill many of these positions, but the government was determined to maintain limitations on their ability to work overtime and to take jobs as night workers. Moreover, the tax system continued to discourage women from taking full-time regular work. These factors served to maintain the gendered labor market, which perpetuated the social roles of women as primarily responsible for the home. Given this evidence, the high state desire for legitimacy cannot fully account for Japan signing and ratifying CEDAW. In contrast, the high state desire for legitimacy that grew out of Japan's identity as an insecure state on the issue of refugees was the sole reason that Japan acceded to the Refugee Convention in 1981. Without strong domestic advocates on this issue, it was impossible to achieve anything more than a low level of compliance.

Identity, Legitimacy, and Civilization: Implications for Compliance

Analysis of the three issues I have studied leads to the conclusion that in the adoption phase Japan often agrees to arrangements that impose obligations without any obvious material benefit on the basis of the state's desire for legitimacy. The state views these actions as necessary for creating a more favorable international identity through which it will gain increased legitimacy. The cues for what kind of identity is acceptable and what kinds of actions are appropriate are rooted in contemporary discourses of civilization, which determine standards of appropriate behavior for members of the international community. I have shown that the power of these logics of appropriateness produces particular interests and identities that may actually clash with domestic norms and identity. This conflict is not necessarily negative; as we saw in the case of CEDAW, it actually opened up political space for domestic advocates to press for change. When domestic advocates are weak, as in the case of the Refugee Convention, change as measured by the level of compliance is also likely to be small. No matter how intensely the state desires legitimacy or how much the government may pursue reform through implementing international norms, domestic advocates are critical for actually mobilizing international norms, taking action to promote their dissemination throughout domestic society, and increasing identification with these norms. This pivotal role is magnified when the international norm in question has a high degree of conflict with domestic norms and identity. The findings in these three cases confirm Finnemore's (1996a) argument that state interests originate in the international structure of meaning and social value. This is partly illustrated by the fact that conflict between state identity and national identity did not play a significant role in the adoption phase of any of the three issues, but were quite significant during the compliance phase. Indeed, they often limited the state's capacity to comply with the international norm in question. This again highlights that implementation of norms and a state's level of compliance depend on domestic advocates.

With regard to adoption or actual ratification of the agreements I have considered, it is clear that Japan's concern for increasing its legitimacy in international society played an important role, especially in the cases of CEDAW and the Refugee Convention. It is remarkable that Japan adopted the Refugee Convention so late in comparison with other countries, considering that if there was a "tipping point" on this agreement, it was certainly in the 1950s, when an overwhelming number of contracting parties signed and ratified it. Because at that time, Japan was just getting its legs back after the war, the U.S. occupation had just recently ended, and Japan was admitted to the United Nations in 1956, one would reasonably expect that Japan—especially with an interest in rebuilding its reputation—would have adopted such an important piece of international law earlier. Japan's adoption of three other international agreements that deal with human rights issues at about the same time—late 1970s and early 1980s—at which the Refugee Convention was adopted is significant.[2] After its amazing economic growth in the 1960s and 1970s, Japan once again faced criticism and the threat of being ostracized from the international community, but this time the charges were unfair trading practices. Understanding Japan as an outsider and often attributing sinister motives to state action is a pattern that has endured since Japan became a part of the international community. These criticisms still abound in some arguments about Japan's motives for adopting some international agreements. This is not to say that some of these actions are not based, at least in part, on instrumental reasoning, but the analysis offered here has shown that this is not a sufficient explanation.

CEDAW was another of the four international rights-based agreements signed during the late 1970s and early 1980s. Initially, adopting CEDAW had less to do with Japan's identity and international legitimacy, partly because there was less pressure from other states for Japan to ratify it. Although there was definitely a movement among governments worldwide to strengthen women's rights, most states viewed this as a fundamentally social and cultural issue. Because most states have room for improvement on this issue, it does not affect international legitimacy to the extent that an issue such as nuclear nonproliferation does. This can in part be because unless a state allowed systematic abuse of women, such as that suffered by women in Afghanistan under the Taliban, discrimination against women was not a key issue in civilization discourses. Although many government actors recognize that women are sometimes oppressed in domestic society, this oppression—especially more recently—has been seen as the result of prejudice based on ignorance as opposed to malignant intent, systematic oppression, or institutionalized practices. Moreover, this issue has traditionally been understood as one better addressed by domestic norms and institutions. Women's rights were by and large viewed as an issue with which all liberal democracies were concerned. Because international concern for women's rights in the 1970s and 1980s was closely tied to concern for their role in economic development, many also viewed this as a problem mostly for third-world, newly independent countries. The fact that Japan's constitution includes a so-called equal rights article also got Japan off the hook internationally. More recent movements by women to press for recognition of women's rights as human rights have challenged these views. Overall respect for human rights is an important part of discourses of civilization today, but this has not always been the case.[3]

Japan's adoption of the Ottawa Convention profoundly implicates both international legitimacy and state identity. From the analysis in Chapter 5, it is clear that the United States pressured Japan to delay ratification, and before ratification Japan was squarely in the U.S.-led blocking coalition. Japan's understanding of itself as a peace nation (*heiwa kuni*) and its long-time goal of a greater international political presence were at stake in this issue. Some have argued that Japan can continue to claim a pacifist identity because it relies on the United States for its security. Thus nothing has to be done to maintain its pacifist identity. Action on this issue was the perfect opportunity for Japan to become actively pacifist and improve its chances of becoming more politically powerful in Asia by becoming less of a threat. At the same time, Japan would also be able to loosen U.S. dominance over its security. Supporting adoption of this norm would serve to increase Japan's overall international legitimacy precisely because of the nature of the issue. As stated earlier, norms on prohibition of weapons of mass destruction are particularly important in contemporary civilization discourses. If advocates of the ban on land mines are successful in their attempt to graft the issue onto prohibitions against use of chemical and nuclear weapons, being a party to the ban treaty will increase a state's legitimacy by identifying it as a civilized state.

The role of domestic advocates on these issues and their influence on adoption of the three conventions must also be considered. On the Refugee Convention, Japanese were working for aid groups in some of the Southeast Asian countries that had the largest numbers of Indochinese refugees. After 1979 the majority of Japanese supported giving assistance to refugees, but there were virtually no domestic advocates for Japan to ratify the Refugee Convention. After it was ratified, few voices within Japan demanded that the country accept refugees, increase the number accepted, or change policies to facilitate resettlement in Japan. During the adoption stage, domestic and international norms were at odds. Japan's state identity as a nonimmigrant country was firmly rooted in its national identity, where understandings of Japaneseness were based on race, biology, culture, and language. Some government actors spoke out on behalf of reforming policies regulating the acceptance of refugees, but they were all but ignored. Analysis of Diet committee records reveals that the Refugee Convention was adopted because members understood that Japan's international role entailed obligations to the international community, and they interpreted acceding to the Refugee Convention as one of these obligations.

The process of implementing international agreements is the area where we see just how much conflict there was between domestic norms and identity and the relevant international norm. When Japan signs an international agreement, the government attempts to reform relevant laws before ratification. This can be explained by the status of international treaties in the domestic legal system. In Japan, treaties supersede domestic law but are subordinate to the constitution. Thus all treaties are immediately implemented upon ratification. However, as we have seen throughout this book, implementation does not ensure compliance. Relevant domestic laws must be reformed in accordance with the treaty or must be created in cases where there is no law. In the area of refugee policy, no laws directly addressed accepting refugees and providing a standardized process for naturalization. In fact, existing laws determining access to social welfare benefits conflicted with the requirements of the Refugee Convention. These laws, which all required that one be a Japanese citizen to receive benefits, were intentionally exclusive and policies that made naturalization difficult and ensured that few non-Japanese would have an opportunity to enjoy the benefits of citizenship. Even after laws governing entitlement to social welfare benefits no longer required citizenship, the process of naturalization remained difficult. Furthermore, the number of asylum seekers accepted remained low; when they were accepted, they often were not given refugee status. Thus the government faced no obligation to extend the protections that come with refugee status. Compliance could be strengthened if the judiciary became more active on this issue, but the disparity between state and national identity on this issue is so great that judges do not have the tools to act.

In contrast, the courts were very active in supporting women's discrimination claims, but since CEDAW has been adopted, this support has waned in recent years even though there is now more legal basis to support these claims. Before CEDAW was adopted, only one law pertained to discrimination in women's employment; it prohibited wage differentials based solely on sex. This law did not address the problem of keeping women in low-wage, low-status jobs, nor did it prevent them from being forced to retire upon marriage or pregnancy. Other laws relating to women's employment were restrictive measures that often served to exclude women from particular jobs while they reflected sociocultural values about women's roles in the workplace and family. Although there was conflict between domestic and international norms on this issue, past judgments of the courts indicate that the domestic norms on this issue were not as entrenched as those related to refugees.

There were very interesting laws on the issue of land mines. Although Japan used land mines to defend its coastline, laws prohibiting export of military weapons and technology prevented Japanese manufacturers from exporting land mines. These laws had to be revised after ratification of the Ottawa Convention because they also prevented export of Japanese land-mine-removal technology, which is the most advanced in the world. The international norm on banning land mines meshed well with Japan's pacifist identity, and laws that conflicted with the Ottawa Convention did not indicate a conflict between international norms and domestic norms, as they did in the cases of refugee policy and women's employment.

Issue Matters

One of my main initial goals was to show how the issue matters in norm adoption. As it turns out, state desire for legitimacy, strength of domestic advocates, and degree of conflict between international norms and domestic norms cannot alone explain norm adoption and compliance. Each of these three variables depends on the specific issue under consideration. More specifically, the issue matters insofar as it is linked to contemporary discourses of civilization and because of the variation of domestic advocates on each issue. These discourses determine standards of appropriate behavior and prescriptions for how these standards should be met; domestic advocates have a key role in whether a state complies with these prescriptions. Discourses of civilization are powerful because they attach certain meanings, values, and significance to particular identities that then influence state identity formation and state behavior. If a state desires to increase its legitimacy, adopting twenty international conventions that no one cares about will not matter if it has not adopted the one that does matter. To some extent, the one that matters is not objectively determined. Instead, it is based on a state's particular relationship to the international community and how that relationship has been constructed historically. Which issues matter also depends to some extent on the identities that are valued in the international system. With the spread of liberalism and increasing globalization, identities such as democracy and free market are more privileged than others.

For Japan in the 1970s and 1980s, adopting treaties based on human rights and disseminating values associated with them was a priority, but this priority had changed over time. Overall, Japan's adoption of international agreements and the norms codified in them is an excellent example of the importance of civilizing discourses because the country was very concerned with being civilized, especially in the late 1970s and early 1980s, when state identity was insecure. The issues considered here are significant because they are all related to contemporary discourses of civilization. CEDAW and the Refugee Convention are part of the international human rights regime; observing human rights is essential for international legitimacy.[4] The issue of AP mines taps into another central contemporary civilizing discourse. The branding of states with such labels as "rogue state" intensified after September 11, 2001, with George W. Bush's phrase "axis of evil." These labels carry value judgments based on appropriate standards of behavior, which again are rooted in civilizing discourses. Thus each label is not just shorthand for use in newspaper articles or the evening news. It is something more profound because it denotes an entire identity construction whose attached meanings signal that particular state's desire for legitimacy in the international community.

Analyzing Japan's adoption of and compliance with the Refugee Convention, CEDAW, and the Ottawa Convention as a set of social and political processes demonstrates that understanding how these processes lead to internalization requires attention to both international and domestic political practices. Because discourses of civilization and state identity change over time, the passage of time is important. One could argue that the difference in Japan's identity from 1981, when it ratified the Refugee Convention, to 1998, when it ratified the Ottawa Convention, can be accounted for by the passage of seventeen years between the two events. However, the passage of time alone does not account for the change in the characterization of Japan's state identity from primarily insecure in 1981 to primarily proactive and responsible in 1998. These identities are linked to specific issues—refugee policy and AP land mines, respectively—and are not necessarily generalizable across issues. Discourses of civilization change over time as they are reconstituted by the values of the international community, shared ideas, and historical context. Because states seek legitimacy in this evolving context, state identity is negotiated in relation to other international actors on specific issues.

Reference Matter

Notes

CHAPTER I

1. Steve Smith, "Forty Years' Detour," 489–93.

2. Kahler, "Legalization as Strategy."

3. Constructivism is an approach to the study of international politics. Although there are many strands of constructivism, they are all united in sharing two basic tenets that Wendt lays out in *Social Theory of International Politics*. Constructivists agree "(1) that the structures of human association are determined primarily by shared ideas rather than material forces, and (2) that the identities and interests of purposive actors are constructed by these shared ideas rather than given by nature" (p. 1).

4. Baldwin, *Neorealism and Neoliberalism*; Keohane and Martin, "Promise of Institutionalist Theory."

5. Some scholars use game theory, specifically the prisoner's dilemma, to support the argument that cheating is the main obstacle to cooperation and can be overcome by institutions that coordinate state behavior. For example, Axelrod, *The Evolution of Cooperation*; Keohane, *After Hegemony*; and Oye, *Cooperation Under Anarchy*.

6. Finnemore and Sikkink, "International Norm Dynamics and Political Change," 902.

7. Ibid., 903.

8. Finnemore, *Defining National Interests in International Society*, 2.

9. Ibid., 15.

10. Miyashita, "Gaiatsu and Japan's Foreign Aid."

11. Honma, *Nanmin mondai to wa nani ka?*

12. Checkel, "Why Comply?" 565; Checkel, "International Institutions and Socialization in Europe," 817.

13. Gamson, *Talking Politics*.

14. I began my document searches from January 1 of the year before each law was ratified.

15. Translations throughout the book are the author's unless otherwise indicated.

16. Broadbent and Kabashima, "Referent Pluralism," 329.
17. Ibid., 330.
18. Flowers, "Failure to Protect Refugees?"
19. Tannenwald, "Nuclear Taboo."

CHAPTER 2

1. Hurd, "Legitimacy and Authority in International Politics"; Franck, "Legitimacy in the International System."
2. Koh, "Why Do Nations Obey International Law?" 2646; Checkel, "Why Comply?" 554.
3. Slaughter Burley, "International Law and International Relations Theory."
4. Downs, Rocke, and Barsoom, "Is the Good News About Compliance Good News About Cooperation?"
5. Kratochwil and Ruggie, "International Organization," 768.
6. Chayes and Chayes, "On Compliance," 176.
7. Ibid., 188.
8. Ibid., 188.
9. Ibid., 194.
10. Geertz, *Negara*; Lindblom, *Politics and Markets.*
11. Raustiala and Slaughter, "International Law," 539.
12. The discussion of power in Liftin, *Ozone Discourses*, 14–23, is helpful here. According to Liftin, power as domination and control is not always appropriate. For example, an actor may be persuaded to revise her interests through evidence or reasoning. Thus a recognition that power ranges from domination and control to mutuality and intersubjective understandings is more fruitful. Legitimacy is important when talking about power based on authority or persuasion. Also see Risse, "Let's Argue!"
13. See Chayes and Chayes, "On Compliance"; and Franck, "Legitimacy in the International System."
14. Koh, "Why Do Nations Obey International Law?" 2656.
15. Ibid., 2656.
16. Ibid., 2634.
17. Raustiala and Slaughter, "International Law," 539.
18. See, for example, Klotz, *Norms in International Relations*; Finnemore, *Defining National Interests in International Society*; Price, *Chemical Weapons Taboo*; Price and Tannenwald, "Norms and Deterrence"; Tannenwald, "Nuclear Taboo"; Keck and Sikkink, *Activists Beyond Borders*; Crawford, "Decolonization as an International Norm."
19. Evangelista, *Unarmed Forces*; Klotz, *Norms in International Relations*; Klotz, "Norms Reconstituting Interests"; Risse-Kappen, "Ideas Do Not Float Freely," 208.
20. Cortell and Davis, "Understanding the Domestic Impact of International Norms," 66.
21. Checkel, "Norms, Institutions, and National Identity"; Checkel, "Why Comply?"

22. Risse-Kappen, "Ideas Do Not Float Freely."

23. Chan-Tiberghien, *Gender and Human Rights Politics in Japan*, 4–5.

24. Risse, Ropp, and Sikkink, *Power of Human Rights*, 38.

25. Hurd, "Legitimacy and Authority in International Politics," 387–89.

26. Campbell, *Writing Security* (1992); Neumann, "Self and Other in International Relations."

27. See, for example, Finnemore, *Defining National Interests in International Society*; Price, "Reversing the Gunsights"; Price and Tannenwald, "Norms and Deterrence"; Risse, Ropp, and Sikkink, *Power of Human Rights*.

28. See, for example, Risse, Ropp, and Sikkink, *Power of Human Rights*; Gurowitz, "Mobilizing International Norms: Domestic Actors, Immigrants and the Japanese State"; Gurowitz, "Mobilizing International Norms: Domestic Actors, Immigrants, and the State"; Gurowitz, "Diffusion of International Norms."

29. Risse, Ropp, and Sikkink, *Power of Human Rights*, 9.

30. Gurowitz (1999a) calls this international identity. Because I agree with Wendt's understanding of state identity as both subjective and intersubjective, I use the term *international identity* only to refer to others' understanding or definition of Japan's identity. Wendt, *Social Theory of International Politics*, 224–32.

31. Risse, Ropp, and Sikkink, *Power of Human Rights*, 10.

32. Miyaoka, *Legitimacy in International Society*, chapter 2.

33. Gong, *Standard of "Civilization" in International Society*, 15.

34. Ibid.

35. Ibid., 10.

36. Ibid., 199.

37. Suzuki, "Japan's Socialization into Janus-Faced European International Society," 139, 149–53.

38. Katzenstein, *Cultural Norms and National Security*; Reus-Smit, *Politics of International Law*.

39. French, "'Japanese Only' Policy Takes Body Blow in Court," *New York Times*, November 15, 1999; Yamanaka, "Ana Bortz' Law Suit and Minority Rights in Japan."

40. Iwasawa, *International Law, Human Rights, and Japanese Law*.

41. Gurowitz, "International Law, Politics, and Migrant Rights," 131.

42. Auslin, *Negotiating with Imperialism*, 17–22.

43. Ibid., 12.

44. Cwiertka, *Modern Japanese Cuisine*, 14.

45. Ibid., 24–34.

46. Gluck, *Japan's Modern Myths*, 90.

47. Cwiertka, *Modern Japanese Cuisine*, 152.

48. Gluck, *Japan's Modern Myths*, 44.

49. Morris-Suzuki, *Re-inventing Japan*, 9–34. In *Multiethnic Japan*, Lie contends that the myth of Japan as a homogeneous nation really developed and took root only in the 1960s. Although I do not disagree with his argument, I do think that there is something to be said for the significance of the idea of homogeneity in

the process of constructing a Japanese national identity prior to 1960. For an argument in support of this point, see Samuels, *Machiavelli's Children.*

50. Morris-Suzuki, *Re-inventing Japan*, 162–67.

51. Katzenstein, *Cultural Norms and National Security.*

52. Gurowitz, "Mobilizing International Norms: Domestic Actors, Immigrants, and the Japanese State."

53. Chan-Tiberghien, *Gender and Human Rights Politics in Japan.*

54. Hirata, *Civil Society in Japan*; Reimann, "Building Global Civil Society."

55. Miyaoka, *Legitimacy in International Society.*

56. Leheny, *Rules of Play*; Leheny, *Think Global, Fear Local.*

57. Leheny, *Rules of Play.*

CHAPTER 3

Portions of this chapter have been previously published in Petrice Flowers, "International Refugee Convention: National Identity as Limitation on Compliance," in *Forced Migration and Global Processes: A View from Forced Migration Studies*, ed. François Crépeau, Delphine Nakache, Michael Collyer, Nathaniel H. Goetz, Art Hansen, Renu Modi, Aninia Nadig, Sanja Špoljar-Vržina, and Loes H. M. van Willigen (Lanham, MD: Lexington Press, 2006), 13–34, reprinted by permission of Rowman & Littlefield Publishing Group; and Petrice Flowers, "Failure to Protect Refugees? Domestic Institutions, International Organizations, and Civil Society in Japan." *Journal of Japanese Studies* 34, no. 2 (2008): 333–61.

1. Raustiala and Slaughter, "International Law," 539.

2. Koizumi, "Refugee Policy Formation in Japan," 123.

3. Takeda, "Japan's Responses to Refugees and Political Asylum Seekers," 445.

4. Honma, *Nanmin mondai to wa nani ka?* 153.

5. Koizumi, "Refugee Policy Formation in Japan," 125.

6. Gurowitz, "Mobilizing International Norms: Domestic Actors, Immigrants, and the Japanese State," 77.

7. Landis, "Human Rights Violations in Japan," 12.

8. United Nations, *Convention Relating to the Status of Refugees.*

9. Hanami, "Japanese Policies on the Rights and Benefits," 225–26.

10. Takeda, "Japan's Responses to Refugees and Political Asylum Seekers," 433. Since 1977 Japan has "repeatedly expanded the number of Indochinese refugees it could accept, from 500 in 1979 to 1,000 in 1980, to 3,000 in 1981, to 5,000 in 1983, and finally to 10,000 in 1985."

11. Human Rights Committee, 12th Session, Document no. CCPR/C/10/Add.1, November 14, 1980, cited in Weiner, *Japan's Minorities*, 40. Japan ratified the International Covenant on Civil and Political Rights in 1979. This comment was made in reference to Article 27 of the covenant.

12. Weiner, "Opposing Visions."

13. For more on this point, see Lie, *Multiethnic Japan*, 125–41.

14. Ohnuki-Tierney, "Conceptual Model"; Morris-Suzuki, *Re-inventing Japan.*

15. Weiner, "Opposing Visions."

16. Ibid., 4.

17. Ibid., 9–10. See also Goodman et al., *Global Japan.*

18. Kajita, "Challenge of Incorporating Foreigners in Japan," 127.

19. Tsuda, *Strangers in the Ethnic Homeland,* finds that contrary to initial expectations, there are sharp identity differences between Japanese workers and *nikkeijin* of Brazilian descent in Japanese workplaces. The experience of these return migrants to Japan often results in them developing a strong ethnic Brazilian consciousness, which they did not have before arriving in Japan.

20. Landis, "Human Rights Violations in Japan," 8.

21. Lie also gives examples of how a discourse of Japan as multiethnic and Japanese as a people from mixed lineage was used to justify Japan's colonial pursuits. For more on this point, see Lie, *Multiethnic Japan,* 111–40.

22. Landis, "Human Rights Violations in Japan," 8.

23. Ibid., 14.

24. Takeda, "Japan's Responses to Refugees and Political Asylum Seekers," 434.

25. Koizumi, "Refugee Policy Formation in Japan," 123. It is important to recognize that the United States and European countries were also facing economic slowdown and increased unemployment; thus tolerance for accepting refugees was low.

26. Ibid., 125.

27. Honma, *Nanmin mondai to wa nani ka?* 31.

28. Ibid., 153–56.

29. Hōmu Iinkai (Judicial Affairs Committee) meeting, November 5, 1980.

30. Editorial, *Asahi Shimbun,* March 14, 1981, "Nihonjin ni totte no nanmin jōyaku" (The Refugee Convention According to Japanese); Editorial, *Asahi Shimbun,* June 4, 1981, "Nanmin jōyaku hikareta nihon ni" (Japan That Is Opened by the Refugee Convention).

31. Yosan Iinkai (Budget Committee) meeting, March 7, 1980.

32. Ibid.

33. Ibid.

34. Ibid.

35. Hōmu Iinkai (Judicial Affairs Committee) meeting, November 5, 1980.

36. Commentary, *Yomiuri Shimbun,* May 29, 1980, Kuahara Shigei, "Hakuryoku kaita nanmin kaigi: daizi kudan no kage ni maibatsushite" (A Refugee Conference That Lacked Force: Buried in the Shadows); Editorial, *Asahi Shimbun,* April 15, 1980, "Heiwa kaifuku na nanmin no kyūsai kara" (Restoring Peace from Refugee Relief); Commentary, *Asahi Shimbun,* June 28, 1980, Kawaguchi, "Nanmin kyūen ni sekkyokuteki kyōryoku o" (Proactively Cooperating in Refugee Assistance); Editorial, *Asahi Shimbun,* March 14, 1981; Editorial, *Asahi Shimbun,* June 4, 1981.

37. Editorial, *Yomiuri Shimbun,* May 29, 1980, "Soren ken mo nanmin kyūsai no buntan o" (The Soviet Union Also Has Burden of Refugee Relief); Commentary, *Asahi Shimbun,* July 1, 1980, "Mazu kanbojia nanmin no kyūsai o" (First, Assistance for Cambodian Refugees).

38. Commentary, *Yomiuri Shimbun*, November 20, 1980, "Nanmin teizyū towareru kokusaisei" (An International Sphere That Also Asks for Refugee Resettlement).

39. Honma, "Nihon no nanmin seido," 15.

40. Ibid., 20.

41. These include the Hōmu Iinkai (Judicial Affairs Committee), Gaimu Iinkai (Foreign Affairs Committee), and Yosan Iinkai (Budget Committee).

42. Opinion, *Yomiuri Shimbun*, January 24, 1981, "Katate ochi no nankakuy-aku" (An Error of the Refugee Convention).

43. Ibid.; Judicial Affairs Committee meeting in the lower house, November 5, 1980, and May 8, 1981.

44. Opinion, *Yomiuri Shimbun*, January 24, 1981.

45. Hōmu Iinkai (Judicial Affairs Committee) meeting, November 5, 1980.

46. Ibid.

47. Ibid.

48. Ibid.

49. Gaimu Iinkai (Foreign Affairs Committee) meeting, March 20, 1981.

50. This problem arose before in the translation of Japan's constitution. Where the Occupation authorities wanted to refer to "the people," the word *minzoku* was originally used, but in discussions to revise the constitution, Japanese Diet members used the word *kokumin*. In contemporary debates, the use of *kokumin* in the constitution is used to justify excluding noncitizens from some legal protections. In my own reading of the Japanese translation of the convention definition of *refugee*, I thought that it was easily understandable.

51. Editorial, *Yomiuri Shimbun*, June 11, 1981, "Nanmin no tame no 'hikareta kuni' ni" (Becoming an "Open Japan" for Refugees).

52. Ibid.

53. For a detailed consideration of Japanese civil society, see Hirata, *Civil Society in Japan*, especially chap. 1; Pekkanen, *Japan's Dual Civil Society*; Chan-Tiberghien, *Gender and Human Rights Politics in Japan*.

54. Author interview, director of research and policy advocacy, Japan Association for Refugees, Tokyo, August 2, 2005.

55. Hirata, *Civil Society in Japan*, 30.

56. I use the term *nongovernmental organization* (NGO) in the way in which it is used in Japan, to refer to nongovernmental organizations that carry out activities overseas; in the international relations literature in the United States, these are referred to as international nongovernmental organizations (INGOs). The term *nonprofit organization* (NPO) refers to domestic nongovernmental organizations.

57. The Japanese government is in the midst of a trend referred to as *kan kara min e*, which translates as "from the public to the private." This trend involves basically trying to reduce government costs by using nonprofit organizations and other citizens' groups to provide services that the government traditionally provided. Economic imperatives have forced the government to relinquish some of its control and take advantage of the growing expertise of the nonprofit sector.

The government has also realized that such organizations can provide the services more cheaply.

58. Editorial, *Yomiuri Shimbun*, June 11, 1981.

59. Lack of legal status even after refugee status is granted remains a problem in Japan.

60. Koizumi, "Refugee Policy Formation in Japan," 128.

61. Honma, *Nanmin mondai to wa nani ka?* 116.

62. Shipper, "Criminals or Victims?"

63. The preceding section is based on Honma, *Nanmin mondai to wa nani ka?* especially pages 116–26.

64. Mizuno, "Refugee Quandary," 93.

65. Fukuoka, *Lives of Young Koreans in Japan*; also see Lie, *Multiethnic Japan*.

66. A related issue was that on Okinawa, which was not returned to Japan until 1972, there were a number of children born of American military men and Okinawan women. Because Japanese women could not transmit citizenship to their children and children of American servicemen and foreign women are not American citizens unless the American father claims the child before she or he reaches the age of eighteen, many of these children were stateless.

67. Landis, "Human Rights Violations in Japan," 5.

68. Augustine-Adams, "Gendered States," 12.

69. Ibid., 14.

70. Ibid., 3.

71. Honma, "Nihon no nanmin seido," 9.

72. Takeda, "Japan's Responses to Refugees and Political Asylum Seekers," 444.

73. Author interview, UNHCR attorney, Tokyo, Japan, August 16, 2001.

74. The government made these facilities available to anyone who had already been granted refugee status by the Japanese government starting in 2003, when twelve refugees took advantage of the program; at the start of fiscal year 2004, however, there was only one such person at the facility in Tokyo. Many argue that because the process of applying for asylum in Japan takes so long, by the time those who are finally recognized as refugees are eligible for the program, their needs are different from the services offered at the center.

75. Author interview, UNHCR attorney, Tokyo, Japan, August 16, 2001.

76. Ministry of Justice Immigration Bureau, 2006 Immigration Report, pt. 1.

77. Honma, "Nihon no nanmin seido," 24.

78. Ibid.

79. Ibid., 21.

80. The May 2002 incident at Japan's embassy in Shenyang, China, has sparked a great debate in Japan and the Japanese Diet about refugee policy in Japan. Chinese officials detained five North Koreans, including two children, after they had already entered the grounds of Japan's embassy in Shenyang. The Japanese government was outraged, and photos of the "invasion" ran in the media for weeks. The incident has resulted in proposals to reform refugee policy in Japan from all the major parties. Eventually reforms to the Immigration Control and Refugee Recognition Act went into effect in 2005.

81. The cabinet, with the agreement of the Interministerial Refugee Policy Coordination Committee, agreed at the end of 2003 to terminate the family reunification program in 2005. Some people have tied the conclusion of this program to the decision to allow convention refugees to take advantage of the settlement program offered at the last remaining center, which is located in Tokyo's Shinagawa ward. This is bolstered by evidence that RHQ delayed the end of the program by accepting groups that were smaller in number than the allowed quota. According to one knowledgeable source, this prolonged the program for an extra one to two years.

82. Watanabe, "Nihon no nanmin jitsumu no genjō," 27–29.

83. Toki, "Kokkyō o koeru NGO no katsudo," 64.

84. Watanabe, "Nihon no nanmin jitsumu no genjō," 29–30.

85. Toki, "Kokkyō o koeru NGO no katsudo," 63.

86. Author interview with an attorney of the Ministry of Justice Immigration Bureau, Refugee Section, Tokyo, August 12, 2005.

87. Watanabe, "Nihon no nanmin jitsumu no genjō," 31; Toki, "Kokkyō o koeru NGO no katsudo," 63.

88. Flowers, "Failure to Protect Refugees?" 341.

89. Watanabe, "Nihon no nanmin jitsumu no genjō," 32. Many advocacy groups assist asylum seekers in addressing these problems. Although finding employment for them is difficult, some organizations have been successful in building relationships with businesses that will hire asylum seekers who do not have work permits. This is technically illegal, but when there are raids, Ministry of Justice officials usually do not detain these people if they show documentation that they have already submitted an application for refugee status. Of course, their illegal status leaves them in a vulnerable position. Organizations that offer counseling to refugees often intervene on their behalf with health-care providers. This usually means that payment plans may be established or bills for care will be deferred; it is not the case that health care is free. There is a doctor in Tokyo who has offered his services by providing free health checks for refugees and referrals when needed, but more specialized care still has to be paid for. On the issue of education, Japanese schools do not have a program in Japanese as a second language, and few schools offer any kind of instruction in languages aside from Japanese. In addition, there is no national policy governing acceptance of refugee children; decisions are left to each local district. It is important to note, however, that as is the case for children of foreign workers in Japan, compulsory education laws do not apply to refugee children. This, along with the lack of second-language programs, often means that children fall through the cracks.

90. Watanabe, "Nihon no nanmin jitsumu no genjō," 33.

91. Ibid., 34.

92. Toki, "Kokkyō o koeru NGO no katsudo," 65.

93. Watanabe, "Nihon no nanmin jitsumu no genjō," 38. For more details and a personal account of detention, see Ali Jane with Ikeda Kayoko, *Okāsan, boku wa ikitemasu* (Mother, I'm Alive) (Tokyo: Magazine House, 2004).

94. Amnesty International, "Japan: Inadequate Protection for Refugees and Asylum-Seekers," 205.

95. Ibid., 216.

96. See, for example, Meyer et al., "World Society and the Nation-State."

97. Flowers, "Failure to Protect Refugees?"

CHAPTER 4

1. Hashimoto Ryutaro, minister of finance of Japan, letter to the editor, *New York Times*, written June 16, 1990, published July 7, 1990; accessed at www.nytimes.com, April 8, 2008.

2. Hashimoto went on to serve as prime minister from January 11, 1996, to July 30, 1998.

3. Fujita, " 'It's All Mother's Fault.' "

4. Japanese women identified three key areas where CEDAW would be useful in their quest for reform: citizenship law, name change upon marriage, and employment. In recent years, women have added goals of ending discrimination against unwed mothers and single women and minority women's rights to their agenda.

5. Garon, *Molding Japanese Minds*; Norgren, *Abortion Before Birth Control*.

6. Risse-Kappen, "Ideas Do Not Float Freely," 210.

7. Checkel, "Norms, Institutions, and National Identity in Contemporary Europe"; Evangelista, *Unarmed Forces*.

8. In addition to tensions over automobiles, there were also tensions over trade liberalization on certain agricultural products under the General Agreement on Tariffs and Trade (GATT).

9. See, for example, Calder, "Japanese Foreign Economic Policy Formation"; Orr, *Emergence of Japan's Foreign Aid Power*.

10. Parkinson, "Japan's Equal Opportunity Law"; Creighton, "Marriage, Motherhood, and Career Management." One exception is Joyce Gelb's *Gender Policies in Japan and the United States*, a comparative study that offers a comprehensive view of the role of Japanese women's movements in adoption of rights policies in Japan; she does not focus on adoption of CEDAW.

11. Parkinson, "Japan's Equal Employment Opportunity Law," 618.

12. Takahashi, "Joshi sabetsu teppai jōyaku no tanjō ni tazusawatte."

13. Creighton, "Marriage, Motherhood, and Career Management," 192.

14. Upham, *Law and Social Change in Postwar Japan*.

15. In later accounts, many women say that it would have been embarrassing for Japan to have a woman ambassador present as its government representative at the mid-decade conference in Copenhagen and not to have signed CEDAW.

16. Robert J. Smith, "Gender Inequality in Contemporary Japan," gives a concise overview of changes in women's lives from 1868 though the mid-1980s, when the EEOL was passed.

17. Iwao, *Japanese Woman*, 5.

18. Lock, "Centering the Household."

19. Uno, "Women and Changes in the Household Division of Labor," 25.

20. Nolte and Hastings, "Meiji State's Policy Toward Women," 153; also see Brinton, *Women and the Economic Miracle*.

21. Quoted in Nolte and Hastings, "Meiji State's Policy Toward Women," 156.

22. Norgren documents similar government-sponsored programs to promote motherhood in the interest of the state in *Abortion Before Birth Control*, chap. 3.

23. Rosenberger, "Fragile Resistance, Signs of Status." We should note that overall, women are getting married and having children at an older age now.

24. United Nations, *Report of the Committee on the Elimination of Discrimination Against Women (Seventh Session)*, 47.

25. "Women who make under 1,000,000 yen per year (about $11,100 at 1995 exchange rates) do not have to pay taxes on their income. In addition, their husbands can still claim them as dependents for spouse deductions of 300,000 yen per year ($3,300). Women's wages need to be well over $10,400 for them to have an incentive to give up this tax benefit." Rosenberger, "Fragile Resistance, Signs of Status," 18.

26. Committee on the Elimination of Discrimination Against Women, *Third Periodic Report of State Party Japan*, 29.

27. I would like to thank Kathryn Sikkink for making this point clear to me.

28. Takahashi was Japan's first female ambassador—she was the ambassador to Denmark—and when she signed CEDAW in 1980, she became the first Japanese woman to sign an international treaty. When Takahashi was an official at the Women's and Young Workers' Bureau, she attended the fourth meeting of the UN Committee on the Status of Women in 1950 as an unofficial observer even before Japan was a member of the UN. She also served as Japan's representative to the International Labor Organization, the Committee on the Status of Women, and General Assembly discussion of the proposed CEDAW.

29. Yamashita, *Report of UN Special Session "Women 2000" and Women's Status in Japan*, 4; author interview with Yasuko Yamashita, Tokyo, Japan, July 23, 2001.

30. Yamashita, *Research on the Convention*, 522.

31. Mackie, *Feminism in Modern Japan*, chap. 7.

32. Yamashita, *Research on the Convention*, 523.

33. Ibid.

34. The Fusen Kaikan publishes *Josei tenbō*, and its contents focus on political issues. Much of the coverage in 1976 reflected on the history and the future direction of the women's movement in Japan.

35. Kokusai Fujinnen Renrakukai (International Women's Year Liaison Group), *Renkei to kōdō: kokusai fujin renrakukai no kiroku* (Cooperation and Action: Record of the International Women's Year Liaison Group) (Tokyo: Ichikawa Fusae Memorial Foundation, 1989), 19.

36. *Josei tenbō* (Women's Perspective), January 1976.

37. Ichikawa Fusae, as quoted in "Minkan yonshūichi dantai kesshū shite kokusai fujinnen nihon taikai hiraku" (Forty-one Citizen's Organizations Gather for the International Women's Year Conference Japan Meeting), *Fujin tenbō* (Women's Perspective), January 1976.

38. Ibid., 138.

39. Ibid., 137.

40. *Josei tenbō*, January 1976.

41. Ogata later served as the UN High Commissioner for Refugees.

42. The chief cabinet secretary also serves as the vice president of the Headquarters for the Promotion of Gender Equality; the prime minister serves as the president of the Headquarters.

43. Kokusai Fujinnen Renrakukai (International Women's Year Liaison Group), 59.

44. Ibid., 140.

45. Takahashi, "Joshi sabetsu teppai jōyaku no tanjō ni tazusawatte," 13.

46. Ibid., 11.

47. Kokusai Fujinnen Renrakukai, 139.

48. Knapp, "Still Office Flowers," 106.

49. Administrative guidance is a process by which the Ministry of Labor tries to persuade employers to adhere to certain standards without using legal sanctions or punishments.

50. Port argues that Japan's government is more likely to implement and comply with international human rights law because the Japanese conception of rights is contextual. This explanation seems relevant in this case, but it does not extend to other kinds of international law, such as the Ottawa Convention that I will consider in the next chapter.

51. Akamatsu and Yamashita, *Josei sabetsu teppai jōyaku and NGO*; Yamashita, "Joshi sabetsu teppai jōyaku no ishiki."

52. Knapp, "Don't Awaken the Sleeping Child," 30.

53. Upham, *Law and Social Change in Postwar Japan.*

54. Knapp, "Still Office Flowers," 103.

55. Ibid., 105; for more detailed discussion of employment discrimination cases, see Upham, *Law and Social Change in Postwar Japan.*

56. Towns, "Status of Women as a Standard of 'Civilization.'"

57. See, for example, Yosan Iinkai (Budget Committee) meeting, February 23, 1985.

58. Honkaigi (lower house) plenary session, June 26, 1984.

59. Ibid.

60. Diet member Tagaya, Shakairōdō Iinkai (Labor and Welfare Committee) meeting, July 17, 1984. See also Yosan Iinkai (Budget Committee) meeting, March 6, 1985, where this issue arises again.

61. Honkaigi (lower house) plenary session, June 26, 1984.

62. Shakairōdō Iinkai (Labor and Welfare Committee) meeting, July 17, 1984. Also see Yosan Iinkai (Budget Committee) meeting, February 23, 1985. Leheny, *Rules of Play*, is an excellent study of Japanese national identity and the significance of the idea that Japan can adopt a norm but tweak it to maintain something uniquely Japanese, thus showing that Japanese are both just like everyone else, "normal," and unique.

63. Shakairōdō Iinkai (Labor and Welfare Committee) meeting, July 17, 1984.

64. Minister Abe, Gaimu Iinkai (Foreign Affairs Committee) meeting, May 24, 1985.

65. Gaimu Iinkai (Foreign Affairs Committee) meeting, May 24, 1985.

66. Shakairōdō Iinkai (Labor and Welfare Committee) meeting, July 17, 1984.

67. Iwasawa, "Impact of International Human Rights Law on Japanese Law"; Iwasawa, *International Law, Human Rights, and Japanese Law.*

68. Minister Abe, Gaimu Iinkai Bunkyō Iinkai Rengō Shinsakai (Foreign Affairs Committee and Education Committee joint hearing), May 30, 1985; see also Shakairōdō Iinkai (Labor and Welfare Committee) meeting, February 26, 1985.

69. Minister Abe, Gaimu Iinkai (Foreign Affairs Committee) meeting, May 24, 1985.

70. Honkaigi (lower house) plenary session, June 26, 1984.

71. United Nations, *Convention on the Elimination of All Forms of Discrimination Against Women.*

72. Nakamura, *Josei deita bukku: seikarada kara seiji sanka made.*

73. Schoppa, *Race for the Exits*, 73–79, 88–97.

74. Ibid., 88–97.

75. Knapp, "Don't Awaken the Sleeping Child," 24.

76. For more on the lack of formal sanctions in Japanese law, see Haley, "Sheathing the Sword of Justice in Japan," 265–81.

77. Creighton, "Marriage, Motherhood, and Career Management," 213.

78. In these relationships the *senpai* is the more experienced person, the mentor, and the *kohai* is the less experienced person, the mentee. In addition, these relationships also include an age component and are sex based.

79. The culture of work in large Japanese firms is changing. Economic recession that has characterized the 1990s and persisted into the first decade of the twenty-first century has led to company restructuring and layoffs. Many Japanese young people are also questioning the desirability of a life dedicated to work. On the other hand, hard economic times have also led to an increase in uncompensated overtime.

80. Schoppa, *Race for the Exits.*

81. Omori, "Gender and the Labor Market."

82. Committee on the Elimination of Discrimination Against Women, *Third Periodic Report of State Party Japan.*

83. Andrews, "National and International Sources," 428. It is important to note that the declining economy of the 1990s and beyond has forced changes in hiring and retention even at large firms.

84. Committee on the Elimination of Discrimination Against Women, *Third Periodic Report of State Party Japan*, 28. The M curve is the pattern of employment described earlier in the chapter where women work until marriage or childbirth, leave work to raise their children, and return to work after the last child enters school.

85. Committee on the Elimination of Discrimination Against Women, *Third Periodic Report of State Party Japan*, 28.

86. Some articles that did make reference to Japan's state and international identity include Editorial, *Yomiuri Shimbun*, August 14, 1984, "Kigyō wa kintōhō ni zenmuki taiō o" (Companies Are Positively Facing the Equal Employment Opportunity Law); Commentary, *Yomiuri Shimbun*, July 27, 1984, "Shizen sōki shikō negau" (Although It Is the Second-Best Policy, There Are Requests to Put It into the Early Stages of Enforcement); Editorial, *Yomiuri Shimbun*, May 11, 1984, "'Kintōhō' made sutaro saseyō" ("Equality Law" Will Probably Be Instituted).

87. Editorial, *Yomiuri Shimbun*, May 11, 1984; Editorial, *Yomiuri Shimbun*, August 14, 1984; Editorial, *Yomiuri Shimbun*, April 15, 1984, "Teichaku saseyō josei byōdō no nagare" (Let's Establish the Trend of Women's Equality).

88. Editorial, *Yomiuri Shimbun*, May 11, 1984.

89. Commentary, *Yomiuri Shimbun*, June 5, 1985, "Josei sabetsu teppai shiren wa kore kara" (From Now On, a Trial on Abolishing Discrimination Against Women).

90. Ibid.

91. Commentary, *Yomiuri Shimbun*, July 27, 1984.

92. Author interview with Akamatsu Ryoko, Tokyo, Japan, August 14, 2001.

93. Editorial, *Yomiuri Shimbun*, June 6, 1984, "Hataraku Josei ni ikujikyū gyōseido o" (A Childcare Leave System for Working Women); Editorial, *Yomiuri Shimbun*, February 26, 1985, "Dō ikasu, josei no sanka iyoku" (How to Utilize Women's Desire to Join Society).

94. In her research on the political lives of Japanese housewives, LeBlanc finds that many women who choose to be housewives are not necessarily content. The women may or may not view their role of housewife as important, but they all, for the most part, feel that society does not value the work of housewives. LeBlanc, *Bicycle Citizens*, 43.

95. For more on the cultural ideology of "mother," see Fujita, "'It's All Mother's Fault,'" 72–80.

96. Editorial, *Yomiuri Shimbun*, February 26, 1985.

97. In addition to the opinions and editorials previously cited, see Editorial, *Yomiuri Shimbun*, April 15, 1985, "Teichaku saseyō josei byōdō no nagare" (Let's Establish the Trend of Women's Equality).

98. Iwasawa, *International Law, Human Rights, and Japanese Law*, 2.

99. Upham, *Law and Social Change in Postwar Japan*, 129–44.

100. Ibid., 130.

101. Andrews, "National and International Sources," 413.

102. Nishimura, "Article 5 and Employment Discrimination," 14.

103. Ibid., 14.

104. Miyachi, "On the Unjust Court Ruling."

105. Ibid., 2–3. Because this decision is consistent with much of international law, there is still the possibility that it will be applied to future cases where the hire took place after CEDAW was ratified.

106. This supports Iwasawa's argument in *International Law, Human Rights, and Japanese Law*, that the courts are reluctant to use international law in deciding cases.

107. Harano, "Cases of Discrimination Against Women at Sumitomo."

108. Committee on the Elimination of Discrimination Against Women, *First Periodic Report of State Party Japan*, 40.

109. Committee on the Elimination of Discrimination Against Women, *Second Periodical Report of State Party Japan*, 4.

110. Risse, Ropp, and Sikkink, *Power of Human Rights*, 29–31.

111. Towns, "Status of Women as a Standard of 'Civilization,'" makes an excellent argument that establishes women's status as a standard of civilization.

CHAPTER 5

1. International Campaign to Ban Landmines, *Landmine Monitor Report 1999: Toward a Mine-Free World*, www.icbl.org/lm/1999/japan.html, accessed April 17, 2008.

2. Chapter 2 of Leheny's *Think Global, Fear Local* is an excellent discussion of the anxiety in 1990s Japan.

3. Miyashita, "Gaiatsu and Japan's Foreign Aid," 702–3.

4. Although the United States was not totally opposed to a limited ban, the treaty negotiators sought an agreement with "no exceptions, no reservations, no loopholes." The United States desired a treaty that would include exceptions for AP mines used in conjunction with antitank mines and for mines used in the demilitarized zone between North and South Korea, as well as a delay in the effective date of the treaty.

5. Christensen, "China, the U.S.-Japan Alliance, and the Security Dilemma in East Asia," 49–52.

6. Michael C. Williams, "Identity and the Politics of Security," 206–9.

7. I would like to thank Helen Kinsella for helping me think differently about pacifism. I think that much of the work that focuses on Japan's identity is easily dismissed because it assumes that pacifism equals a fixed passive identity, and therefore it cannot account for Japan's behavior.

8. Kenneth Anderson, "Ottawa Convention Banning Landmines."

9. Politis, "Regulation of an Invisible Enemy," 465, 471.

10. Ibid., 474–75; Shawn Roberts, "No Exceptions, No Reservations, No Loopholes," 371, 377.

11. Shawn Roberts, "No Exceptions, No Reservations, No Loopholes," 374.

12. Ibid., 376.

13. The remainder of this section is based on information from Williams and Goose, "International Campaign to Ban Landmines"; Cameron, Lawson, and Tomlin, "To Walk Without Fear"; Dolan and Hunt, "Negotiating in the Ottawa Process"; Shawn Roberts, "No Exceptions, No Reservations, No Loopholes"; and Politis, "Regulation of an Invisible Enemy."

14. Williams and Goose, "International Campaign to Ban Landmines," 36.

15. I would like to thank Kristin Willey for her "skeptics" reading of this chapter.

16. Dolan and Hunt, "Negotiating in the Ottawa Process," 415.

17. Price, "Reversing the Gun Sights"; Rutherford, "Evolving Arms Control Agenda."

18. Cameron, "Democratization of Foreign Policy."

19. Mekata, "Building Partnerships Toward a Common Goal," 168.

20. For a discussion of Japan's civil society, see Pekkanen, *Japan's Dual Civil Society*. See Broadbent, *Environmental Politics in Japan*, for a discussion of environmental groups. It is important to acknowledge, however, that the status of NGOs has been improving since passage of a new nonprofit law in the mid-1990s.

21. Risse-Kappen, "Ideas Do Not Float Freely," 208.

22. Gaimu Iinkai (Foreign Affairs Committee) meeting, September 18, 1998.

23. Flowers, "Crossing Borders: Transnationalism, Civil Society, and Post-9/11 Refugee Policy in Japan."

24. Nanmin o Tasukerukai, "NGO Tokyo jirai kaigi '98."

25. Osa, "Keynote Report," 174.

26. Kitagawa, "Mine Ban Policy of the Japanese Government," 9.

27. Adachi, "Why Japan Signed the Mine Ban Treaty," 407, 409.

28. The discussions of the Shōkō Iinkai (Commerce and Industry Committee) meeting on September 25, 1998, include several references to Jody Williams and the ICBL winning the Nobel Peace Prize.

29. Gaimu Iinkai (Foreign Affairs Committee) meeting, February 13, 1998.

30. Ibid.

31. Author interview, Tokyo, Japan, July 28, 2001. Another interviewee also reported a lack of outside pressure from foreign governments; Tokyo, August 1, 2001.

32. Author interview, Tokyo, Japan, July 28, 2001.

33. Rutherford, "Evolving Arms Control Agenda," 87.

34. Commentary, *Asahi Shimbun*, October 15, 1997, Fukiura Tadamasu, "Jirai jōyaku to nihon no gimu" (Land-Mine Convention and Japan's Duty).

35. Ibid.

36. Ibid.

37. See, for example, Editorial, *Asahi Shimbun*, March 8, 1997, "Taijin jirai o chijō kara nakuse" (Remove Antipersonnel Land Mines from the Ground); Commentary, *Asahi Shimbun*, May 12, 1997, Bushita Yukihisa, "Taijin jirai kinshi e seifu wa genkō icchi o" (The Government Moves Toward an Agreement on Banning Antipersonnel Land Mines).

38. Commentary, *Asahi Shimbun*, August 4, 1998, Mekata Motoko, "Jirai shomei no Obuchi-san, tsugi wa hijun desu" (Mr. Obuchi Who Signed the Land Mine Treaty, Next Is Ratifying).

39. The suggestion that Japan make a contribution to mine removal is not trivial because it involves policy change on what is considered a military issue. Japanese law prohibits export of military goods manufactured in Japan and technology required for this manufacture. Because the SDF is prohibited from participating in mine clearance, a policy change would be required to allow this technology to be exported for use by other militaries, NGOs, or private companies.

40. Editorial, *Yomiuri Shimbun*, September 25, 1997, "Taijin jirai haizetu ni hazumi tuku ka" (Is There Momentum Toward Banning Land Mines?).

41. Editorial, *Yomiuri Shimbun,* December 4, 1997, "Taijin jōyaku shomei de fukaketsu na shiten" (An Indispensable Point for Signing the Land-Mine Treaty).

42. Mekata, "Building Partnerships Toward a Common Goal," 168.

43. Anzen Hoshō Iinkai (Security Committee) meeting, March 12, 1998.

44. Satoh, *Evolution of Japanese Security Policy.*

45. The Yosan Iinkai (Budget Committee) meeting of March 19, 1998, offers examples, including one where Obuchi's leadership is mentioned in connection with the possibility of reclaiming the Northern Territories from Russia, in the context of discussions of exporting Japanese repair technology to India, and in the general context of Official Development Assistance funding discussions.

46. Sato won the Nobel Peace Prize in 1974 for instituting the three nonnuclear principles.

47. Edström, "Japan's Foreign Policy and Human Security," 219.

48. UNDP, *Human Development Report,* 1993; UNDP, *Human Development Report,* 1994.

49. Ibid., 212–17.

50. Cameron, Lawson, and Tomlin, *To Walk Without Fear,* 465.

51. Ibid., 466.

52. Ibid.

53. Ibid., 470.

54. Ibid., 474.

55. De Larrinaga and Sjolander, "(Re)presenting Land Mines from Protector to Enemy," 378.

56. Gaimu Iinkai (Foreign Affairs Committee) meeting, September 25, 1998.

57. Tannenwald, "Nuclear Taboo," 437.

58. Shōkō Iinkai (Commerce and Industry Committee) meeting, September 25, 1998; Gaimu Iinkai (Foreign Affairs Committee) meeting, September 18, 1998.

59. Yosan Iinkai (Budget Committee) meeting, August 17, 1998.

60. Price and Tannenwald, "Norms and Deterrence," 134.

61. Shōkō Iinkai (Commerce and Industry Committee) meeting, September 25, 1998; Plenary Session (meeting of the entire lower house), September 24, 1998.

62. Price, "Reversing the Gun Sights," defines grafting as "the mix of genealogical heritage and conscious manipulation involved in . . . normative rooting and branching," 628.

63. This parallels the omission of linking use of nuclear weapons on Japan to later aversion to the weapon in Tannenwald, "Nuclear Taboo."

64. Berger, "Norms, Identity, and National Security," 317.

65. Drifte, *Japan's Foreign Policy for the 21st Century,* 50–51.

66. Anzen Hoshō Iinkai (Security Committee) meeting, March 12, 1998.

67. Shōkō Iinkai (Commerce and Industry Committee) meeting, September 25, 1998.

68. Anzen Hoshō Iinkai (Security Committee) meeting, September 28, 1998. The *fushinsen* incidents where suspicious boats were detected in Japanese coastal

waters in the 1990s certainly helped perpetuate this fear. See Leheny, *Think Global, Fear Local*, for a detailed discussion of how the government used international norms against terrorism to deal with domestic threat posed by the suspicious boats.

69. Price, "Compliance with International Norms and the Mines Taboo," 341.

70. Although Prime Minister Sato and his cabinet committed to the three non-nuclear principles—not to possess, introduce, or manufacture nuclear weapons—and Sato won a Nobel Peace Prize for this repudiation of the weapon in 1974, this is another illustration of the conflict between security and identity, given more recent evidence that the U.S. military actually stored nuclear weapons in Japan with the Japanese government's knowledge.

71. Price, "Compliance with International Norms and the Mines Taboo," 360.

72. Diet member Ito Shigeru, Gaimu Iinkai (Foreign Affairs Committee) meeting, September 25, 1998.

CHAPTER 6

1. See Table 1 in Chapter 1.

2. The four human rights conventions adopted in the late 1970s and early 1980s include the Refugee Convention and CEDAW. The other two, the International Covenant on Civil and Political Rights and the International Covenant on Economic, Social, and Cultural Rights, along with the Universal Declaration of Human Rights, constitute the core of the international human rights regime. Both the ICCPR and the ICESC were adopted in 1979.

3. Peters and Wolper, *Women's Rights / Human Rights*.

4. Donnelly, *Universal Human Rights in Theory and Practice*, 38.

Bibliography

Abe, Kohki. "Protecting Whom? Japanese Refugee Policies Revisited." *Kanagawa Law Journal* 36, no. 3 (2003): 1–39.

Adachi, Kenki. "Why Japan Signed the Mine Ban Treaty: The Political Dynamics Behind the Decision." *Asian Survey* 45, no. 3 (2005): 397–413.

Akamatsu Ryoko and Yasuko Yamashita, eds. *Josei sabetsu teppai jōyaku and NGO*. Tokyo: Meiseki, 2003.

Allison, Anne. "Producing Mothers." In *Re-imaging Japanese Women*, edited by Anne E. Imamura, 135–55. Berkeley: University of California Press, 1996.

Amnesty International. "Japan: Inadequate Protection for Refugees and Asylum-Seekers." *International Journal of Refugee Law* 5, no. 2 (1993): 205–39.

AMPO Review—Japan Asia Quarterly, ed. *Voices from the Japanese Women's Movement*. Armonk, NY: M. E. Sharpe, 1996.

Anderson, Benedict. *Imagined Communities*. London: Verso Press, 1991.

Anderson, Kenneth. "The Ottawa Convention Banning Landmines, the Role of International Non-governmental Organizations and the Idea of International Civil Society." *European Journal of International Law* 11, no. 1 (2000): 91–120.

Andrews, Jill. "National and International Sources of Women's Right to Equal Employment Opportunities: Equality in Law Versus Equality in Fact." *Journal of International Law and Business* 14 (1994): 413–40.

Arakaki Osamu. *Aratana nanmin nintei seido no kakuritsu: Fueanesu no kochō toshite.* jiyū to segi, 2002.

Augustine-Adams, Kif. "Gendered States: A Comparative Construction of Citizenship and Nation." *Virginia Journal of International Law* 41 (2000): 93–139.

Auslin, Michael R. *Negotiating with Imperialism: The Unequal Treaties and the Culture of Japanese Diplomacy*. Cambridge, MA: Harvard University Press, 2004.

Axelrod, Robert. *The Evolution of Cooperation*. New York: Basic Books, 1984.

Baldwin, David. *Neorealism and Neoliberalism: The Contemporary Debate*. New York: Columbia University Press, 1993.

Barkin, Samuel, and Bruce Cronin. "The State and the Nation: Changing Norms and the Rules of Sovereignty." *International Organization* 48, no. 1 (1994): 107–30.

Barnett, Michael, and Martha Finnemore. *Rules for the World: International Organizations in Global Politics.* Ithaca, NY: Cornell University Press, 2004.

Barnett, Robert. *Beyond War: Japan's Concept of Comprehensive National Security.* Washington, DC: Pergamon-Brassey's International Defense Publishers, 1984.

Barnhart, Michael A. *Japan Prepares for Total War: The Search for Economic Security, 1919–1941.* Ithaca, NY: Cornell University Press, 1987.

Berger, Thomas U. "Norms, Identity, and National Security in Germany and Japan." In *The Culture of National Security: Norms and Identity in World Politics,* edited by Peter J. Katzenstein, 317–56. New York: Columbia University Press, 1996.

Bernstein, Ann, and Myron Weiner, eds. *Migration and Refugee Policies: An Overview.* London: Pinter Press, 1999.

Bernstein, Gail Lee, ed. *Recreating Japanese Women, 1600–1945.* Berkeley: University of California Press, 1991.

Boulding, Elise. *Building a Global Civic Culture.* Syracuse, NY: Syracuse University Press, 1990.

Bridges, Brian. *Japan: Hesitant Superpower.* London: Research Institute for the Study of Conflict and Terrorism, 1993.

Brinton, Mary. *Women and the Economic Miracle: Gender and Work in Postwar Japan.* Berkeley: University of California Press, 1993.

Broadbent, Jeffrey. *Environmental Politics in Japan: Networks of Power and Protest.* New York: Cambridge University Press, 1998.

Broadbent, Jeffrey, and Ikuo Kabashima. "Referent Pluralism: Mass Media and Politics in Japan." *Journal of Japanese Studies* 12, no. 2 (1986): 329–61.

Brown, Catherine. "Japanese Approaches to Equal Rights for Women: The Legal Framework." *Law in Japan: An Annual* 29 (1979).

Brown, Michael E., and Sumit Ganguly, eds. *Depoliticizing Ethnicity: Government Policies and Ethnic Relations in Asia and the Pacific.* Cambridge, MA: MIT Press, 1997.

Buckley, Sandra. *Broken Silence: Voices of Japanese Feminism.* Berkeley: University of California Press, 1997.

Bull, Hedley. *The Anarchical Society.* New York: Columbia University Press, 1977.

Calder, Kent. "Japanese Foreign Economic Policy Formation: Explaining the 'Reactive State.'" *World Politics* 40 (1988): 517–41.

Cameron, Maxwell A. "Democratization of Foreign Policy: The Ottawa Process as a Model." In *To Walk Without Fear: The Global Campaign to Ban Landmines,* edited by Maxwell A. Cameron, Robert J. Lawson, and Brian W. Tomlin, 424–47. Toronto: Oxford University Press, 1998.

Cameron, Maxwell A., Robert J. Lawson, and Brian W. Tomlin. "To Walk Without Fear." In *To Walk Without Fear: The Global Campaign to Ban Landmines,* edited by Maxwell A. Cameron, Robert J. Lawson, and Brian W. Tomlin, 1–19. Toronto: Oxford University Press, 1998.

———, eds. *To Walk Without Fear: The Global Movement to Ban Landmines.* Toronto: Oxford University Press, 1998.

Campbell, David. *Writing Security: United States Foreign Policy and the Politics of Identity.* Minneapolis: University of Minnesota Press, 1992.

Carlsnaes, Walter, Thomas Risse, and Beth Simmons, eds. *Handbook of International Relations.* London: Sage, 2002.

Chafetz, Glenn, Michael Spirtas, and Benjamin Frankel. "Introduction: Tracing the Influence of Identity on Foreign Policy." *Security Studies* 8, nos. 2/3 (1999): vii–xxii.

Chan-Tiberghien, Jennifer. *Gender and Human Rights Politics in Japan.* Stanford, CA: Stanford University Press, 2004.

Chayes, Abram, and Antonia Handler Chayes. "On Compliance." *International Organization* 47, no. 2 (1993): 175–205.

Checkel, Jeffrey T. "The Constructivist Turn in International Relations." *World Politics* 50, no. 2 (1998): 324–48.

———. "International Institutions and Socialization in Europe: Introduction and Framework." *International Organization* 59 (2005): 801–826.

———. "International Norms and Domestic Politics: Bridging the Rationalist-Constructivist Divide." *European Journal of International Relations* 3 (1997): 473–95.

———. "Norms, Institutions, and National Identity in Contemporary Europe." *International Studies Quarterly* 43 (1999): 83–114.

———. "Why Comply? Social Learning and European Identity Change." *International Organization* 55, no. 3 (2001): 553–88.

Christensen, Thomas J. "China, the U.S.-Japan Alliance, and the Security Dilemma in East Asia." *International Security* 23, no. 4 (1999): 49–80.

Committee on the Elimination of Discrimination Against Women. *Consideration of Reports Submitted by States Parties Under Article 18 of the Convention. First Periodic Report of State Party Japan.* New York: United Nations, 1988.

———. *Consideration of Reports Submitted by States Parties Under Article 18 of the Convention. Second Periodic Report of State Party Japan.* New York: United Nations, 1992.

———. *Consideration of Reports Submitted by States Parties Under Article 18 of the Convention. Third Periodic Report of State Party Japan.* New York: United Nations, 1993.

Copeland, Dale C. "The Constructivist Challenge to Structural Realism." *International Security* 25, no. 2 (2000): 187–212.

Cortell, Andrew P., and James W. Davis. "Understanding the Domestic Impact of International Norms: A Research Agenda." *International Studies Review* 2, no. 1 (2000): 65–87.

Crawford, Neta. "Decolonization as an International Norm: The Evolution of Practices, Arguments, and Beliefs." In *Emerging Norms of Justified Intervention: A Collection of Essays from a Project of the American Academy of Arts and Sciences,* edited by Laura W. Reed. Cambridge, MA: American Academy of Arts and Sciences, 1993.

Creighton, Millie R. "Marriage, Motherhood, and Career Management in a Japanese 'Counter Culture.'" In *Re-imaging Japanese Women*, edited by Anne E. Imamura, 192–220. Berkeley: University of California Press, 1996.

Curtis, Gerald. *The Logic of Japanese Politics: Leaders, Institutions, and the Limits of Change*. New York: Columbia University Press, 2000.

Cwiertka, Katarzyna J. *Modern Japanese Cuisine: Food, Power and National Identity*. London: Reaktion Books, 2006.

de Larrinaga, Miguel, and Claire Turenne Sjolander. "(Re)presenting Landmines from Protector to Enemy: The Discursive Framing of a New Multilateralism." In *To Walk Without Fear: The Global Movement to Ban Landmines*, edited by Maxwell A. Cameron, Robert J. Lawson, and Brian W. Tomlin, 364–91. Toronto: Oxford University Press, 1998.

Destler, Irving. *Managing an Alliance: The Politics of U.S.-Japanese Relations*. Washington, DC: Brookings Institution, 1976.

Dobson, Hugo. *Japan and United Nations Peacekeeping: New Pressures, New Responses*. London: Routledge Curzon, 2003.

Dolan, Michael, and Chris Hunt. "Negotiating in the Ottawa Process: The New Multilateralism." In *To Walk Without Fear: The Global Campaign to Ban Landmines*, edited by Maxwell A. Cameron, Robert J. Lawson, and Brian W. Tomlin, 392–423. Toronto: Oxford University Press, 1998.

Donnelly, Jack. *Universal Human Rights in Theory and Practice*. Ithaca, NY: Cornell University Press, 2003.

Downs, George W., David M. Rocke, and Peter N. Barsoom. "Is the Good News About Compliance Good News About Cooperation?" *International Organization* 50, no. 3 (1996): 379–406.

Drifte, Reinhard. *Japan's Foreign Policy for the 21st Century: From Economic Superpower to What Power?* 2nd ed. Oxford: St. Anthony's College, 1998.

Edström, Bert. "Japan's Foreign Policy and Human Security." *Japan Forum* 15, no. 2 (2003): 209–25.

Evangelista, Matthew. "The Paradox of State Strength: Transnational Relations, Domestic Structures, and Security Policy in Russia and the Soviet Union." *International Organization* 49, no. 1 (1995): 1–38.

———. *Unarmed Forces: The Transnational Movement to End the Cold War*. Ithaca, NY: Cornell University Press, 1999.

Finnemore, Martha. *Defining National Interests in International Society*. Ithaca, NY: Cornell University Press, 1996a.

———. "Norms, Culture, and World Politics: Insights from Sociology's Institutionalism." *International Organization* 50, no. 1 (1996b): 325–47.

———. *The Purpose of Intervention: Changing Beliefs About the Use of Force*. Ithaca, NY: Cornell University Press, 2003.

Finnemore, Martha, and Kathryn Sikkink. "International Norm Dynamics and Political Change." *International Organization* 52, no. 4 (1998): 887–917.

Flowers, Petrice R. "Crossing Borders: Transnationalism, Civil Society, and Post-9/11 Refugee Policy in Japan." In *Inescapable Transnationalisms: Japan, Foreign Aid, and the Search for Global Solutions*, edited by David Leheny and Kay Warren. London: Routledge, forthcoming.

———. "Failure to Protect Refugees? Domestic Institutions, International Organizations, and Civil Society in Japan." *Journal of Japanese Studies* 34, no. 2 (2008): 333–61.

———. "The International Refugee Convention: National Identity as a Limitation on Compliance." In *Forced Migration and Global Processes: A View from Forced Migration Studies*, edited by François Crépeau, Delphine Nakache, Michael Collyer, Nathaniel H. Goetz, Art Hansen, Renu Modi, Aninia, Nadig, Sanja Špoljar-Vržina, and Loes H. M. van Willigen. Lanham, MD: Lexington Books, 2006.

Franck, Thomas M. "Legitimacy in the International System." *American Journal of International Law* 82, no. 4 (1988): 705–59.

Fujimori-Fanselow, Kumiko, and Atsuko Kameda. *Japanese Women: New Feminist Perspectives on the Past, Present, and Future*. New York: Feminist Press at the City University of New York, 1995.

Fujita, Mariko. " 'It's All Mother's Fault': Childcare and the Socialization of Working Mothers in Japan." *Journal of Japanese Studies* 15, no. 1 (1989): 67–91.

Fukuoka, Yasunori. *The Lives of Young Koreans in Japan*. Translated by Tom Gill. Melbourne, Australia: Trans Pacific Press, 2000.

Fukutake, Tadashi. *The Japanese Social Structure*. Translated by Ronald Dore. Tokyo: Tokyo University Press, 1989.

Gamson, William. *Talking Politics*. New York: Cambridge University Press, 1992.

Garon, Sheldon. *Molding Japanese Minds: The State in Everyday Life*. Princeton, NJ: Princeton University Press, 1997.

Geertz, Clifford. *Negara: The Theatre State in Nineteenth-Century Bali*. Princeton, NJ: Princeton University Press, 1980.

Gelb, Joyce. *Gender Policies in Japan and the United States: Comparing Women's Movements, Rights, and Politics*. New York: Palgrave Macmillan, 2003.

Gills, Barry. "The Hegemonic Transition in East Asia: A Historical Perspective." In *Gramsci, Historical Materialism and International Relations*, edited by S. Gill. Cambridge: Cambridge University Press, 1993.

Gladney, Dru C., ed. *Making Majorities: Constituting the Nation in Japan, Korea, China, Malaysia, Fiji, Turkey, and the United States*. Stanford, CA: Stanford University Press, 1998.

Gluck, Carol. *Japan's Modern Myths: Ideology in the Late Meiji Period*. Princeton, NJ: Princeton University Press, 1985.

Goldstein, Judith, Miles Kahler, Robert O. Keohane, and Anne-Marie Slaughter, eds. *Legalization and World Politics*. Cambridge, MA: MIT Press, 2001.

Goldstein, Judith, and Robert Keohane, eds. *Ideas and Foreign Policy: Beliefs, Institutions, and Political Change*. Ithaca, NY: Cornell University Press, 1993.

Goodman, Roger, Ceri Peach, Ayumi Takanaka, and Paul White. 2003. *Global Japan: The Experience of Japan's New Immigrants and Overseas Communities*. New York: RutledgeCurzon.

Gong, Gerrit W. *The Standard of "Civilization" in International Society.* New York: Oxford University Press, 1984.

Gries, Peter Hays. *China's New Nationalism: Pride, Politics, and Diplomacy.* Berkeley: University of California Press, 2004.

Gurowitz, Amy. "The Diffusion of International Norms: Why Identity Matters." *International Politics* 43 (2006): 305–41.

———. "International Law, Politics, and Migrant Rights." In *The Politics of International Law,* edited by Christian Reus-Smit, 131–50. Cambridge: Cambridge University Press, 2004.

———. "Mobilizing International Norms: Domestic Actors, Immigrants, and the Japanese State." *World Politics* 51, no. 3 (1999a): 413–45.

———. "Mobilizing International Norms: Domestic Actors, Immigrants, and the State." Ph.D. diss., Cornell University, Ithaca, New York, 1999b.

Guzzini, Stefano. "A Reconstruction of Constructivism in International Relations." *European Journal of International Relations* 6, no. 2 (2000): 147–82.

Haley, John O. "Governance by Negotiation: A Reappraisal of Bureaucratic Power in Japan." *Journal of Japanese Studies* (1987): 343–57.

———. "Sheathing the Sword of Justice in Japan: An Essay on Law Without Sanctions." *Journal of Japanese Studies* 8 (1982): 265–81.

Hanami, Tadashi. "Japanese Policies on the Rights and Benefits Granted to Foreign Workers, Residents, Refugees, and Illegals." In *Temporary Workers or Future Citizens? Japanese and U.S. Migration Policies,* edited by Myron Weiner and Tadashi Hanami. New York: New York University Press, 1998.

Harano, Sachiko. "Cases of Discrimination Against Women at Sumitomo." Osaka: Working Women's International Network, 2001.

Hastings, Sally Ann. "Women Legislators in the Postwar Diet." In *Re-imaging Japanese Women,* edited by Anne E. Imamura, 271–300. Berkeley: University of California Press, 1996.

Hathaway, James C. *The Law of Refugee Status.* Toronto: Butterworths, 1991.

Hathaway, Oona. "Do Human Rights Treaties Make a Difference?" *Yale Law Journal* 111 (2001–2002): 1942–55.

Heginbotham, Eric, and Richard J. Samuels. "Mercantile Realism and Japanese Foreign Policy." *International Security* 22, no. 4 (1998): 171–203.

Helwig, Diana. "Japan's Equal Employment Opportunity Act: A Five-Year Look at Its Effectiveness." *Boston University International Law Journal* 9 (1991): 293–320.

Hirata, Keiko. *Civil Society in Japan: The Growing Role of NGOs in Tokyo's Aid Development Policy.* New York: Palgrave Macmillan, 2002.

Honma Hiroshi. *Nanmin mondai to wa nani ka?* Tokyo: Iwanami Shoten, 1990.

———. "Nihon no nanmin seido." In *Nanmin to jinken,* edited by Nanmin Kenkyū Foramu. Tokyo: Gendaijinbunsha, 2001.

Hopf, Ted. *Social Construction of International Politics: Identities and Foreign Policies, Moscow, 1955 and 1999.* Ithaca, NY: Cornell University Press, 2002.

Hurd, Ian. "Legitimacy and Authority in International Politics." *International Organization* 53, no. 2 (1999): 379–408.

Hurrell, Andrew, and Benedict Kingsbury. *The International Politics of the Environment: Actors, Interests, and Institutions.* Oxford: Clarendon Press, 1992.

Imamura, Anne E., ed. *Re-imaging Japanese Women.* Berkeley: University of California Press, 1996.

Iwao, Sumiko. *The Japanese Woman: Traditional Image and Changing Reality.* Cambridge, MA: Harvard University Press, 1993.

Iwasawa, Yuji. "The Impact of International Human Rights Law on Japanese Law: The Third Reformation for Japanese Women." *Japanese Annual of International Law* 34 (1991): 21–68.

———. *International Law, Human Rights, and Japanese Law: The Impact of International Law on Japanese Law.* Oxford: Clarendon Press, 1998.

Japanese Association of International Women's Rights, ed. *International Women.* Tokyo: Japanese Association of International Women's Rights, 2000.

———, ed. *Kokusai josei.* Tokyo: Japan Association of International Women's Rights, 1993.

Japanese Government. "Fourth Periodic Report on Implementation of Convention of the Elimination of All Forms of Discrimination Against Women." Tokyo, 1998.

———. "Response to the Questionnaire to Government on Implementation of the Beijing Platform for Action." Tokyo, 1999.

Johnson, Chalmers. *Japan: Who Governs? The Rise of the Developmental State.* New York: W. W. Norton & Company, 1995.

Kahler, Miles. "Legalization as Strategy: The Asia-Pacific Case." In *Legalization and World Politics*, edited by Judith Goldstein, Miles Kahler, Robert O. Keohane, and Anne-Marie Slaughter, 165–88. Cambridge, MA: MIT Press, 2001.

Kaino, Michiatsu. "Some Introductory Comments on the Historical Background of Japanese Civil Law." *International Journal of the Sociology of Law* 16, no. 3 (1988): 383–93.

Kajita, Takamichi. "The Challenge of Incorporating Foreigners in Japan: 'Ethnic Japanese' and 'Sociological Japanese.'" In *Temporary Workers or Future Citizens? Japanese and U.S. Migration Policies*, edited by Myron Weiner and Tadashi Hanami. New York: New York University Press, 1998.

Kamiya, Masako. "Women in Japan." *University of British Columbia Law Review* 20 (1986): 447–69.

Kataoka, Tetsuya, and Ramon H. Myers. *Defending an Economic Superpower: Reassessing the U.S.-Japan Security Alliance.* London: Westview Press, 1989.

Katzenstein, Peter J. *Cultural Norms and National Security: Police and Military in Postwar Japan.* Ithaca, NY: Cornell University Press, 1998.

———, ed. *The Culture of National Security: Norms and Identity in World Politics.* New York: Columbia University Press, 1996.

Katzenstein, Peter J., and Nobuo Okawara. *Japan's National Security: Structures, Norms and Policy Responses in a Changing World.* Ithaca, NY: Cornell University East Asia Program, 1993.

Katzenstein, Peter J., and Yutaka Tsujinaka. *Defending the Japanese State: Structures, Norms and the Political Responses to Terrorism and Violent Social Protest in the 1970s and 1980s.* Ithaca, NY: Cornell University East Asia Program, 1991.

Keck, Margaret E., and Kathryn Sikkink. *Activists Beyond Borders: Advocacy Networks in International Politics.* Ithaca, NY: Cornell University Press, 1998.

Keely, Charles B. "How Nation-States Create and Respond to Refugee Flows." *International Migration Review* 30, no. 4 (1996): 1046–67.

Kenney, Sally J. *For Whose Protection? Reproductive Hazards and Exclusionary Policies in the United States and Britain.* Ann Arbor: University of Michigan Press, 1992.

Keohane, Robert. *After Hegemony: Cooperation and Discord in the World Political Economy.* Princeton, NJ: Princeton University Press, 1984.

———, ed. *Neorealism and Its Critics.* New York: Columbia University Press, 1986.

Keohane, Robert, and Lisa Martin. "The Promise of Institutionalist Theory." *International Security* 29 1995: 39–64.

Kerbo, Harold R., and John A. McKinstry. *Who Rules Japan? The Inner Circles of Economic and Political Power.* Westport, CT: Praeger, 1995.

Kitagawa, Yasuhiro. "Mine Ban Policy of the Japanese Government, 1994–2004." Vancouver: University of British Columbia, 2005.

Klotz, Audie. *Norms in International Relations: The Struggle Against Apartheid.* Ithaca, NY: Cornell University Press, 1995a.

———. "Norms Reconstituting Interests: Global Racial Equality and U.S. Sanctions Against South Africa." *International Organization* 49, no. 3 (1995b): 451–78.

Knapp, Kiyoko Kamio. "Don't Awaken the Sleeping Child: Japan's Gender Equality Law and the Rhetoric of Gradualism." *Columbia Journal of Gender and Law* 8 (1999): 143–95.

———. "Still Office Flowers: Japanese Women Betrayed by the Equal Employment Opportunity Law." *Harvard Women's Law Journal* 18 (1995): 86–137.

Koh, Harold Hongju. "Why Do Nations Obey International Law?" *Yale Law Journal* 106 (1997): 2599–2659.

Koizumi, Koichi. "Refugee Policy Formation in Japan: Developments and Implications." *Journal of Refugee Studies* 5, no. 2 (1992): 123–35.

Kondo, Dorinne. *Crafting Selves: Power, Gender, and Discourses of Identity in a Japanese Workplace.* Chicago: University of Chicago Press, 1990.

Kowert, Paul. "National Identity: Inside and Out." *Security Studies* 8, nos. 2/3 (1999): 1–34.

Kowert, Paul, and Jeffrey Legro. "The Causes and Consequences of Norms in International Politics." In *The Culture of National Security: Norms and Identities in World Politics,* edited by Peter J. Katzenstein, 451–97. New York: Columbia University Press, 1996.

Krasner, Stephen D., ed. *International Regimes.* Ithaca, NY: Cornell University Press, 1983.

Kratochwil, Friedrich. "Constructing a New Orthodoxy? Wendt's 'Social Theory of International Politics' and the Constructivist Challenge." *Millennium: Journal of International Studies* 29, no. 1 (2000): 73–101.

Kratochwil, Friedrich, and John Gerard Ruggie. "International Organization: A State of the Art on the Art of the State." *International Organization* 40, no. 4 (1986): 753–75.

Lafer, Celso. "Brazilian International Identity and Foreign Policy: Past, Present, and Future." *Daedalus* 129, no. 2 (2000): 207–28.

Landis, Crane Stephen. "Human Rights Violations in Japan: A Contemporary Survey." *Detroit College of Law Journal of International Law and Practice* 5 (1996): 53–85.

LeBlanc, Robin. *Bicycle Citizens: The Political World of the Japanese Housewife.* Berkeley: University of California Press, 1999.

Legro, Jeffrey W. "Which Norms Matter? Revisiting the 'Failure' of Internationalism." *International Organization* 51, no. 1 (1997): 31–64.

Leheny, David. *The Rules of Play: National Identity and the Shaping of Japanese Leisure.* Ithaca, NY: Cornell University Press, 2003.

———. *Think Global, Fear Local: Sex, Violence, and Anxiety in Contemporary Japan.* Ithaca, NY: Cornell University Press, 2006.

Lie, John. *Multiethnic Japan.* Cambridge, MA: Harvard University Press, 2001.

Liftin, Karen T. *Ozone Discourses: Science and Politics in Global Environmental Cooperation.* New York: Columbia University Press, 1994.

Lindblom, Charles. *Politics and Markets.* New York: Basic Books, 1977.

Lipschutz, Ronnie. "Reconstructing World Politics: The Emergence of Global Civil Society." *Millennium: Journal of International Studies* 21, no. 3 (1992): 389–420.

Liu, Dongxiao, and Elizabeth Heger Boyle. "Making the Case: The Women's Convention and Japanese Equal Employment Opportunity." *International Journal of Comparative Sociology* 42, no. 4 (2001): 389–404.

Lock, Margaret. "Centering the Household: The Remaking of Female Maturity in Japan." In *Re-imaging Japanese Women*, edited by Anne E. Imamura, 73–103. Berkeley: University of California Press, 1996.

———. "Ideology, Female Midlife, and the Greying of Japan." *Journal of Japanese Studies* 19, no. 1 (1993): 43–77.

London, Nancy. *Japanese Corporate Philanthropy.* New York: Oxford University Press, 1991.

Long, Susan Orpett. "Nurturing and Femininity: The Ideal of Caregiving in Postwar Japan." In *Re-imaging Japanese Women*, edited by Anne E. Imamura. Berkeley: University of California Press, 1996.

Lumsdaine, David Halloran. *Moral Vision in International Politics.* Princeton, NJ: Princeton University Press, 1993.

Mackie, Vera. *Feminism in Modern Japan.* Cambridge: Cambridge University Press, 2003.

Maniruzzaman, Talukder. *Japan's Security Policy for the Twenty-First Century.* Dhaka: University Press Limited, 2000.

Matthews, Ron, and Keisuke Matsuyama, eds. *Japan's Military Renaissance?* New York: St. Martin's Press, 1993.

McIntosh, Malcolm. *Japan Re-armed.* New York: St. Martin's Press, 1986.

Mearsheimer, John J. "The False Promise of International Institutions." *International Security* 19, no. 3 (1995): 5–49.

Mekata, Motoko. "Building Partnerships Toward a Common Goal: Experiences of the International Campaign to Ban Landmines." In *The Third Force: The Rise of Transnational Civil Society*, edited by Ann M. Florini, 143–76. Washington, DC: Carnegie Endowment for International Peace, 2000.

Mercer, Jonathan. "Anarchy and Identity." *International Organization* 49, no. 2 (1995): 229–52.

Meyer, John. "The World Polity and the Authority of the Nation-State." In *Studies of the Modern World System*, edited by A. Bergesen. New York: Academic Press, 1980.

Meyer, John, John Boli, George M. Thomas, and Francisco O. Ramirez. "World Society and the Nation-State." *American Journal of Sociology* 103, no. 1 (1997): 109–37.

Miyachi, Mitsuko. "On the Unjust Ruling over the Sumitomo Electric Gender-Based Wage Discrimination Case." Osaka: Working Women's International Network, 2001.

Miyake, Yoshiko. "Doubling Expectations: Motherhood and Women's Factory Work Under State Management in Japan in the 1930s and 1940s." In *Recreating Japanese Women, 1600–1945*, edited by Gail Lee Bernstein, 267–95. Berkeley: University of California Press, 1991.

Miyaoka, Isao. *Legitimacy in International Society: Japan's Reaction to Global Wildlife Preservation*. Oxford: Palgrave Macmillan, 2004.

———. "More Than One Way to Save an Elephant: Foreign Pressure and the Japanese Policy Process." *Japan Forum* 10 (1998): 167–79.

Miyashita, Akitoshi. "Gaiatsu and Japan's Foreign Aid: Rethinking the Reactive-Proactive Debate." *International Studies Quarterly* 43 (1999): 695–732.

Mizuno, Takaaki. "The Refugee Quandary." *Japan Quarterly* 37, no. 1 (1990): 89–93.

Mochizuki, Mike M., ed. *Toward a True Alliance: Restructuring U.S.-Japan Security Relations*. Washington, DC: Brookings Institution Press, 1997.

Molony, Barbara. "Activism Among Women in the Taisho Cotton Textile Industry." In *Recreating Japanese Women, 1600–1945*, edited by Gail Lee Bernstein, 217–38. Berkeley: University of California Press, 1991.

Moravcsik, Andrew. "Introduction: Integrating International and Domestic Theories of International Bargaining." In *Double-Edged Diplomacy: International Bargaining and Domestic Politics*, edited by Harold K. Jacobson, P. B. Evans, and Robert B. Putnam. Berkeley: University of California Press, 1993.

Morris-Suzuki, Tessa. *Re-inventing Japan: Time, Space, Nation*. Armonk, NY: M. E. Sharpe, 1998.

Muller, Viana. "The Formation of the State and the Oppression of Women: Some Theoretical Considerations and a Case Study in England and Wales." *Review of Radical Political Economics* 9 (1977): 7–21.

Nagy, Margit. "Middle-Class Working Women During the Interwar Years." In *Recreating Japanese Women, 1600–1945*, edited by Gail Lee Bernstein, 199–218. Berkeley: University of California Press, 1991.

Nakamura Kumiko. *Josei deita bukku: seikarada kara seiji sanka made.* Tokyo: Yūhikaku, 1995.

Nanmin Jigyō Honbu. *Nanmin Jigyō Honbu annai.* Tokyo: Nanmin Jigyō Honbu, 2001.

Nanmin o Tasukerukai. "NGO Tokyo jirai kaigi '98: Ima watashitachi ni dekiru koto." Tokyo: Nanmin o Tasukerukai, 1998.

——. "Taijin jirai zenmen kinshi ni mukete: Ima watashitachi ni dekiru koto." Tokyo: Nanmin o Tasukerukai, Nihon Shōgaisha Kyōgikai, 1997.

Neumann, Iver B. "Self and Other in International Relations." *European Journal of International Relations* 2, no. 2 (1996): 139–74.

Neumann, Iver B., and Jennifer M. Welsh. "The Other in European Self-Definition: An Addendum to the Literature on International Society." *Review of International Studies* 17 (1991): 327–48.

Nishimura, Katsumi. "Article 5 and Employment Discrimination: Japan." In *Culture, Custom and Women's Human Rights: CEDAW Convention Article Five,* edited by Marsha Freeman, 12–15. Minneapolis: International Women's Rights Action Watch, 1999.

Nolte, Sharon H., and Sally Ann Hastings. "The Meiji State's Policy Toward Women, 1890–1910." In *Recreating Japanese Women, 1600–1945,* edited by Gail Lee Bernstein, 151–74. Berkeley: University of California Press, 1991.

Norgren, Tiana. *Abortion Before Birth Control: The Politics of Reproduction in Postwar Japan.* Princeton, NJ: Princeton University Press, 2001.

Ogasawara, Yuko. *Office Ladies and Salaried Men: Power, Gender, and Work in Japanese Companies.* Berkeley: University of California Press, 1998.

Ohnuki-Tierney, Emiko. "A Conceptual Model for the Historical Relationship Between the Self and the Internal and External Others: The Agrarian Japanese, the Ainu, and the Special-Status People." In *Making Majorities: Constituting the Nation in Japan, Korea, China, Malaysia, Fiji, Turkey, and the United States,* edited by Dru C. Gladney, 31–54. Stanford, CA: Stanford University Press, 1998.

Omori, Maki. "Gender and the Labor Market." *Journal of Japanese Studies* 19 (1993): 79–101.

Orr, R. M. *The Emergence of Japan's Foreign Aid Power.* New York: Columbia University Press, 1990.

Osa, Yukie. "Keynote Report: NGO Tokyo Conference '98 on Anti-personnel Landmines." Tokyo, 1998.

Osaka Prefectural Government. *Osaka no josei deita bukku 2000.* Osaka: Osaka Prefectural Government, 2000.

Oye, Kenneth, ed. *Cooperation Under Anarchy.* Princeton NJ: Princeton University Press, 1986.

Painter, Andrew A. "The Telerepresentation of Gender in Japan." In *Re-imaging Japanese Women,* edited by Anne E. Imamura, 46–72. Berkeley: University of California Press, 1996.

Parkinson, Loraine. "Japan's Equal Employment Opportunity Law: An Alternative Approach to Social Change." *Columbia Law Review* 89 (1989): 604–36.

Pekkanen, Robert. *Japan's Dual Civil Society: Members Without Advocates*. Stanford, CA: Stanford University Press, 2006.

Peng, Y. "The Earth Summit and Japan's Initiative in Environmental Diplomacy." *Futures* 25 (1993): 379–91.

Peters, Julie, and Andrea Wolper, eds. *Women's Rights / Human Rights: International Feminist Perspectives*. New York: Routledge, 1995.

Peterson, V. Spike, and Ann Sisson Runyan. *Global Gender Issues*. Boulder, CO: Westview Press, 1993.

Pettman, Jan Jindy. "Nationalism and After." *Review of International Studies* 24 (1998): 149–64.

Pharr, Susan J. *Political Women in Japan: The Search for a Place in Political Life*. Berkeley: University of California Press, 1981.

Politis, Yvette. "The Regulation of an Invisible Enemy: The International Community's Response to Land Mine Proliferation." *Boston College International and Comparative Law Review* 22 (1999): 465–93.

Port, Kenneth L. "The Japanese International Law 'Revolution': International Human Rights Law and Its Impact in Japan." *Stanford Journal of International Law* 28, no. 1 (1991): 139–72.

Price, Richard M. *The Chemical Weapons Taboo*. Ithaca, NY: Cornell University Press, 1997.

———. "Compliance with International Norms and the Mines Taboo." In *To Walk Without Fear: The Global Campaign to Ban Landmines*, edited by Maxwell A. Cameron, Robert J. Lawson, and Brian W. Tomlin, 340–63. Toronto: Oxford University Press, 1998a.

———. "A Genealogy of the Chemical Weapons Taboo." *International Organization* 49, no. 4 (1995): 73–103.

———. "Reversing the Gun Sights: Transnational Civil Society Targets Land Mines." *International Organization* 52, no. 3 (1998b): 613–44.

Price, Richard, and Nina Tannenwald. "Norms and Deterrence: The Nuclear and Chemical Weapons Taboos." In *The Culture of National Security: Norms and Identity in World Politics*, edited by Peter J. Katzenstein. New York: Columbia University Press, 1996.

Ramseyer, J. Mark, and Frances McCall Rosenbluth. *Japan's Political Marketplace*. Cambridge, MA: Harvard University Press, 1997.

Raustiala, Kal, and Anne-Marie Slaughter. "International Law, International Relations, and Compliance." In *Handbook of International Relations*, edited by Walter Carlsnaes, Thomas Risse, and Beth Simmons. London: Sage, 2002.

Reimann, Kim. "Building Global Civil Society from the Outside In? Japanese International Development NGOs, the State, and International Norms." In *The State of Civil Society in Japan*, edited by Frank J. Schwartz and Susan J. Pharr, 298–315. Cambridge: Cambridge University Press, 2003.

Reus-Smit, Christian. "The Politics of International Law." In *The Politics of International Law*, edited by Christian Reus-Smit, 14–44. Cambridge: Cambridge University Press, 2004.

Risse, Thomas. "Let's Argue! Communicative Action in World Politics." *International Organization* 54 (2000): 1–39.

Risse, Thomas, Stephen C. Ropp, and Kathryn Sikkink, eds. *The Power of Human Rights: International Norms and Domestic Change.* Cambridge Studies in International Relations. Cambridge: Cambridge University Press, 1999.

Risse-Kappen, Thomas. *Bringing Transnationalism Back In: Non-state Actors, Domestic Structures and International Institutions.* Cambridge: Cambridge University Press, 1995.

———. "Ideas Do Not Float Freely: Transnational Coalitions, Domestic Structures, and the End of the Cold War." *International Organization* 48, no. 2 (1994): 185–214.

Rittberger, Volker, ed. *Regime Theory and International Relations.* Oxford: Clarendon Press, 1993.

Roberts, Glenda S. "Careers and Commitment: Azumi's Blue-Collar Women." In *Re-imaging Japanese Women*, edited by Anne E. Imamura, 221–43. Berkeley: University of California Press, 1996.

Roberts, Shawn. "No Exceptions, No Reservations, No Loopholes: The Campaign for the 1997 Convention on the Prohibition of the Development, Production, Stockpiling, Transfer, and Use of Anti-personnel Mines and on Their Destruction." *Colorado Journal of International Law and Policy* 9 (1998): 371–91.

Rodd, Laurel Rasplica. "Yosano Akiko and the Taisho Debate over the 'New Woman.'" In *Recreating Japanese Women, 1600–1945*, edited by Gail Lee Bernstein, 175–98. Berkeley: University of California Press, 1991.

Rosenau, James N. *Turbulence in World Politics: A Theory of Change and Continuity.* Cambridge: Cambridge University Press, 1990.

Rosenberger, Nancy R. "Fragile Resistance, Signs of Status: Women Between State and Media in Japan." In *Re-imaging Japanese Women*, edited by Anne E. Imamura, 12–45. Berkeley: University of California Press, 1996.

Ross, Robert S. "The Geography of the Peace: East Asia and the Twenty-first Century." *International Security* 23, no. 4 (1999): 81–118.

Ruggie, John Gerard. "What Makes the World Hang Together? Neo-utilitarianism and the Social Constructivist Challenge." *International Organization* 52, no. 4 (1998): 855–85.

Rumelili, Bahar. *Constructing Regional Community and Order in Europe and Southeast Asia.* New York: Palgrave Macmillan, 2008.

———. "Liminality and Perpetuation of Conflicts: Turkish-Greek Relations in the Context of Community-Building by the EU." *European Journal of International Relations* 9, no. 2 (2003): 213–48.

Rutherford, Kenneth. "The Evolving Arms Control Agenda: Implications of the Role of NGOs in Banning Antipersonnel Landmines." *World Politics* 53 (2001): 74–114.

Said, Edward. *Culture and Imperialism.* New York: Vintage Books, 1993.

Samuels, Richard J. *Machiavelli's Children: Leaders and Their Legacies in Italy and Japan.* Ithaca, NY: Cornell University Press, 2005.

————. *Rich Nation, Strong Army: National Security and the Technological Transformation of Japan.* Ithaca, NY: Cornell University Press, 1994.

Satoh, Yukio. *The Evolution of Japanese Security Policy.* London: International Institute for Strategic Studies, 1982.

Schoppa, Leonard. *Race for the Exits: The Unraveling of Japan's System of Social Protection.* Ithaca, NY: Cornell University Press, 2006.

————. "Two-Level Games and Bargaining Outcomes: Why Gaiatsu Succeeds in Japan in Some Cases but Not Others." *International Organization* 47, no. 3 (1993): 353–86.

Schwartz, Frank J., and Susan J. Pharr, eds. *The State of Civil Society in Japan.* Cambridge: Cambridge University Press, 2003.

Shipper, Apichai W. "Criminals or Victims? The Politics of Illegal Foreigners in Japan." *Journal of Japanese Studies* 31, no. 2 (2005): 299–327.

Sievers, Sharon. *Flowers in Salt: The Beginnings of Feminist Consciousness in Modern Japan.* Stanford, CA: Stanford University Press, 1983.

Sims, Calvin. "World Business Briefing: Asia; Japan's Joblessness Still at High." *New York Times,* September 1, 1999.

Slaughter Burley, Anne-Marie. "International Law and International Relations Theory: A Dual Agenda." *American Journal of International Law* 87, no. 2 (1993): 205–39.

Smith, Robert J. "Gender Inequality in Contemporary Japan." *Journal of Japanese Studies* 13, no. 1 (1987): 1–25.

Smith, Steve. "The Forty Years' Detour: The Resurgence of Normative Theory in International Relations." *Millennium: Journal of International Studies* 21, no. 3 (1992): 489–506.

Soguk, Nevzat. *States and Strangers: Refugees and Displacements of Statecraft.* Minneapolis: University of Minnesota Press, 1999.

Spurr, David. *The Rhetoric of Empire: Colonial Discourse in Journalism, Travel Writing, and Imperial Administration.* Durham, NC: Duke University Press, 1994.

Suzuki, Shogo. "Japan's Socialization into Janus-Faced European International Society." *European Journal of International Relations* 11, no. 1 (2005): 137–64.

Tabb, William K. *The Postwar Japanese System: Cultural Economy and Economic Transformation.* New York: Oxford University Press, 1995.

Takahashi Nobuko. "Joshi sabetsu teppai jōyaku no tanjō ni tazusawatte." In *Sekai kara nihon e no messeji,* edited by Kokusai jorsei no chii kyōkai, 4–17. Tokyo: Shogakusha, 1989.

Takeda, Isami. "Japan's Responses to Refugees and Political Asylum Seekers." In *Temporary Workers or Future Citizens? Japanese and U.S. Migration Policies,* edited by Myron Weiner and Tadashi Hanami. New York: New York University Press, 1998.

Tannenwald, Nina. "The Nuclear Taboo: The United States and the Normative Basis of Nuclear Non-use." *International Organization* 53, no. 3 (1999): 433–68.

Taylor, Jonathan. "Japan's Global Environmentalism: Rhetoric and Reality." *Political Geography* 18 (1999): 535–62.

Thomas, Nicholas. *Colonialism's Culture: Anthropology, Travel and Government.* Princeton, NJ: Princeton University Press, 1994.

Tilly, Charles. *Big Structures, Large Processes, Huge Comparisons.* New York: Russell Sage Foundation, 1984.

Toki Hinako. "Kokkyō o koeru NGO no katsudo." In *Nanmin to jinken,* edited by Nanmin Kenkyū Foramu. Tokyo: Gendaijinbunsha, 2001.

Towns, Ann. "Paradoxes of (In)equality: Something Is Rotten in the Gender Equal State of Sweden." *Conflict and Cooperation* 37, no. 2 (2002): 157–79.

———. "The Status of Women as a Standard of 'Civilization.'" *European Journal of International Relations* (forthcoming).

Tsuda, Takeyuki. *Strangers in the Ethnic Homeland: Japanese Brazilian Return Migration in Transnational Perspective.* New York: Columbia University Press, 2003.

United Nations Committee on the Elimination of Discrimination Against Women. *Report of the Committee on the Elimination of Discrimination Against Women (Seventh Session).* New York: United Nations, 1988.

———. *Report of the Committee on the Elimination of Discrimination Against Women (Thirteenth Session).* New York: United Nations, 1994.

United Nations Development Program (UNDP). *Human Development Report, 1993.* New York: Oxford University Press, 1993.

———. *Human Development Report, 1994.* New York: Oxford University Press, 1994.

Uno, Kathleen. "Women and Changes in the Household Division of Labor." In *Recreating Japanese Women, 1600–1945,* edited by Gail Lee Bernstein. Berkeley: University of California Press, 1991.

Upham, Frank. *Law and Social Change in Postwar Japan.* Cambridge, MA: Harvard University Press, 1987.

Walker, R.B.J. *Inside/Outside: International Relations as Political Theory.* Cambridge: Cambridge University Press, 1993.

Watanabe Shogo. "Nanmin jōyaku no kokunaiteki jisshi: Nanmin nintei tetsuzuki." In *Gaikokujin hō to rōyaringu,* edited by Shigeo Miyagawa. Tokyo: Gendaijinbunsha, 2005.

———. "Nihon no nanmin jitsumu no genjō—Bengoshi no tachiba kara." In *Nanmin to jinken,* edited by Nanmin Kenkyū Foramu. Tokyo: Gendaijinbunsha, 2001.

Weiner, Michael. *Japan's Minorities: The Illusion of Homogeneity.* London: Routledge, 1997.

———. "Migration and Refugee Policies: An Overview." In *Migration and Refugee Policies: An Overview,* edited by Ann Bernstein and Myron Weiner. London: Pinter Press, 1999.

———. "Opposing Visions: Migration and Citizenship Policies in Japan and the United States." In *Temporary Workers or Future Citizens? Japanese and U.S. Migration Policies,* edited by Myron Weiner and Tadashi Hanami. New York: New York University Press, 1998.

Weiner, Myron, and Tadashi Hanami, eds. *Temporary Workers or Future Citizens? Japanese and U.S. Migration Policies.* New York: New York University Press, 1998.

Weinstein, Martin E. *Japan's Postwar Defense Policy, 1947–1968.* New York: Columbia University Press, 1971.

Weldes, Jutta, Mark Laffey, Hugh Gusterson, and Raymond Duvall, eds. *Cultures of Insecurity: States, Communities, and the Production of Danger.* Minneapolis: University of Minnesota Press, 1999.

Wendt, Alexander. "Anarchy Is What States Make of It: The Social Construction of Power Politics." *International Organization* 46, no. 2 (1992): 391–425.

———. "Collective Identity Formation and the International State." *American Political Science Review* 88, no. 2 (1994): 384–96.

———. "Constructing International Politics." *International Security* 20, no. 1 (1995): 71–81.

———. *Social Theory of International Politics.* Cambridge: Cambridge University Press, 1999.

Williams, David. *Japan: Beyond the End of History.* New York: Routledge, 1994.

Williams, Jody, and Stephen Goose. "The International Campaign to Ban Landmines." In *To Walk Without Fear: The Global Campaign to Ban Landmines,* edited by Maxwell A. Cameron, Robert J. Lawson, and Brian W. Tomlin. Toronto: Oxford University Press, 1998.

Williams, Michael C. "Identity and the Politics of Security." *European Journal of International Relations* 4, no. 2 (1998): 204–25.

Williams, Michael C., and Iver B. Neumann. "From Alliance to Security Community: NATO, Russia, and the Power of Identity." *Millennium: Journal of International Studies* 29, no. 2 (2000): 357–87.

Working Women's International Network. *Jyosei sabetsu teppai jōyaku wa nihon de ikasareteiru ka.* Osaka: Working Women's International Network, 2000.

———. *Kokuren josei 2000 nen kaigi to WWN.* Osaka: Working Women's International Network, 2000.

———. *Public Echo Reaction's References: Sumitomo's Litigation Information's Material.* Osaka: Working Women's International Network, 2001.

———. *WWN Went to the ILO: To Submit a Report on the Real Situation of Japanese Wages Based on Our Experience in the Work Place and to Eliminate Wage Discrimination Between Men and Women by Using "Convention 100 and 156."* Osaka: Working Women's International Network.

Yamanaka, Keiko. "Ana Bortz' Law Suit and Minority Rights in Japan." *Japan Policy Research Institute at the University of San Francisco Center for the Pacific Rim,* 2002. www.jpri.org/publications/workingpapers/wp88.html, accessed January 9, 2009.

Yamashita Yasuko. "Joshi sabetsu teppai jōyaku no ishiki." In *Sekai kara nihon e no messeiji,* edited by Kokusai josei no chii kyōkai, 18-29. Tokyo: Shogakusha, 1989.

———. *Report of UN Special Session "Women 2000" and the Women's Status in Japan.* Tokyo: Japanese Association of International Women's Rights, 2000.

————. *Research on the Convention for the Elimination of All Forms of Discrimination Against Women*. Translated by E. A. Leicesterz. Tokyo: Dougakusha, 1996.

Yoshino, Kosaku. "Culturalism, Racialism, and Internationalism in the Discourse on Japanese Identity." In *Making Majorities: Constituting the Nation in Japan, Korea, China, Malaysia, Fiji, Turkey, and the United States*, edited by Dru C. Gladney. Stanford, CA: Stanford University Press, 1998.

The letter *f* following a page number denotes a figure; the letter *t*, a table.